Praise for *We Have Plenty*

Wealth and the Gospel do not mix. Wealth is oil; the Gospel is water. The two can coexist, even peacefully, but they can never become one. Lorena M. Parrish's treatment of this conundrum, especially challenging in the capitalistic plutocracy the United States is becoming, offers a womanist perspective on this ancient dilemma. When that happens, new ideas and new hope emerge. I came away from *We Have Plenty* with a better understanding of the Gospel and money, of womanist theology, and of the world in which we live.

Sarah B. Drummond, founding dean, Andover Newton Seminary at Yale Divinity School

Lorena M. Parrish aims to foster communal liberation and wholeness by adeptly probing the power and promise of God's salvation. Discerning between contemporary theologies of prosperity and Jesus's teachings on wealth renunciation, redistribution, and call for a radical reversal, Parrish lays a clear path to communal abundance built on tangible models of resistance and transcendence that face poverty and oppression foursquare faithfully.

Emilie M. Townes, Martin Luther King, Jr. Professor of Religion and Black Studies, Boston University School of Theology, and author of *Womanist Ethics and the Cultural Production of Evil*

Lorena M. Parrish provides us with new strategies to take seriously the suffering of prosperity theology that we choose to ignore. Adding her voice with Abisoye Ajayi-Akinfolarin, Majora Carter, and William Barber, Parrish explores the devastating challenges of wealth and poverty with keen insight and substantive womanist prowess concerning the unique harms to Black women, Black churches, and all communities. Parrish's fluid writing disturbs – provoking action and insisting upon social change and theological re-imagination. With this very accessible resource, no more should theologies of prosperity go unchecked in our theological and religion classrooms.

Nancy Lynne Westfield, director, Wabash Center for Teaching and Learning in Theology and Religion, and author of *Glimpses of Me and Mine*

We Have Plenty is a groundbreaking work that challenges the Black Church to reimagine abundance beyond the limits of prosperity gospel ideology. With womanist theological depth and prophetic urgency, Lorena M. Parrish examines the historical ambivalence toward Jesus's teachings on wealth and poverty and presents a compelling vision of communal plenty rooted in justice, redistribution, and radical love. This is a timely must-read for scholars, clergy, and anyone seeking to align faith with liberation.

Reggie Blount, Murray H. Leiffer Associate Professor of Formation, Leadership, and Culture, and director, Center for the Church and the Black Experience, Garrett-Evangelical Theological Seminary

We Have Plenty should be read by all. It is particularly attuned to ongoing Black longing for abundant living that resides in practices of Black faith—from some community's attraction to empty prosperity preaching to other Black faith community's commitment to sharing and caring as hallmarks of religious practice. Importantly, this book was birthed from the womb of first-generation womanist theology, which was both an academic project and a movement of Black women scholars who gathered at tables of abundance—abundant hospitality and belonging among each other, abundant experience of loving God and Black people, abundant concern for the godly and daily survival of Black women. It is a gift to the reader that the teaching and inspiration of Delores Williams rings clearly throughout this text. This book is Lorena M. Parrish's twenty-first century encounter and expansion of first-generation womanist thought. In offering models of resistance and transcendence centered in Black Christian women's experience, *We Have Plenty* points toward models that can sustain us in continuously treacherous times for Black lives.

P. Kimberleigh Jordan, Minister for Spiritual Formation, Community Ministries and Creative Arts, St. Luke's Episcopal Church, Atlanta

WE HAVE **PLENTY**

WE HAVE PLENTY

A Womanist Theology of Communal Abundance for the Black Church

LORENA M. PARRISH

Fortress Press
Minneapolis

WE HAVE PLENTY
A Womanist Theology of Communal Abundance for the Black Church

31 30 29 28 27 26 25 1 2 3 4 5 6 7 8 9

Library of Congress Control Number: 2024061913 (print)

Cover design: Kris E. Miller
Cover illustration: Digital collage with Getty Images

Print ISBN: 978-1-5064-9931-4
eBook ISBN: 978-1-5064-9932-1

Printed in China.

Dedicated to the woman to whom, besides God, I owe my very existence—my late great-grandmother Posey Mazyck-Warren

CONTENTS

ACKNOWLEDGMENTS

My heart is filled with profound appreciation, deep gratitude, and so much love for the many who have helped me in a multitude of ways to complete this book. Thank you to those of you who showered me with acts of loving-kindness, words of encouragement, prayers, admonishments, and support, all of which sustained me in my most depleted times.

I begin with the woman to whom this work is dedicated and to whom, besides my God, I owe my very existence—my late great-grandmother Posey Mazyck-Warren. Determined that "her babies" would advance well beyond her sixth-grade education to acquire the highest level of academic achievement available, she created my first classroom and study hall at the kitchen table and served as my first teacher and sage. Her sacrifice, support, steadfast faith, and abundance of love were my lifeline. And I know she still watches over me from her heavenly seat. Thank you, Mama.

Thank you, my beloved sisters, Dorothy, Nellie, and Ellie, and all of my family for having high expectations of my work and encouraging me to keep pushing forward.

At Union Theological Seminary, it was the late Dr. Delores S. Williams who introduced me to womanist theology, nurtured my theological development, and mentored me on this journey. I will remain forever grateful to her for extending her brilliance, guidance, patience, unwavering support, demand for scholarly excellence, couch on which I and others sat many a day, and acknowledgment of my intellectual potential.

To Dr. Serene Jones, thank you for stepping in when Dr. Williams retired and for encouraging me to keep going. This book, which began as my dissertation, is the result of your encouragement. Thank you, Drs. Emilie Townes, Christopher Morse, Chung Hyun Kung, and Vincent Wimbush, and all the brilliant scholars who took time to instruct, challenge, and shape me as an activist-scholar and preacher. I am also grateful to have been blessed by the late Dr. James Hal Cone, the late Dr. James Melvin Washington, and the late Dr. Annie Ruth Powell.

Words can barely express my gratitude to the friends and colleagues whom I met in the academic halls of Union Seminary in New York City and who helped me to traverse the sometimes thrilling, sometimes lonely academic journey with their intellectual engagements, constructive criticism, random acts of kindness, unconditional love, and moments of comic relief during times of stress.

Thank you to the special gems in my life—my sisters in the spirit from Union and beyond—the late Rev. Dr. Mariah Ann Britton, Rev. Dr. Lisa M. Weaver, Rev. Dr. Kanyere Eaton, Dr. Andrea Smith, Rev. Dr. Kimberleigh Jordan, Rev. Cathlin Baker, Rev. Dr. Joy Bostic, Dr. Martha Wiggins, Rev. Dr. JoAnne Marie Terrell, Rev. Dr. Violet Dease-Lee, Rev. Dionne Boissière, Lisa Anderson, Dr. Teresa Delgado, Rev. Dr. Sally McNichol, Rev. Adriene Thorne, Rev. Yvette Vanterpool, and Zenobia Gray. Your love, encouragement, kitchen-table conversations, and sisterly attention throughout my academic journey and the writing process have been immeasurably sustaining and more important than you can ever know.

Thank you, Susan L. Taylor for being a dear sister-friend and believing in my work.

To my brother Dr. Adam Clark, who throughout my matriculation at Union and beyond has kept me focused and inspired, and to all my beloved brothers—Rev. Dr. (Senator) Raphael Warnock, Rev. Dr. Mark V. C. Taylor, Rev. Anthony Lee, Rev. Eugene Palmore, Rev. Dr. John Vaughn, Rev. Melvin Miller, and Dr. Sylvester Johnson—I owe my deepest gratitude.

Thank you to my editor, Yvonne D. Hawkins, and to Fortress Press for believing in this project and making this a reality. I am grateful that you saw fit to publish this manuscript. I have been abundantly blessed with an incredible tribe. But all glory and honor and praise belongs to God.

INTRODUCTION

We are living in extraordinary times that are calling for extraordinary measures. The disproportionately high rates of COVID-19 infections, hospitalizations, and deaths among African Americans, the unrest and protests provoked by the exorbitant number of Black women and men killed by police officers since George Floyd's murder in 2020,[1] and the vast wealth gap between Blacks and whites, driven by segregation, redlining, evictions, and exclusion, all highlight structural racism as a fundamental root cause of so many of the disparities in America that remain largely unaddressed. These challenges also point to a long-standing economic ethic that continues to disenfranchise Black women, men, and children, and other marginalized groups—an ethic that prizes individual wealth acquisition, ignores dynamics that generate inequality, and fosters an ambivalence toward Jesus's teachings on poverty, wealth acquisition, and material redistribution. Such an ethic has yet to be fully interrogated by the Black Church. This is a plea and a call to action for the Black Church to engage in such an interrogation.

It has been well established that the Black Church has played a pivotal role in advocating for various social justice issues within the African American community as it looked to the ministry of Jesus to confront oppression and "build beloved community."[2] It has also been well established that, in the past few decades, successive generations of African American Christians have outwardly displayed an ambivalence toward Jesus's teachings on wealth, poverty, and communal sharing, as significant numbers have come to embrace the message and ministry of prosperity gospel churches. As stadium-sized to storefront churches spewing prosperity messages have sprung up across Black America, drawing millions into their fold, little can be heard about Jesus's identifying with and concern for the poor and oppressed. Instead of the prophetic messages that impart the Black Church's traditional understanding of its responsibility to address systems of oppression, including the hegemonic economic policies and programs that perpetuate poverty and inequality, one finds sermons that ignore this charge and endorse an individualistic responsibility to seek a better quality of life through acquiring personal wealth and prosperity. Yet, there is no question in the minds of these African American ministers who espouse their various strands of prosperity gospel that they are indeed within the Christian tradition in preaching a God-sanctioned message of personal financial empowerment and social advancement.

For instance, the 2006 issue of *Black Enterprise* magazine published a special report, entitled "The Business of Faith," highlighting the multimillion-dollar enterprises of Eddie Long, Thomas D. (T. D.) Jakes, and Kirby Caldwell, and the role that these "CEOs" play in their Black megachurches and multiple businesses. Emphasizing the community development aspects of their ministries, the article also cites these ministers' understanding of their entrepreneurial endeavors and the resultant material rewards they receive as part and parcel of their answering God's call. Indeed, they see their multimillion-dollar homes, luxury cars, and private jets not just as material rewards that are socially accepted but material blessings that are theologically expected as God's tangible gifts for their faithfulness.

Researchers of prosperity gospel churches have argued that the sermonic messages, lifestyles, financial empires, branding, and marketed merchandise of these and other celebrated Black prosperity preachers, such as Reverend Frederick K. C. Price, Reverend Creflo Dollar, and Bishop Kenneth Ulmer, can in large part be credited for the explosive growth of prosperity preaching. Modern technological resources of all kinds, from around-the-clock televised services, movies, and plays to podcasts, books, digital properties, conferences, and other live events, have not only provided megachurch prosperity preachers with celebrity status but also with devoted followers whose numbers rival those of world-renowned musicians, actors, and athletes.

While these religious elites have played a central role in proffering contemporary theologies of prosperity among Black American Christians, they are not alone. Countless less popular prosperity gospel preachers with much smaller congregations and preaching platforms can be included within their ranks. These faith leaders from across a spectrum of independent and denominationally affiliated churches may defy organizational and denominational categorization. They may offer diverse versions of the prosperity gospel message of faith-fueled abundant living, or what one scholar calls various versions of "hard prosperity" (a prosperity that perceives and appears to judge people's faith by their immediate circumstances) and "soft prosperity" (a kinder, gentler, less ostentatious message that speaks of internal blessings as well as living your best life, which of course includes financial wealth and health).[3]

What these prosperity preachers do have in common with each other, and with Western Christianity as a whole, is a valuation of wealth and poverty that, from the patristic period onward, has bred an ambivalence toward Jesus's revolutionary revaluation of wealth acquisition and a radical new understanding of who and what are to be revered as "blessed" in the material world—that is, the poor and those who practice redistribution and renunciation of prioritizing individual wealth acquisition in ways that foster communal well-being.

This widespread influence of the prosperity gospel movement and the seismic shift it has created in the landscape of African American Christianity should not only prompt us to question whether prosperity theologies reflect the teachings of Jesus. This phenomenon should also raise for us other important questions such as: Is the sociohistorical trajectory used to trace the contemporary prosperity gospel movement adequate for explaining the rise of prosperity theologies in Western Christianity in general and the Black Church in particular? Is this new prosperity gospel indeed something "new," birthed in contemporary times, or can it be said to belong to a trajectory that has existed in the Christian tradition since the time of the patristic fathers? What is the relationship between contemporary theologies of prosperity and the long-standing ambivalence toward Jesus's teachings on wealth renunciation, redistribution, and his call for a radical reversal? Can the prosperity gospel message be said to represent what Christ had in mind regarding salvation? And, if indeed prosperity is an indication of one's salvation, then what does this notion of salvation, aligned with America's hypercapitalistic economic system and its myth of equality for all, have to say to Black folks in general, and Black women in particular, who continue to suffer under the weight of entrenched poverty, gender discrimination, racial oppression, and economic exploitation?

What This Book Provides

This book provides a critical theological analysis of the long-running ambivalent attitudes toward Jesus's teachings on wealth and poverty within the Christian tradition and the impact of this ambivalence upon Black Church soteriology and praxis. This ambivalent attitude toward Jesus's teachings on poverty and wealth has fostered, from the patristic period onward, what I call a "legacy of a theology of prosperity," and this legacy has vital implications for constructing a womanist theology of communal plenty—that is, a soteriological perspective that at once addresses Black women's and men's longing for abundant living and takes seriously Jesus's teachings on material redistribution.

Jesus's call for a revolutionary radical devaluation of wealth, consistently expressed in the Synoptic Gospels, is a call to initiate faithful acts and redemptive responses that renounce stratified power, privilege, and wealth inequity. It is a call that ushers into being a new human paradigm that values nonhierarchical relations, radical egalitarianism, and a culture of sharing and hospitality. It is a call to trust in God's infinite hospitality and God's vision for a redeemed humanity, which is characterized by the absence of unjust hierarchies of privilege and domination. Jesus describes it as a world where "the last are first and the first are last" (Mark 10:31). These words do not foretell merely a reversal of fortunes within an existing established power structure. Rather, they signify a time when the first are last and the last are first because they are literally indistinguishable. The reversal is that there are no rich, there are no poor, and there are no unjust hierarchies of privilege and domination. Yet, there exists in the Western Christian tradition, from the patristic period onward, ambivalent attitudes toward Jesus's thoughts on wealth acquisition.

It has often been the Black Church, energized by the divine mandates for liberation found in the biblical texts of Exodus 9 and John 3:16, that has served as a prophetic voice to speak against the hypocrisies of Western Christianity, including its acceptance of the degradations of slavery, the defeat of Reconstruction, Jim and Jane Crow and the codified system of racial apartheid, and the persistent, pervasive, structural nature of white supremacy. Yet, the Black Church has been less of a prophetic voice in upholding Jesus's views on wealth, poverty, and material redistribution.

This book also offers a womanist way forward for the Black Church. A concern for biblical interpretation, social justice, the prophetic voice of the Black Church, and the well-being of Black women, men, and children are at the heart of this project. As theology always emerges from life itself, my interest in addressing the spiritual and material needs of Black women in particular and disenfranchised communities in general is not only the result of my identity as a womanist theologian and former pastor of predominantly Black and Latinx working-class and poor congregations. My desire to foster communal liberation and wholeness was initiated by my own family's poverty and attraction to prosperity preaching that, in valuing wealth acquisition over communal sharing and associating material riches with being more faithful and blessed by God, rendered us, as it does all poor persons, less favored, less blessed, and spiritually deficient.

I begin my discourse on a way forward in chapter 1, "Black Folks, Prosperity Gospels, and a Legacy of Longing," by providing a womanist analysis of how and why the Black Church has appropriated oppressive and substantive elements of white Western Christianity, including a theology of ambivalence toward wealth accumulation, poverty, and materialism. Here I discuss the contours of contemporary theologies of prosperity being heard today in the Black Church and how these theologies are situated within the long-standing legacy of both valuing wealth and spiritualizing poverty in the Christian tradition. I examine how and why the Black Church has appropriated oppressive and substantive elements of white Western Christianity, including a theological ambivalence toward Jesus's position on wealth accumulation, poverty, and materialism. I explore why this has been the case in spite of the failure of prosperity gospel messages to eradicate America's wealth and poverty divide or address African Americans' longing for a better quality of life. I then discuss the contours of these contemporary prosperity theologies and how today's prosperity gospel movement in the Black Church is situated within a long-standing legacy of both valuing wealth and spiritualizing poverty in the Christian tradition that is counter to Jesus's call for a new valuation of both poverty and wealth.

Chapter 2, "Jesus, Wealth, and Poverty," examines Jesus's position on poverty and wealth and further explains how prosperity theologies and practices in the Black Church are far from Jesus's perspectives. Certain texts in the

Old Testament/Hebrew Bible reveal that poverty and wealth were either seen as part of the natural and divine order or poverty was seen as a scandal caused by the wealthy or injustice. Analysis of specific texts in the Gospels characterizes Jesus as having negative attitudes about individual wealth and positive attitudes toward the poor, emphasizing communal sharing, redistribution, and equality, and ushering in a new valuation of both wealth and poverty. In other words, one can certainly find a plurality of voices in the Old Testament/Hebrew Bible that speak of poverty and wealth, some of which appear to contradict each other. Pondering the significance of such conflicting texts—from those that portray poverty and wealth as part of the natural and divine order to those texts that portray poverty as a scandal caused by the wealthy or injustice—has been an ongoing task within the Christian Church. However, specific texts in the Gospels characterize Jesus's valuation of wealth and poverty as less ambiguous and more aligned with the radical trajectory of the prophets who cautioned against wealth acquisition and emphasized justice.

In chapter 3, "The Valuation of Poverty and Wealth in the Early Church," I trace what I deem the anatomy of a theology of prosperity, through the particular sermons and writings of St. Augustine of Hippo and John Calvin, two highly influential theologians in the Western tradition. Augustine's theology enunciated in *City of God* and his letters addressed to wealthy landowners are an excellent window into his and the Western world's valuation of material possession, inequality, human responsibility, and the religious life. Calvin's views on wealth and poverty in his *Institutes of the Christian Religion* and his exegesis of select biblical texts clarify his position on Jesus's teachings on wealth and poverty. Thus, the chapter outlines a theological genealogy and historical treatment of Western Christianity's long-standing ambivalence toward Jesus's teachings on poverty and wealth accumulation. I explore not only how Calvin's and Augustine's views have informed Western Christianity's ideas concerning the valuation of wealth, poverty, material possession, inequality, human responsibility, and the religious life, but also how mainline Christianity's long-standing ambivalence toward Jesus's teachings on poverty and wealth has fostered, from the patristic period onward, *a legacy of a theology of prosperity*.

Chapter 4, "The Legacy of a Theology of Prosperity on American Soil," traces this prevailing Christian attitude toward wealth and poverty on American soil by examining the theologies of John Wesley and Walter Rauschenbusch. Here I explore these theologians' positions on wealth and poverty through an analysis of their sermons and Rauschenbusch's argument for a revaluation of wealth and poverty based on what he saw as a new social order inaugurated by Jesus. Examining Wesley's and Rauschenbusch's theological thoughts uncovers important but often overlooked articulations about wealth, poverty, and redistribution, and doing so helps us to further interrogate this anatomy of a theology of prosperity.

Chapter 5, "Womanist Sources for a Redemptive Response," offers context that can be accessed to build a constructive response to this legacy by presenting a new theology—a womanist theology of communal plenty—that shifts the Black Church's allegiance to wealth and material acquisition to an allegiance with a theology (and praxis) that aligns with Jesus's radical teachings on wealth, poverty, and material redistribution while advancing a communal vision of abundant living.

Chapter 6, "Redemptive Models of Resistance and Transcendence," provides for readers' consideration some models that embody womanist practices of fostering communal abundance, beginning with the life and work of US civil rights activist Fannie Lou Hamer, whose work was based on her interpretation of economic justice, wealth redistribution, and Jesus's teachings.

Important Terms

Ambivalence

Throughout this text, I use the word "ambivalence" to describe an indecisive or compromised attitude toward Jesus's call for a radical devaluation of wealth acquisition. Such a compromised attitude allows for less focus on the material realm and a tendency to spiritualize his teachings on wealth renunciation and redistribution.

My probing Christianity's long-standing ambivalence toward Jesus's revolutionary revaluation of wealth renunciation, redistribution, and communal sharing and the resultant legacy of a theology of prosperity that has infiltrated the Black Church is intimately tied to my desire to offer a womanist way forward to resist the perpetuation of this legacy and offer a constructive theological approach that replaces a theology of individual entitlement with a theology that takes seriously Jesus's teachings, and addresses Black women's and men's longings for abundant living.

Theology of prosperity

My use of the term "theology of prosperity" here refers to the way in which wealth accumulation has come to be understood in the Christian faith as part of God's divine order. A theology of prosperity legitimizes linking individual prosperity, social power, mobility, and material acquisition to God's blessings. The notion that Jesus required a radical renunciation or redistribution of material goods is set aside, as is his radical revaluation of wealth and poverty. The storing up and accumulation of wealth is no longer antithetical to salvation. Instead, it is seen as an intrinsic blessed state, and its renunciation and redistribution are not required as acts of faith.

The Black Church

It is important to define what is meant here by the term "Black Church." While renowned scholars of the Black religious experience C. Eric Lincoln and Lawrence Mamiya acknowledged that the term "Black Church" may include smaller Black denominations, Black congregations within white denominations, and independent nondenominational churches, they set the stage for limiting the definition of the Black Church to seven large historic Black independent mainline denominations within the Methodist, Baptist, and Pentecostal traditions.[4] Yet, as Kelley Brown Douglas and Ronald E. Hopson contend:

> *The black church is a multitudinous community of churches, which are diversified by origin, denomination, doctrine, worshipping culture, spiritual expression, class, size and other less obvious factors. Yet, as disparate as black churches may seem, they share a special history, culture, and role in black life, all of which attest to their collective identity as the black church.*[5]

Distinguishing between what Williams calls the visible Black denominational churches that inflict "a multitude of sins against black women . . . on a daily basis"[6] and the "invisible black church" that "God works through . . . [on] behalf of the survival, liberation and positive, productive quality of life of suffering people"[7] and challenges the former to live up to the promise of its highest liberationist ideals, Delores Williams has argued:

> *The black church does not exist as an institution. Regardless of the sociological, theological, historical and pastoral attempts, the black church escapes precise definition. . . . Some believe it to be rooted deeply in the soul of the community memory of black folk. Some believe it to be the core symbol of the four-hundred-year-old African American struggle against white oppression with God in the struggle providing black people with spiritual and material resources for survival and freedom. Others believe it to be the places where black people come to worship God without white people being present. I believe the black church is the heart of hope in the black community's experience of oppression, survival struggle and its historic efforts toward complete liberation. . . . The black church is invisible, but we know it when we see it.*[8]

While I concur with Williams that the Black Church exists both in its visible and invisible forms, when I refer to the Black Church in this text I am speaking of the varied *visible* ecclesial groups of Christians of African descent, both inside and outside Black and white denominations, informed by the legacy of slavery and segregation in America and a suffering Jesus who revealed a preferential option for the oppressed. While this phenomenon has deep roots in the independent Black Church movement, the common tragedy and depth of racism experienced by Christians of African descent ensures its import for Black congregations and ecclesial groupings of various configurations that, consciously and unconsciously, live within the conflicting intersections of being Black and Christian in America.

Methodology

The methodology used in this book is descriptive, analytical, comparative, and constructive. Through a descriptive approach, I describe and situate each theologian's thoughts regarding Jesus's teachings on wealth and poverty within their historical contexts. However, it is through critical analysis of select writings of these theologians that the reader is further apprised of the ways in which each theologian's response to Jesus's position on poverty, wealth, and material redistribution either advances such a position or fosters what I call "a legacy of a theology of prosperity."

By comparing the views of these theologians with each other regarding their valuation of wealth and poverty, I have attempted to chronologically trace an ambivalent attitude toward Jesus's teachings on the subject of wealth and poverty in the Western Christian tradition from the patristic period onward. While comparative and analytical strategies are employed to test the validity of my claim, the constructive intent of this project is to build on the claim that this legacy has significance for the construction of a womanist soteriological perspective that at once addresses Black communities' and in particular Black women's, longing for "abundant living" and takes seriously Jesus's teaching on material redistribution.

Part One

A LEGACY OF LONGING, HISTORY OF LACK, AND THE PROBLEM FOR THE BLACK CHURCH

1

BLACK FOLKS, PROSPERITY GOSPELS, AND A LEGACY OF LONGING

SITUATING PROSPERITY PREACHING that is heard today in Black churches within Western Christianity's tradition of valuing wealth and spiritualizing poverty starts with understanding the contours of theologies of prosperity. There is a genealogy of African American theological ambivalence toward wealth accumulation, poverty, and materialism that is connected to Western Christianity's long-standing history of viewing the wealthy as divinely favored and the poor as less blessed. Various themes, streams of thought, and praxis have helped to sustain that ambivalence, while social, economic, and religious realities have held such ambivalence in place and the concept of power has served as its driving force.

Examining the genealogical connection between Black churchgoers' espousal of prosperity theologies and Western Christianity's long-standing embrace of wealth accumulation as divinely sanctioned is fundamental to offering a soteriological vision that addresses Black people's multifaceted oppression and legacy of longing for a better quality of life.

The Black Church and Black Life in America

Though its impact is oftentimes minimized by mainstream society, the Black Church has been the most prominent institution in the African American community. Whether as the "invisible institution"[1] of the United States antebellum period or as independent African American denominational churches, the Black Church has played a critical role in providing African Americans with the spiritual, social, political, and economic resources essential to their survival in a hostile, anti-Black, racist America. It served as a much-needed shelter in the time of storm. From the time of US slavery to the period of legalized racial segregation, to the 1950–1960 US Civil Rights Movement, and through the continuing psycho-emotional, sociopolitical, and economic assaults, African Americans have turned to the Black Church for refuge, leadership, and the agency to counter oppressive religious narratives and practices of white America.

Born during the period of Black enslavement, the Black Church signified Black resistance to an enslaving and dehumanizing white culture as it testified to God's affirmation of Black people's humanity. It rendered educational, health, banking, legal, and other services by establishing schools, clinics, banks, credit unions, insurance companies, low-income housing, and institutions within the Black community. It often served as a launchpad for Black sociopolitical involvement. It was the place in which African Americans developed their leadership skills and found the encouragement to forge ahead.

However, the Black Church did not always respond well to the Black community's complex needs. Theologian Gayraud Wilmore points out the Black Church's peaks and valleys of providing liberative leadership for the Black community. Chapter titles in Wilmore's *Black Religion and Black Radicalism* hint at the church's high and low points: "The Black Church Freedom Movement," "Black Religion and Black Nationalism," "The Deradicalization of the Black Church," "The Dechristianization of Black Radicalism," and "Black Power, Black People, and Theological Renewal."[2] At times, the church may have been ill-equipped to meet the complex needs of congregants and the Black community. At other times, the church showed an unwillingness to stray from views and strategies that were antithetical to Jesus's teachings and the Black community's well-being. While there are marked differences and dissimilarities between the religious orientations of African American and European American Christians, as Wilmore points out, the Black Church does indeed possess some substantive and oppressive features of white Western Christianity.[3] For instance, Black churches have a long and distinctive history of opposing Pauline "slave texts" and white supremacy. However, this opposing consciousness did not extend to critiquing the relationship between Christianity's theological ruminations about wealth and poverty and the vast economic inequality in the United States.

Given the pressure for subordinated groups to conform to the social norms of the dominating architects of a systemically oppressive culture, a marginalized group oftentimes internalizes aspects of oppressive ideologies into its own systems and structures. When this happens, a decisive blow is struck in favor of perpetuating prevailing systems of oppression. The blow is even more substantial when such oppressive systems are infused with religious and theo-ethical meaning because these ideologies become embedded with sacred authority. One can argue that such is the case with many African Americans' embrace of prosperity gospel in particular and Western Christianity's valuation of wealth, poverty, material acquisition, and the American economy as a whole.

Black Longings and the Rise of Prosperity Theologies

After the Atlantic slave trade era and continental phase from 1808 to 1906, the heritage of slavery would remain a defining reality for African Americans as they found themselves locked into second-class citizen status—legally, politically, and economically. The brief period of Reconstruction seemed to suggest that national standards of equal citizenship might finally prevail. However, by 1905, when legal segregation had been firmly established in both law and practice, most African Americans had become permanently trapped on the physical and social terrain of slavery's legacy. The religious life of African Americans would be fundamentally shaped by these realities as African Americans invested much time, energy, and resources to build religious institutions and reckon with the religious meaning of their experiences.

As Protestant evangelicalism was adapted to the traditions and realities of African American life, it gradually became the dominant form of religion among Blacks in America. Black Methodist and Baptist churches led the way in creating independent African American denominations. Black evangelicals also became part of a wide range of predominantly white denominations, though oftentimes they were relegated to segregated Black congregations. As a result, significant differences of religious belief, style, and organization could be found not only within Black evangelicalism, but also between it and its white religious counterpart.[4]

These Black congregations drew upon and interpreted differently a common stock of biblical images,[5] including the image of Christ. White evangelical Christology was fixated upon understanding the human and divine nature of Jesus as delineated in the Council of Chalcedon. African Americans grappled with the liberative significance of Jesus for a suffering, persecuted people. As such, they constructed an understanding more reflective of Jesus as their deliverer, co-sufferer, and reason for hope in the struggle for a resurrected, liberated existence.

Still, despite Black evangelicals' rejection of the racist posture of white evangelicalism,[6] Black evangelicalism shared with white evangelicalism interpretations of the Bible that provided both an account of God's past dealings with the world and a set of clues for deciphering the meaning of their current situation. While they drew differently on a common stock of biblical images and engaged in questioning their history, destiny, and all things human and divine, African Americans fell short of moving toward a critical analysis of Western Christianity's understanding of poverty and wealth acquisition propagated by prominent theologians of the early Church and later supported by the capitalist, classist economic and political structure of American society. This they did even as they argued against the inequitable appropriation of material resources. As womanist theologian Jacquelyn Grant notes, this may have been the case because "our fore parents were essentially poor by virtue of their race, [and] there was no real need for them to address classism as a separate reality."[7]

Instead, buying into "the American Success Syndrome,"[8] the Black Church endeavored to balance its pursuit of social justice with abundant living through economic gain. Indeed, abundance as a biblical image that included material acquisition has long been emphasized in African American religion. The image is connected with the idea of the church as an authoritative agent in the pursuit of economic uplift, righteousness, justice, and equity for all.[9] According to Lincoln and Mamiya, it was under the national leadership of Booker T. Washington that the economic role of Black churches gained traction. Washington, who was closely connected to Black churches and whose views on economics closely resembled those of many Black preachers, argued that Blacks could gain acceptance in America through economic gain and the "cultivation of morality."[10] Few Black clergy would take a more radicalized approach to address racial prejudice, discrimination, and economic inequity.

Black churches were also instrumental in promoting economic cooperation in Black communities; they played a central role in the creation of the first major Black-owned financial institutions.[11] Espousing strategies for both survival and liberation, the churches relied on extended kinship networks, bartering, and forming financial institutions and mutual aid societies. These churches served both as a protest against white racist practices and a means to meet the socioeconomic needs of African Americans. Thus, Black churches promoted communalism while trying to address their adherents' longing to be part of the American mainstream. As Lincoln and Mamiya state:

> *The survival strategy in the everyday economic life of black people [stressed] just get[ting] by or "survivin' one day at a time." It meant to stay alive "until my chance comes." Nevertheless, as important as the stage of survival economics was for poor people, it was inevitably marked by extreme dependence, uncertainty and insecurity. The liberation strategy in the black community, on the other hand, focused on gaining both upward mobility from poverty and eventual economic independence. There was an understanding that real freedom only comes with the attainment of a measure of economic base. [While] upward mobility or becoming middle class was not an end in itself . . . it was important because it allowed for the possibility of devising strategies for a greater economic independence in the future."*[12]

The Black Church played a crucial role in espousing an ethos of cooperative economic advancement and a liberation perspective that was critical of the dehumanizing and oppressive economic aspects of the American economy. Still, it largely accepted capitalism as a viable economic system. Indeed, the church failed to develop any serious critique of either the basis of American capitalism or the major values of the Protestant ethic: frugality, hard work, and individual achievement through self-help.

What was espoused was the idea that socioeconomic uplift demanded not a revaluation of wealth acquisition, but an opportunity to experience acceptance through wealth acquisition. Rather than challenging the system of American capitalism, most Black people and their churches wanted to be part of it. While the Black Church and its leadership furthered Black survival and liberation strategies, along with a Black cooperative self-help tradition, to address the existence of economic inequity, Black people did not see wealth acquisition or the inequitable social arrangements that resulted from such as the problem. Rather, they saw as problematic the inability to have equal access to acquiring financial resources.

Even the majority of Black Church leaders during the Civil Rights Movement who offered a formidable challenge to racial injustice failed to turn their critique toward the liberal capitalist economic system that exacerbates gross inequality. The aim was to dismantle structural barriers such as Jim Crow so that African Americans could have greater access to America's economic pie. Aside from the latter years of Martin Luther King Jr.'s life,[13] the ways in which the pie was being distributed were not necessarily a concern of most leaders within the Black Church. As Black people continued to combat the increasingly complex and myriad forms of marginalization, many Black preachers attempted to help their constituents re-vision the cognitive dissonance between their lived realities and the promise of American society. Addressing the longing for sociocultural and financial deliverance in the Black community, Black religious leaders maintained an ambivalence toward Jesus's teachings on wealth and poverty. Even as they challenged Jim Crow laws, political disenfranchisement, and other forms of bigotry and economic deprivation, they acquiesced to capitalistic notions of economic gain.

As concerns about how to address the oppression and disenfranchisement of Black Americans lingered, twentieth-century African Americans, able to soak up the intellectual, ideological, and spiritual life of the country as never before, engaged with many new religious movements. Whether they sought personal or socioeconomic power, tools with which to resist natal alienation and other forms of social death, or a way to work for the greater good, a number of African Americans explored and adopted into their own religious thinking new religious ideologies that promised a better of quality of life. These included New Thought, founded in 1840 by Phineas Quimby, who professed the mind's ability to heal the body; Unity School of Christianity, developed in 1903 by Myrtle and Charles Fillmore, who contended that positive thinking brought one close to divinity and that a person creates her own reality through her thinking; Science of Mind or Religious Science, founded by Ernest Holmes, who combined the ideas of Quimby and the Fillmores; and the Word of Faith movement, founded by Essek

William Kenyon, whose theological orientation was later made known to the contemporary charismatic community through the works of Kenneth E. Hagin Sr.[14]

Perhaps these ideas resonated with or affirmed the concepts that Blacks already held about the power of the Divine to manifest herself in the daily lives of faithful adherents. Perhaps they experienced these theological ideas as welcome responses to their persistent longing and genuine search for a remedy to their impoverished and oppressed segregated lives. Womanist theologian Stephanie Mitchem notes, "the stresses from economic deprivation, lack of control, and domination [were] not new in black communities. Nor [were] religious responses that can be termed 'prosperity preaching.'"[15] As Mitchem points outs, African Americans have a long history of seeking ways to remedy economic deprivation, racial oppression, and lack of political/sociocultural control.

Furthermore, theologies that incorporated a prosperity theme of "name it and claim it" were not totally foreign to them. Indeed, theological concepts about the power of God to become manifest in and through the daily lives of Black people had long been embraced and depended upon, whether that embrace and dependence was due in part to a lingering African-derived understanding of the Divine or a desire to break the chains of racism, injustice, and deprivation. What prosperity theology in contemporary times did introduce into the Black religious scene is a profoundly different way of understanding God as one who is bound to bestow blessings upon all who partake in aggressive tithing, positive confession, and an unerring belief in the right to increased personal prosperity as part of one's inheritance from God. These theologies of prosperity not only proffer that the acquisition of wealth is sanctioned by God and linked to God's favor, but also that wealth is the defining factor to experience abundant living or "the good and righteous life."

Contours of Today's Theologies of Prosperity

At its core, what is known today as prosperity theology—also known as word-of-faith theology, faith formula theology, positive confession theology, or prosperity gospel—involves the belief that God intends for Christians to be prosperous with worldly possessions and capital. A theology of prosperity legitimizes linking individual prosperity, social power, mobility, and the acquisition of material goods and capital to God's blessings. That Jesus required a radical renunciation or redistribution of material goods is, at minimum, set aside, if not altogether denounced. Instead, the ability to acquire wealth is an intrinsic blessed state, and renouncing and redistributing wealth is neither observed nor appreciated as an act of faith.

Prosperity theology not only sees wealth acquisition as sanctioned by God, it maintains that all who are faithful can obtain financial success. This theology argues that what is needed is not reform of inequitable economic, political, and social systems. Rather, what is needed is the right amount of faith, since an individual's faith can change her circumstances. Prosperity theology affirms a theological anthropology[16] that values not one's humanity but one's capacity to acquire and accumulate wealth and materiality. It sets aside serious analysis of or active engagement in dismantling systematic disenfranchisement and directs individuals to re-envision themselves, their self-worth, and what it means to live the higher Christian life. Adherents are taught that as a new creation in Christ, adherents are entitled to and capable of reaping immeasurable material and immaterial benefits while avoiding a "defeated life" or living "beneath their privileges."[17] Abundant life is and has already been made available. The task is simply to faithfully name what one wants, boldly claim it, and trust in God's promises of earthly rewards. Conversely, the inability to transcend poverty or lack of wealth is due to one's disobedience and lack of faith.

Prosperity theology is often spoken of as a twentieth-century phenomenon proffered by the Word of Faith movement. That movement grew out of nineteenth-century New England's New Thought movement which was led by Phineas Parkhurst Quimby. Quimby was a practitioner of mesmerism, a fusion of healing practices and metaphysical thought based on Franz Anton Mesmer's discovery of hypnosis. Quimby made two assertions: that the mind could overcome illness through mental and spiritual alignment and that he had uncovered Jesus's healing technique in discovering the connection between the mind and disease.[18] Quimby's teachings would influence other healing, positive-thinking, and deliverance movements to proffer the mind's ability to heal the body and impact one's living and sense of well-being.[19] These movements include Neo-Pentecostalism, with its stress upon the power of the Holy Spirit for healing and prosperity in every aspect of one's life. Likewise, new forms of evangelical, charismatic Christianity that developed in the United States since World War II arose to play a critical role in furthering prosperity theologies, especially in Black prosperity preaching.[20]

However, the core beliefs and practices regarding materialism and wealth, which are central to prosperity theologies, have a history within Western Christian thought that dates back well beyond these more recent moments. These beliefs and practices hinge on the understanding of wealth as a blessing or reward from God, individual acquisition of capital as a Divine right, and the spiritualization of wealth and poverty. Christianity has traditionally resolved this agitation by allegorizing Jesus's statements on wealth and poverty and transforming them into statements on interior attitudes—aligning true poverty with piety and humility—and deeming discussions of external poverty to be irrelevant, missing the point, or spiritually immature.

Core Beliefs, Practices, Values, and Messages

There are essentially three core beliefs and practices associated with the contemporary prosperity gospel message. The first affirms that to live the higher Christian life believers must know who they are in Christ. This understanding of Christian identity is premised upon the professed spiritual laws of the biblical text, which is viewed as a contract between believers and God. Because God is understood to be faithful and just, the believer must uphold her end of the covenant relationship to receive all of God's promises and blessings that come with salvation.[21] This type of faith allows one to exercise spiritual authority and walk in divine favor.

The result is the capacity to engage the second core belief and practice—to name whatever one wants and to claim possession of it by faith. This act of naming and claiming it—known as the ritual practice of positive confession—is critical to prosperity theology. Once believers have a clear understanding of who they are in Christ, states Milmon,

> *They are able to speak the same words about themselves that God has spoken about them in the Bible. This allows them to access and exercise the power vested in them through their identification with Christ's finished work on the cross. According to this notion,*

> *believers can "think God's thoughts after him and speak his words after him" as well. In the biblical account of creation, God spoke and there was light . . . the Faith Message [prosperity gospel] teaches believers the same word-creating power is theirs as born-again Christians . . . and that it is a spiritual law that the spoken word sets creative (or destructive) forces in motion.*[22]

The argument goes like this: naming and claiming what you desire and rightfully deserve as a born-again Christian prepares your heart and mind to receive the seeds of knowledge that will allow you to reap your harvest—the financial and material prosperity that God wishes to confer upon you as a righteous, confessing member of the body of Christ.

These believe it, conceive it, and receive it confessions include "I'll never be broke another day in my life," "I am expecting supernatural increase," and "I am expecting supernatural debt-cancellation this week." Likewise, adherents are expected to offer replies such as "blessed and highly favored" or "blessed on the top and rising" to the question "How are you?" A believer is dissuaded from replying "I am fine" and discouraged from professing "I'm not feeling well" or "things are not going well," since faith is a confession and since the power of faith manifests through the spoken word. Thus, believers are encouraged to speak only in the positive regarding their life circumstances. Negative statements indicate a lack of faith. An example of this is the refusal of the pastor of a prosperity gospel and deliverance church in Sacramento, California, to use the term "poor" to describe those who are impoverished. Instead, the pastor employs the term "persons between blessings" to refer to those who are economically disadvantaged.[23]

The third core belief of the prosperity gospel message is a worldview that emphasizes material prosperity and physical health as the divine right of every Christian.[24] Such a worldview rejects that Jesus was poor. Rather, adherents reason that Jesus was financially prosperous and that he desires the same for all believers. Jesus and his disciples "were not poor but had houses and a common treasury from which Judas Iscariot embezzled funds."[25] Even the teaching that Christians are called to identify with the poor is understood as an inaccurate reading of the biblical text.

Proponents of prosperity theology argue that once believers know who Christ is and who they are in Christ, and once they confess their divine right to prosperity and memorize Scriptures that support such beliefs, they can shun poverty and control their physical and financial fate. The practices of seeing oneself as entitled to what one desires materially and naming and claiming one's rightful blessings not only are part of a person's spiritual salvation, but they are also critical to and symbolize the person's faith walk. Divine health and wealth are not merely the fruits of the higher life, they are synonymous with the higher life.

Just as one's faith in Christ can be measured by one's prosperity, one's lack of wealth and health is an indictment against one's faith in Christ. Poverty and illness are no longer social realities for those in Christ. They are instead a mindset and spiritual curse upon those who do not know "who they are in Christ" and those who fail to uphold their contractual agreement with God as set forth in the Bible.[26]

Consequently, it is through faith and positive confessions that an individual can transcend her physical state of being and the world's systems of oppression, reaching a metaphysical existence in the physical world. Prosperity theologies use here a pseudo-Platonic understanding of reality mediated through the writings of the Apostle Paul. Plato's conception of the two realms—visible and intelligible—is used to articulate two levels of existence, the lower and the higher levels of life. Humanity is born into this lower level of existence, the carnal realm. But unlike Plato's philosophical construction, prosperity theology does not trap humanity in an allegorical cave of existence. An exit from the lower level into a higher level of existence is extended by Jesus.[27] In this higher level, persons are no longer bound to the laws of the carnal realm. Here, the laws of nature no longer apply to the believer.

Because of the belief that people can reach a metaphysical state of being, churches that embrace prosperity theology are not as concerned with addressing socioeconomic inequality and systems of domination as they are with personal material gain. Initiating community development corporations, job training, health clinics, educational programs, or programs that seek to change social structures that are dehumanizing and oppressive is not a high priority. Biblical passages such as "as a man thinketh, so he is" (Prov 23:7) are interpreted literally. Therefore, advocating for policy changes or social programs and resources is not seen as helpful to those who are not walking in their anointing because they are unclear about who they are in Christ. To overcome negative social factors such as racism, sexism, classism, and poverty, one must overcome one's internalized negative mindset that unleashes these dynamics into the world.

Prosperity theology also devalues those individuals who continue to experience poverty and sickness at the same time as it elevates the propertied and capital-rich, particularly those from formerly impoverished conditions who successfully overcame socioeconomic hardship. Having a rich lifestyle is associated with truly being saved and blessed by God, while the poor are defined as cursed and presumed to be living in sin, according to the explicit and implicit lessons contained in prosperity teaching.[28] God neither sides with nor has a preferential option for the poor.

In this sense, a theology of prosperity maintains a preferential option for the wealthy—those who own the most property and capital—even as it appears to speak to the desires of the poor who seek relief from their impoverished existence. Although a theology of prosperity can appear to support the desires of persons who are marginalized and who long for a better quality of life, it never questions the systems that support and sustain the rich–poor divide and the unjust distribution of power, privilege, and wealth.

Erasing the idea that an individual is linked to, defined by, accountable to, and responsible for others within their community or world, a person is free to reorient herself and her sense of self-worth to pursue individual gain regardless of the well-being of others. The acquisition and accumulation of personal wealth to experience human fulfillment is bolstered by a focus on the self for the self. Thus, a utilitarian view of the world where people, places, and things are stepping-stones toward personal gain is understood as the way to liberate oneself from poverty and hardships.

Sociologist Milmon Harrison notes that contemporary prosperity theology draws its message and core values from evangelicalism, neo-Pentecostalism or the charismatic movement, and New Thought metaphysics or the psychology of positive thinking.[29] From its evangelical roots, prosperity theology adopts the emphasis on personal conversion through spiritual rebirth—being born again—and its high regard for biblical inerrancy and authority over every aspect of one's life. From its neo-Pentecostal or charismatic roots comes the emphasis upon the Holy Spirit's role in empowering Christians to live healthy, vital, prosperous, and productive lives.[30]

While Black Pentecostalism is often considered a US creation,[31] it cannot easily be separated from white Pentecostalism that grew out of the Holiness movement and has roots in John Wesley's thought, Methodism, and those who carried Wesleyan theology onto American soil.[32] Neo-Pentecostalism refers to a contemporary form of the traditional charismatic or Pentecostal movement, which emerged in the later part of the twentieth century, that puts less stress upon baptism of the Holy Spirit and speaking in tongues and more emphasis upon the power of the Holy Spirit for healing, prophetic utterances, vibrant worship and music, and prosperity for believers. Traditionally, Pentecostals in general adhere to strict prohibitions against pleasures—such as consuming alcohol, playing cards, dancing, listening to secular music, dating, and other so-called worldly activities—and a puritanical asceticism. However, neo-Pentecostals are more lenient with their emphasis on a Christian's freedom to be led by the Spirit in every aspect of life.

Thus, neo-Pentecostals are known for having lavish sanctuaries and an unapologetic attitude toward material possessions. Furthermore, there is an emphasis on personal experiences over communal concerns and even doctrinal authority. While neo-Pentecostals appeal to the Bible as the authoritative source for Christian living, they tend to emphasize scriptural texts that support personal blessings and deliverance rather than Scriptures that speak of communal responsibility and judgment. Sociologist Shayne Lee asserts,

> *The underlying assumption is that the death and resurrection of Jesus Christ provided Christians with the ability to live in total victory, financial prosperity, and perfect health. However, God's "hands are tied" from blessing many Christians who lack faith and misappropriate biblical principles, thus explaining why all Christians are not experiencing prosperous and healthy lives.*[33]

Finally, it is New Thought metaphysics that offered prosperity theology the belief that material prosperity and other earthly rewards are available if believers apply certain principles to realize God's blessings in every situation of their everyday lives. What began as a movement fixated on the generative power of the mind to exact healing through positive thinking became a component central to metaphysical Christianity and prosperity gospel theologies. New Thought mind-over-matter principles helped to create a form of metaphysical Christianity that prioritized an individual's spiritual power to, when rightly aligned with God's power, reimagine, control, and create the material world they desired. Proponents believe that memorizing Scriptures, thinking positively, meditating correctly, professing positive thoughts, and speaking accordingly gives them access to a power directly from God to control their physical well-being and financial fortune.

Early Leaders of Prosperity Theology in the Black Community

At the turn of the twentieth century, the New Thought movement and metaphysical religion permeated almost every aspect of the American sociocultural landscape. Bestselling self-help books, plays, radio broadcasts, advice columns, and street corner pamphlets popularized metaphysical religious concepts about the mind, body, self-actualization, and access to prosperity and the Good Life. New Thought messages also promulgated from lecture halls and churches, promising religious and metaphysical answers to pressing social problems.

These messages caught the attention of several Black spiritualists, prophets, and preachers who were intent on offering a gospel of hope, uplift, prosperity, and opportunity. These religious leaders adopted and adapted New Thought metaphysical ideals into their theologies of materialism. A significant number of Black migrants who made their way to northern and midwestern cities during the Great Migration would come to embrace these new hope-infused self-help messages that guaranteed spiritual and material deliverance. These new Black transplants sought a faith that could provide a better quality of life in an anti-Black America.

It is difficult to pinpoint exactly when African Americans began to engage with New Thought metaphysics,[34] as various forms of metaphysical religion including New Thought attracted the attention of African Americans from across a spectrum of religious ideologies and social classes. However, examining the ministries and impact of three religious leaders who played a major role in introducing metaphysical religion to large numbers of African Americans gives us insight into how early New Thought Christian practitioners set the stage for contemporary prosperity theologies in the Black Church. These leaders were: Reverend Major Jealous Divine, or "Father Divine"; Johnnie Colemon, referred to in the African American New Thought circles as "the First Lady of New Thought"; and Frederick "Reverend Ike" Eikerenkoetter. Their large ministries preceded the ministries of today's Black prosperity gospel preachers and inspired new directions in African American Christianity.

Father Divine

At a time when African Americans were struggling to eke out a living, Father Major Jealous Divine, born George Baker Jr. in 1879 in Rockville, Maryland, encouraged them to desire more for themselves and to believe that with God's help they could do more than merely survive; they could thrive. Baker grew up during the post-Reconstruction era when the federal government had stopped assistance to former slaves, and in a state where, though Blacks suffered segregation and discrimination, they nonetheless enjoyed limited opportunities unavailable to Blacks in other states. Baker's experience was unique. Black landownership was common and Black men participated in the electoral process because of the 1870 ratification of the Fifteenth Amendment.[35] Although entrenched social, political, and economic barriers kept Blacks disenfranchised, Black citizens of Montgomery County, where Baker lived, organized and agitated for legal protection against disenfranchising laws including voter restrictions. For Baker, whose life was not qualitatively different from his enslaved ancestors, but whose family could claim to be self-supporting landowners, the community's emphasis upon individualism, self-help, and self-reliance was a means of achieving a better quality of life.[36]

The most influential factor upon Baker's life was religion, notably the Methodist Church. Methodism espoused the belief that spirituality came from the heart rather than from laborious study. Consequently, the Black Methodist church that he attended selected preachers who demonstrated inspirational speaking ability, not just those who possessed formal clerical training. Thus, Baker discovered a loving community where he found acceptance and respect. Through participating in worship services and Sunday school, he found a place that afforded him admiration, power, and opportunities for success.[37]

Baker would also find inspiration from other religious traditions, including Quakerism. However, at the root of Baker's early religious experiences was Black religion, the combination of traditional African religions and Black Christianity passed down through generations of African American slaves. This experience provided Baker not only with specific rituals and theological tenets but a legacy of syncretism.

As Baker approached early adulthood, external and internal forces began to erode the place that mainline denominational Black churches held for him as the primary originator and agent of Black radicalism and resistance to racism. Thus, as changing economic and social formations in the South and North invigorated the northward relocation of millions of African Americans to what they conceived as the "Promise Land" for Black people,[38] mainline denominational Black churches became less able to adequately address the needs of these emerging African American poor migrant communities. The decline of mainline denominational Black churches as the central, most powerful institution in Black communities can be attributed to rigid hierarchies, new requirements for formal training for ministry, and the inability to provide social relief to the growing number of urban poor.[39] While preachers appeared content with maintaining a moralistic focus, asserting the benefits of the afterlife, "a religious alternative for working class Blacks evolved—the independent storefront church."[40]

Baker continued his spiritual development through Black storefront churches, gaining leadership training, refining his preaching skills, and blending several religious ideologies from Methodism, Catholicism, and Black storefront church traditions to formulate his own theology. To this blend he would later add Charles and Myrtle Fillmore's brand of New Thought. As historian Jill Watts notes:

> *[The Fillmores'] brand of New Thought provided a formula for the acceptance and inclusion of African Americans without altering or threatening the structure of American society. Exercising mind-power and oneness with God, anyone, regardless of race, had the potential to achieve spiritual and social equality. Blacks possessed just as much divinity as whites and, by applying mind-power, could overcome oppression and reap the benefits of American*

> *enterprise. [Thus] Positive thinking allowed African Americans to assert control over their destiny and to combat their feelings of powerlessness in white America. If it was the Race Mind that held Blacks in bondage, then by following [the Fillmores'] guidelines, African Americans could conquer white oppression. The solution to racism was quite clear; it rested on a spiritual cleansing of the American mind.*[41]

As New Thought spread, some of its disciples, such as Baker, added the Protestant work ethic to their teachings, contending that positive thinking also brought financial and material rewards. Like Charles and Myrtle Fillmore's theology, Baker's theology retained a strong capitalistic tone. Baker warned followers not to become enslaved to money, but he also encouraged them to strive for prosperity, purchase property, and buy nothing on credit. There was no righteousness in poverty because God's kingdom held sufficient riches for all. Likewise, poverty, a product of negative thinking, was an indication of estrangement from God's presence.[42]

With his new theology that opposed excessive wealth and greed but endorsed wealth acquisition and affluence as a reflection of a state of grace, Baker moved to Harlem in New York City in 1917. There he began the Father Divine Peace Mission and changed his name to Reverend Major Jealous Divine, reinforcing through his name his claim that he was God. His followers addressed him simply as Father Divine. Despite the adoption of New Thought, the Peace Mission movement closely resembled the traditional African American church with which Harlem's Black community was familiar. Father Divine required his followers to follow a strict code of ethics that included no drinking or smoking. He also prohibited racial discrimination among his adherents and established Black businesses and urged congregants to patronize those businesses. He encouraged his followers to commit to social justice and a "righteous government" in which Jim Crow would be repealed, lynching ended, and equality for all realized.[43]

What set Father Divine's church apart from the traditional Black Church was its unapologetic emphasis on prosperity and self-help within a religious context. This was supplemented by Father Divine's Holy Communion banquets and other community-focused programs that were meant to counter scarcity and racial oppression and challenge the impoverishment and destitution foisted on Blacks in the United States.[44] Father Divine furnished lavish meals, clothing, and shelter to destitute Blacks and offered a theology that promised a better life and brighter future in the here and now, regardless of economic status.[45]

Johnnie Colemon

Johnnie Colemon is another important although little-known figure who paved the way for the infusion of the New Thought message and prosperity theology into the African American community.[46] Colemon was the founder of Christ Universal Temple in Chicago, the first predominantly African American Unity (New Thought) Church,[47] and several organizations in the African American New Thought movement. A former schoolteacher, Colemon was raised as a Methodist in the rural southern town of Columbus, Mississippi, and was introduced to the Unity (New Thought) faith by her mother. After refusing to accept a medical diagnosis that gave her six months to live, Colemon turned to Unity's New Thought literature as a means of recovery. At the urging of her mother, she enrolled in the Unity School of Christianity founded by the Fillmores.[48] Like the Fillmores, who both attributed their recovery from illnesses to practicing New Thought principles, Colemon would also confess being physically healed as a result of attending the Unity School and practicing her new-found faith. A trailblazer in the New Thought movement, Colemon would initiate a number of firsts, including being the first African American student to live on the school's campus at Unity Village, and the first Black to serve as president of the Association of Unity Churches.[49]

Coleman's experience at the Unity School was not without challenges. While the Unity School's literature professed that all people are divine, equal, and made in God's image, its segregated campus life told a different story. The school welcomed Black students to Unity Village to enroll in classes with one caveat: They could not live in campus housing. While Black students could participate in courses and other activities, they were not allowed to stay overnight or eat with their white classmates. The third Black student to study at Unity, Colemon was the first to challenge the school's discriminatory practices. After commuting thirty miles to and from her classes for two years, Colemon threatened to leave the school because of its housing discrimination. Her threat prompted the school to change its housing policy and offer her a place to live in Unity Village. However, the facility that she was offered, and later told to share with other Black students, was a subpar cottage in a distant corner of the campus set apart from the cottages of the white residents. Housing for Black students at the Unity School remained unequal for years to come and Colemon continued to confront the racist practices of the Unity School and its associational arm, the Association of Unity Churches.

In 1956, Colemon founded Chicago's Christ Unity Temple. In 1974, she left the Association of Unity Churches because of its pervasive racism and, using the Christ Unity Temple congregation, founded the Christ Universal Temple for Better Living, taking "Unity" out of the name.[50] During that same year, she founded the Universal Foundation for Better Living, an association of African American New Thought metaphysical congregations led primarily by ministers trained at her institute, and the Johnnie Colemon Institute, a school of metaphysics. By the late 1980s, the Universal Foundation for Better Living would boast more than twenty-three member churches.[51] The foundation also serves as the parent organization to the largest metaphysical bookstore in the Midwest, the Colemon Academy elementary school, a banquet facility, a restaurant, and a multimedia center. A media televangelist pioneer, Colemon began appearing weekly with her show, *Better Living with Jonnie Colemon*, which aired in thirteen markets. By 1981, Colemon's broadcast reached a greater audience than she could through the three services held at her church.[52] Her message was clear:

> *heaven and hell are not places; but they are states of mind . . . when you are sick; you are in hell, when you are broke; you are in hell. To be in heaven is to enjoy prosperity, and prosperity does not just mean money. . . . [It] means love, health, joy, and peace—all the good things. But it does include money . . .*

For Colemon, "money is God in action. God is my source of supply . . ."[53] Her argument that money can be the instrument through which God's message is heard on earth is the argument that believers use to answer detractors who warn against being enamored with wealth and ignoring Jesus's warnings against trusting in earthly treasures. For Colemon's followers, better living includes helping oneself to all forms of physical, social, emotional, and material prosperity. It calls for individuals to practice living a better life through changing their thoughts and speech to manifest positive outcomes. Here having faith and experiencing a better life is seen as an individual decision. Little is said about confronting social systems, structures, and environmental realities that impede a community's quality of living. Nor is the link between individual well-being and communal well-being explored.

Still, Colemon's prescriptive gospel of wealth—a self-help gospel that is meant to be followed and not simply studied—captured the attention of an expanse of African Americans seeking to reimagine themselves as inwardly divine and outwardly empowered. Moreover, her leadership in New Thought gave particular license to the religious imaginations of African American women. As the founder and pastor of one of the largest churches in Chicago, Colemon presented a new narrative regarding the religious leadership of Black women that ran counter to the generally accepted portrayal of them as the backdrop, support, and secondary members of a ministry team headed by men. Her ordaining and mentoring Black women paved the way for others to become founders of congregations and institutions in the New Thought movement, including singer-actress Della Reese-Lett, who founded Understanding Principles for Better Living Church in Los Angeles and Mary A. Tumpkin, who, in collaboration with Colemon, founded the Johnnie Colemon Theological Seminary.

Although Coleman is a forerunner to today's Black prosperity preachers engaged in spreading a prosperity gospel message that synthesizes New Thought metaphysics with evangelical, charismatic Christianity, her story is often overlooked. Yet her emphasis on Holy materialism[54] and insistence that God's intention is for adherents to prosper regarding "health, love, peace of mind, all that God is, all the good things of life"[55] clearly marks her as an important contributor.

Reverend Ike

Frederick J. Eikerenkoetter II, better known as Reverend Ike, founded the United Church and Science of Living Institute in 1969. Eikerenkoetter was known for his custom-tailored suits, diamond rings, fleet of Rolls-Royces adorned with mink, and charismatic ability to impel the most socially downtrodden to walk with the gait of a millionaire. He was also among the first African American preachers to use an amphitheater as a place of worship, build an in-house video production center, and package and distribute his brand of prosperity preaching to a national audience via television and radio. Eikerenkoetter blazed a trail whose path contemporary Black prosperity preachers currently tread.

Eikerenkoetter was born on June 1, 1935, in Ridgeland, South Carolina. His parents separated when he was five years old, and the separation plunged young Eikerenkoetter and his mother into deep poverty. Eikerenkoetter commonly evoked and embraced the image of a shoeless and shirtless boy who followed his mother to the one-room schoolhouse where she worked as a teacher and was paid $65 a month.[56] Later, Eikerenkoetter followed his father's footsteps into the ministry and began preaching at the age of fourteen at a Holiness-Pentecostal church. Within a year, Bible Way Baptist Church of Ridgeland, where Eikerenkoetter was raised, appointed him as pastor.[57]

Eikerenkoetter left the rural South for the North. For many Black people like Eikerenkoetter who moved to cities such as Chicago, Detroit, Philadelphia, and New York, there was a spiritual dimension to the Great Migration. As historian Milton Sernett points out, the religious imagery that framed the migration for African Americans was bound in the conceptualization of the North as the Promised Land.[58] This of course was coupled with the pull of a stimulated northern industrial economy resulting from the wars and the increased demand for labor.

Eikerenkoetter returned to Ridgeland just long enough to organize the United Church of Jesus Christ for All People, then moved back to Boston and established the Miracle Temple in 1965. Here, he attempted to find his niche as a faith healer, once confessing in an interview that,

> *Faith healing, that was the big thing at the time, and I was just about the best in Boston, snatching people out of wheelchairs and off their crutches, pouring some oil over them while I commanded them to walk or see or hear. I don't know if I cured many folks—it's a wonder I didn't kill somebody, though.*[59]

Within a year, Eikerenkoetter would relocate to New York City and renovate the dilapidated Sunset Theater in Harlem in 1966. He shortened his name to make it easier to become well known, donned custom-tailored suits and expensive jewelry, and in 1969 bought the historic Palace Auditorium, a five-thousand-seat abandoned theater in Washington Heights where he established the United Church and Science of Living Institute. After massive renovations, the United Church's theater boasted gold-plated ornamentation, crystal chandeliers, seating for five thousand people, and recording and production studios that enabled Eikerenkoetter to broadcast his services nationally over television and to more than eighty-nine radio stations.

Eikerenkoetter's theological and ideological shift seemed to coincide with his new surroundings. Discarding much of his Baptist and Pentecostal roots and evangelical posture, he adopted a thaumaturgical—the ability to change one's reality—posture that he called *The Science of Living*. This message promulgated:

- The notion that salvation must be achieved in the here and now.
- Positive thinking.
- The notion that God dwells in everyone.
- The notion that thoughts govern behavior.
- The belief that healing emanates from individual desire.
- A rejection of the devil as a tangible entity.
- An approval of monetary and material acquisitiveness.
- A rejection of the traditional Christian idea of sin.[60]

Envisioning his theological message as a message of self-awareness, Eikerenkoetter stated,

> *My philosophy may be described as self-image psychology. The ultimate goal is to teach the individual to be master of his own mind and affairs by changing his own self-image. Through positive self-awareness, the individual can change the conditions and circumstances in his life. I teach the individual that he can be what he wants to be, can do what he wants to do and that he can have what he wants to have, through the presence and power of God which is within each person.*[61]

Like Father Divine and Colemon, Eikerenkoetter was influenced by New Thought because it placed greater power and responsibility upon the individual to affect the course of her or his life. Eikerenkoetter taught that to concern oneself with the nature and being of God was to concern oneself with oneself. The human mind is the only real God in the universe, and that God is in the possession of every individual. "God is not someone else, somewhere else, sometime else. God is here and now and living, sometimes dormant in everyone."[62] His theology also shunned traditional conceptions of heaven and hell.

Eikerenkoetter's theological formation was also shaped by the syncretization of religious forms. The conversionist strand of the Black evangelical tradition of the rural South, which emphasized rigid behavioral codes for proving parishioners "holy and acceptable before God" (Rom 12:1), had a great impact on Eikerenkoetter's theology. Likewise, Eikerenkoetter drew from the Pentecostal healing revivalism that flourished in the post–World War II period and was spread by a new cadre of healing revivalists such as the Reverend Oral Roberts.[63]

Eikerenkoetter was the first to package this new gospel of prosperity within the African American religious ethos and successfully market it to the Black community on a national platform. He taught that "the lack of money is the root of all evil"[64] and proclaimed, "I like money. I need money. I want money . . . money is not sinful in its right place. Money is good."[65]

African American Women and Today's Prosperity Theologies

Ultimately, Black prosperity churches seek an opening that exploits the longing for sociocultural and financial deliverance within the Black community. Black mainline churches have failed to counter such exploitations with theologies or praxes that address Black longings and embrace Jesus's teachings on wealth acquisition and equity. Instead, mainline churches offer little more than nostalgic understandings of the historical form and function of the Black Church in the United States. Few offer a liberative theology that leaves Black women and men hopeful of being delivered from lives constrained—physically, socially, economically, and politically—by oppressive systems and practices. As Black Christians continue to look for ways to address, as womanist theologian

Delores Williams states, "black women's issues and life struggles and . . . the black community's historic struggle to survive and develop a positive productive quality of life in the face of death . . .,"[66] many flock to churches preaching a gospel of prosperity. These churches espouse a myth of equal opportunity and equate God's transformative movement with material acquisition and socioeconomic gain. Feeling able to glimpse an alternate kingdom where "the last shall be first and the first shall be last" (Matt 20:16) in the here and now, Black Christians embrace a soteriology of capitalism.

For African American women, in particular, who live under what womanist theologian Jacquelyn Grant refers to as the "triple Jeopardy" of racism, classism, and sexism, feeling able to transcend the dominance and oppression that is projected upon their bodies is deeply desired.[67] No longer would Black women be reduced to being single mothers, divorcees, hoes, or bitches as they take on more socially accepted and God-sanctioned roles of "God's leading lady," "anointed woman of God," or "Daddy's little girl."[68] These so-called proper roles are viewed as conferring holiness, redemption, respect, and a rightful place in the Black Church and society upon Black women.

While these theologically sanctioned roles may help Black women feel a sense of belonging in the Black faith community, they also are part of the construction of gender roles that privilege male patriarchy at the expense of female agency. According to prosperity worldviews, Black women's submission to patriarchal privilege allows them—and Black men—to be in the will of God and the African American family to experience God's anointing. This submission also allows Black women to find and be in a right relationship with their holy Black Prince Charming or "Sanctified Strong Black Man." Black women's acceptance of these roles signals their submission to the male coverings of the Father God, father in their family, and all other male authorities. Likewise, submission involves rejecting anything—Black women's agency, affinity to matriarchy, lesbian, transgender, and nonbinary orientations, or a hermeneutic of resistance—that makes Black women deviate from these roles. Open conversations about mutuality and gender inequities are unnecessary, according to this worldview, unless they help someone accept these God-sanctioned roles.

The writings of contemporary prosperity preacher Bishop Thomas "T. D." Jakes, arguably the leading international televangelist, espouse this worldview.

Jakes's affirmation of women and his willingness to address women's concerns make it difficult to dismiss him as a raving patriarch. Compared to other leading figures in the prosperity circles, Jakes is seen as a Black male feminist.

T. D. Jakes

An ordained preacher in the Apostolic church, Jakes was born in South Charleston, West Virginia, and raised in poverty. After preaching throughout West Virginia in small storefront churches, Jakes organized his first congregation, Greater Emmanuel Temple of Faith in Montgomery, West Virginia, and shortly after met and married Serita Ann Jamison, a local coal miner's daughter. The couple lived in poverty for some time and repeatedly relocated Jakes's congregation until they finally came to the affluent suburb Cross Lanes, where Jakes began his successful women's Sunday school class, "Woman, Thou Art Loosed." The class offered a message of hope and healing to Black women dealing with issues that African American mainline denominational churches often ignore—sexual, physical, and mental abuse, child molestation, and domestic violence.

In 1992, Jakes was invited to preach by Bishop Carlton Pearson of the Azusa Fellowship at Higher Dimension Ministries at a regional conference. An excerpt of Jakes's sermon, "Behind Closed Doors,"[69] which was aimed at healing women's hurts, was aired on Pearson's Sunday evening service on the Trinity Broadcast Network (TBN) to advertise the conference's videotape series. Paul Crouch, TBN president and owner, aired the hour-long sermon in its entirety for the next eight weeks. When Pearson invited Jakes to be the keynote preacher at the Azusa conference in 1993, over twelve thousand people showed up and Jakes preached his infamous sermon based on his women's Bible study class, "Woman, Thou Art Loosed."[70]

Jakes's publication of *Woman, Thou Art Loosed* as a book soon followed. The book's wide exposure coupled with Jakes's presence at the Azusa conference helped to draw thousands nationwide to his Woman, Thou Art Loosed and Man Power conferences. Within two years of headlining Azusa, Jakes was a national figure and a millionaire. His conspicuous consumption, however, inflamed some members in his working-class community, and he departed West Virginia in 1996 with his personal staff and fifty other families for Dallas, Texas, to establish the Potter's House church.

Although Jakes emphasizes economic empowerment, he distinguishes his theological perspective, and even social and economic agenda, from the prosperity gospel and Word of Faith movement. He situates himself between the ascetic dimensions of Pentecostalism that eschew worldly goods and faith teachers who delineate wealth as a sign of godliness. While regarding both deficiency and excess as vices to overcome, Jakes maintains that poverty must not be equated with godliness because impoverished Christians have limited possibilities of affecting change in society. Jakes maintains that Christians should not look to the monastic tradition of material denial nor demonize material success as a response to their own inability to advance materially in society.[71] A believer has a duty to pursue and exploit an opportunity to make a profit as fulfillment of one's duty to glorify God with one's labor. This pursuit, however, does not mean that wealth is a sign of one's faith.

While Jakes has publicly labeled prosperity gospel as "magic . . . [and] a simple solution to a long-term problem,"[72] along with those who espouse and believe in it as people who "believe their identity and acceptance by God is seen in the acquisition of things," his public protestation against the gross materialism of prosperity gospel has not altered his aesthetic embrace of its luxurious accoutrements. With his seven-figure publishing contract with Penguin Putnam Publishers, a highly successful annual summer Megafest gathering, a multimillion-dollar spiritual enterprise that produces books, audios, videos, movies, music, and plays, and web and conference services, Jakes has become one of America's financial elite. He is also seen as a voice of dispossessed, violated Black women whose churches had long ignored their hurts and blamed them for being abused. Believed by some to be a male supremacist, Jakes is regarded by millions of others as someone who is in tune with the concerns of struggling Black women.

Because Jakes appears to champion the cause of Black women in every sector of society, he appears to dismantle the myth of the Strong Black Man.[73] But a critical look at his writings, particularly his early work, uncovers essentialist themes of manhood that promote the Strong Black Man myth. In *Loose That Man & Let Him Go*, Jakes calls for male restoration to a place of authority and purpose, often employing hypermasculine metaphors to explain the essence of manhood. Using phrases like "there is a hunter in you whether you are stalking a contract, a deer, or a woman," he reinforces themes of male domination and female subjugation.[74] Jakes asserts that Black men need to take pride in being men, and he contrasts male indifference with a stereotypical depiction of women. He states,

> *Women, for the most part, enjoy being women. They surround themselves with beautiful things—flowers and lacy, delicate things that help to frame and enhance the beauty of their femininity.*[75]

Jakes's gendered understanding of men and women affirms the power dynamics that place African American women on the underside of Strong Black Male agency. Even the passive acceptance of liberation signified by *Woman, Thou Art Loosed*[76] contrasts the agency encoded in *Man Power.*[77] Similarly, the challenge he presents to men in *So You Call Yourself a Man?*[78] and *Real Men Pour In*[79] is different than that offered to women in *The Lady, Her Lover, and Her Lord*[80] or *Daddy Loves His Girls.*[81] While the books directed at African American men present a call to responsibility, the books directed at African American women insinuate a parasitic womanhood that is essentially connected to a loving God at best and an earthly male figure at worst. These roles, Black women are told, are salvific for women to counter a life of hopelessness and despair.

Creflo Dollar

Creflo A. Dollar Jr., senior pastor of World Changers Church International in College Park, Georgia and New York City, does not speak of his two churches as being rooted in or particularly concerned with the Black community. Yet the overwhelming majority of his nearly forty thousand members—99 percent—are African American, most of whom are poor and working class. Dollar's ministry is part of the predominantly white neo-Charismatic Word of Faith movement and ecclesiastical perspective that emerged as part of the post–World War II charismatic revivals in the United States. This movement is wedded to views of US world dominance, capitalism, and patriarchy. Dollar developed his prosperity theology alongside white preachers Kenneth E. Hagan Sr. and Kenneth Copeland of Fort Worth, Texas. The three core Word of Faith beliefs that Dollar espouses are: (1) Scripture is a contract between believers and God that binds the believer and God into a covenant relationship; (2) believers are called to exercise the positive confession or practice; and (3) believers are called practice the law of "seed time and harvest," that is, they are to see God's Word as the seed that produces a prosperous life.[82] Acting according to these three core beliefs and principles unleashes divine health and material wealth.

Born in College Park, Georgia, a predominantly African American suburb, Dollar attended West Georgia College on a football scholarship and answered the call to the ministry after a football injury. In 1983, while in his third year at West Georgia, he was ordained at the Shiloh Missionary Baptist Church. After graduating in 1984, he taught public school and worked as an occupational therapist. In 1986, Dollar married Taffi Bolton, a classmate at West Georgia who had accepted Christ at one of Dollar's college Bible study classes, and the same year he started the World Changers Church in the elementary school cafeteria where his mother had once served lunches.

Within three years, World Changers had grown to five hundred members, and the church moved from the school cafeteria to an abandoned Baptist church in College Park. Although he was ordained Baptist, he did not claim such an affiliation either for himself or for his church. Information is sketchy on how he came under Copeland's tutelage, but Dollar's time spent under Copeland's counsel is undeniable. His preaching style, sermonic cadence, and voice intonations mirror Copeland's. Dollar refers to Copeland as his father in the ministry.

The father of a white son whom the couple adopted before having their four biological children, Dollar purports there is no Black or white—only *The Color of Love*.[83] Still, Dollar's change in his ecclesiastical alignment from the Black Church to what he perceives as an interracial one has proven to be materially prosperous due to his mostly Black followers.

Within five years of founding World Changers, Dollar was constructing the World Dome, a state-of-the-art eight-thousand-seat worship center, and flying across country in his personal Learjet, reportedly a gift from Copeland. By 2007, the ministry reported having thirty thousand members and an annual budget of about $70,000,000. Its headquarters is located in a renovated strip mall adjacent to the World Dome. On its 81-acre campus is a children's academy, publishing house, television studio, gospel record label, bookstore, and health club. To spread his message to an international audience, Dollar founded Creflo Dollar Ministries, a global ministry under the umbrella of World Changers Church International, with offices in Australia, Canada, Nigeria, South Africa, and the United Kingdom, spread to "nearly one billion homes around the world."[84]

For Dollar, according to the core beliefs of Word of Faith theology, just as poverty is essentially in one's mind, so too is racism. Racism is a sin that African Americans as well as whites must reconcile. Reconciliation has nothing to do with addressing corrupt social systems or power relations but with individual cross-cultural exchanges. For African Americans, overcoming racism consists of not only overcoming discriminatory actions but denouncing any emphasis put upon cultural distinctions. Thus Dollar, who claims to be color-blind, can instruct his predominantly African American congregation to be reconciled to white cultural norms.

Word of Faith theology is based on a Platonized understanding of a dualistic reality. This reality consists of the lower life, that is, the earthly realm into which humanity is born and where Satan has dominion, and the higher life which is accessible to the believer through God's grace and favor and through Jesus conquering sin and death. In the higher life social structures and social ills are inconsequential and the laws of nature no longer apply to the believer, as God's love and eternal grace provides for, empowers, and liberates one from the laws of the natural world. No longer subject to the law of sin and death, a believer has the ability, through life in Christ, to change the laws of the flesh and make those laws subject to the law of Spirit by recognizing herself as an heir of God and using the power of her tongue.[85]

It is the practice of positive confession, or naming and claiming it, that controls the demonic spirits which would prevail over a person's life and keep that person from receiving one's blessings. Positive confession is not only demonstrative of a person's inner faith and confidence in Scripture. It is also demonstrative of her power, and it is the tool by which she opens the windows of heaven and unleashes for herself divine health and material wealth.

While Dollar's individualist theology borders on a profession of human divinity, it can be attractive to people who live on society's margins. For many African Americans, the ability to change their circumstances without having the burden of challenging the political realities, racist ideologies, and patriarchal oppressive structures that shape and inform their lives can seem like a long-awaited, long-sought answer to their prayers for a better quality of life. Ethnographer Marla Frederick, in her text, *Between Sundays: Black Women and Everyday Struggles of Faith*, which records African American women's testimonies and faith practices, shares the story of a woman named Gloria who maintains that she was able to overcome her financial anxieties by incorporating Dollar's teachings into her daily practice. Frederick states of Gloria's professed experience:

> *During one message Dollar challenged the congregation to believe that "you will never be broke again in your life." She said that she received his prophetic word, and "from that day to this, whether it's five dollars or ten dollars, or one dollar, I always have money in my pocket." This testimony in itself keeps her from worrying constantly about bills and the possibility of ever being broke. She simply trusts God to provide when funds are insufficient. Although she and her husband are now financially stable and paying for her youngest to complete college, Gloria has long had a tendency to worry about money, especially after she left her first husband and began raising their children on her own. Dollar's teachings about financial prosperity . . . at the very least encouraged her not to worry about financial matters. This sense of peace and security, she explains, is leaps and bounds above where she used to be.*[86]

A hegemonic hypermasculinity also is central to Dollar's ministry. That is to say, a so-called real man, Black or white, embraces the ideology that a man has and must assume control over women. Dollar's commitment to an economic reordering of society is based on his reading of white male-dominated corporate America and on his patriarchal understanding of the family. Women must succumb to their place if they are to be blessed and if the family is to prosper. Thus, educating African American women into the role of the virtuous woman and away from the roles that support matriarchy is a significant part of Dollar's ministry.

Dollar's wife and partner in his ministry, Taffi, takes the lead in making sure that Black women understand that a man can only be who he is called to be when a woman submits to who she is called to be: "a woman after

God's own heart . . . honorable, truthful, intelligent, confident, capable and supportive . . . [with a] primary focus on the well-being of her household."[87] However, supporting and focusing on a woman's household is not enough. A woman also must take instructions from her husband. Proclaiming that she had to learn to do so, Taffi Dollar states, "I humbled myself to receive God's instructions and became more accountable to my husband."[88] Such instructions for women included learning when and how much to talk, when to listen, and how to dress.[89] A woman's refusal to submit to male headship and an inability of a man to control his household are outside the will of God.

In sum, the ministries of prosperity gospel preachers, like Jakes's and Dollar's ministries, highlight two important trajectories among prosperity theologies. First, their ministry success and consumerist lifestyles serve as a model for contemporary prosperity preachers and their congregants who long to find the road to abundance. Second, the semblance of hope their ministries offer is tied not to liberation but to accommodationism. Prosperity gospel ministries are concerned with personal advancement and economic empowerment at the individual level. There is little concern for or belief in the existence of capitalist exploitation, patriarchal domination, or white supremacy. Concern for communal liberation and social transformation is decentralized. Instead, their theological ethic accommodates the norms, principles, and practices that legitimize and leave in place social systems and structures that foster inequity along economic, gender, racial, political, and cultural lines. As anthropologists Hans A. Baer and Merrill Singer state, an economic ethic of accommodation creates an acquiescent space for African American women and men in a racist, and, I would add, hyperconsumerist, economically unjust, and gender-biased society.[90] The rhetoric of self-choice, controlling one's own destiny, and promoting economic empowerment also assumes that wealth accumulation is salvific. Thus, silence about racism, sexism, and social injustice, as well as belief in the myth of American success, is all a person needs to possess buckets of mammon and material accoutrements.

The Cost of Living the Good Life

In the context of the United States, African American women and men have always longed for ways to counter disenfranchisement, poverty, and despair while experiencing personal and spiritual growth, words of hope, and an economically fulfilled life. Hearing prosperity preachers claim unlimited personal possibilities for their social and economic problems, health, and spiritual well-being, many Black people flock to these preachers' churches in pursuit of freedom and happiness. Often their decision to join these congregations is preceded by years of struggling to feed, clothe, house, and educate themselves and their families on a daily basis. Some feel the sermon message of practicing perseverance and steadfastness that is preached by many Black ministers outside the prosperity gospel circles does not heal Black people's poverty fatigue or adequately address their longing for economic justice. On the other hand, prosperity churches profess to have the answers to address poverty, access socioeconomic success, and ultimately achieve the good life.

For Black women to achieve the good life, they must be willing to embrace oppressive social models such as male headship and social submission. They must also being willing to ignore systemic racist, sexist, and economic structures and practices within society and their own community. Through prosperity gospels, Black women must see their humanity as secondary to men's and deny that they are indeed made in the image of God. Ultimately, a Black woman is called to forfeit any liberative understanding of what it means to be a Black woman in Christ even as she experiences the church as a community of spiritual transcendence, courage, and hope.

Both Jakes and Dollar have managed with astute business savvy and unrestrained ambition to propel themselves toward the front of the economic line in Black America, but neither Jakes's nor Dollar's success within America's capitalist economy has proven to be available to all. Jakes's and Dollar's ability to control their destinies and secure economic prosperity has more to do with acquiescing to accommodationist Christian economic ethics than dismantling systems and practices that take advantage of Black people's longing for economic equity and a better quality of life. An analysis of the Synoptic Gospel's portrayal of Jesus in Matthew, Mark, and Luke can help the Black Church as a whole better align itself with Jesus's teachings about wealth, poverty, and materialism, as it seeks to address Black women's and men's longing for economic empowerment.

2

JESUS, WEALTH, AND POVERTY

IN ALL FOUR gospels, Jesus makes liberal and discriminating use of the Old Testament writings in his teaching and speaking about his mission in the world. Thus, an examination of Jesus's position on wealth, poverty, material possession, and redistribution must begin with an analysis of the Hebrew Bible's understandings of each subject, which was familiar to Jesus and would have informed his position.

First, it's important to acknowledge that the Old Testament holds a plurality of voices or traditions about poverty, wealth, material acquisition, and redistribution. Some are contradictory and occupy different spaces on the Hebraic social stratum. In the Hebrew tradition the notion that wealth reflects divine favor and poverty divine retribution is clearly present. But also, within that heritage is the prophetic view of poverty as a scandal, as something abnormal that was to be addressed through redistributive systems and acts of kindness. And, while they may all be part of the inherited tradition of Jesus, Jesus adopts the more radical trajectory passed on to him from the prophets, with its emphasis on justice for the most oppressed.[1] Only, Jesus does not merely adopt this trajectory, he radically transforms it—identifying with the poor, the outsider, and the disenfranchised to call his followers to also claim such identification as a way of divesting themselves of the status-quo "way of being in the world." This includes practicing the renunciation of material possessions as a redemptive act of faith.

Second, it's important to note that there is also a diversity of perspectives among scholars on the subject of both Jesus's socioeconomic status and his position on poverty and wealth. A sampling of these contradictory perspectives illustrates this point. In his book, *The Wealth of Christians*, Redmond Mullin argues that Jesus and his disciples were not poor but rather tradesmen, craftsmen, and small businessmen who chose an itinerant life as preachers who shared a common purse and who could return to their original vocations if they needed to do so.[2] New Testament scholar Martin Hengel goes as far as saying Jesus belonged to the middle class of Galilee.[3] In direct opposition to this, Wolfgang Stegemann in *The Gospel of the Poor* puts forth two possible viewpoints. The first being that,

> *The "representatives" of the "gospel of the poor" are themselves poor . . . we know about them via the allegedly oldest tradition of Jesus of Nazareth, which is preserved in the Synoptic Gospels, as well as via the Sayings Source (Q).*

Another possibility, Stegemann states, may also be that,

> *Apart from a few wealthy persons, the "representatives" of the gospel are Christian groups outside Palestine who are not ptôchoi (poor/destitute) but are predominantly penêtes (powerless/weak/lowly "little people"). Rudiments of this gospel are evident in the Pauline letters but are most prominent in the Gospels according to Matthew and Luke (see also the Letter of James).*[4]

Stegemann argues that the apparent discrepancy within the tradition as set forth in the text is resolved by the fact that the two situations are part of earlier and later branches of the tradition and different geographical locations of "The movement within Judaism in Palestine [which] associated with the name of Jesus a movement 'of the poor for the poor.'"[5]

> *Apart from the son of a certain carpenter from Nazareth (Mk 6:3), its figureheads are some fishermen from Galilee (Mk 1:16–20), a minor customs employee (Mk 2:13–14), and a zealot (Mk 3:18). Women, too, belonged from the very beginning (Mk 15:40–41) . . .*
>
> *The fact that Jesus, as the son of a carpenter, was probably a carpenter is often used as evidence that he himself was not among the poor. Thus, his solidarity with them was supposedly of "ethical" and "partisan" origin. And, indeed, an important proof for this is the indisputable fact that the occupation of carpenter was not*

> *a despised one. It proves nothing, however, about the material circumstances of a carpenter.*[6]

Thus, Stegemann rightly points out that the social circumstances of a carpenter in as insignificant a Galilean hamlet as Nazareth in Roman-occupied Palestine, with its system of heavy taxation bordering on extortion, must be assessed accordingly. Indeed, according to theologian John Dominic Crossan, an artisan was more of a day laborer, and a step below the peasant farmers[7] (because they owned no land). But New Testament scholars Sharon Ringe and Brian Blount both make the critical point that in the Synoptic Gospels the evangelists use the language "poor" as a descriptive whose range includes and extends well beyond matters of economics. According to Ringe,

> *These [synoptic] contexts [that mention the poor] underline the importance of "the poor" in Jesus' ministry and in his identity as the Christ. They also expand the meaning of "the poor" to include people who are social outcasts and physically disabled, as well as people who are economically disadvantaged.*[8]

Blount states, "In the Greco-Roman world, wealth and poverty were elements of relationship rather than exclusively matters of money. One would therefore think in terms of status, which turns the discussion in the thematic direction of power."[9] The concern of Jesus is above all with those who are defined by their dishonorable status, those who are outside the circles of power and privilege. Thus, poverty must not be merely understood in economic terms but must also be grasped in terms of one's social standing, which embraces wealth but also family heritage, ethnicity, vocation, religious purity, and gender.[10]

Wealth and Poverty in Ancient Israel

In the life of ancient Israelites, poverty was a painful fact experienced as dependence, oppression, and humiliation. Nonetheless, the phenomenon of poverty provoked different views among the Israelites, as indicated by the writers of the Hebrew Bible, and led to different explanations and approaches to the poverty and wealth divide. An examination of the biblical text suggests that three major views of poverty and wealth existed side by side: poverty and wealth as a fact of life; poverty as retribution and wealth as a blessing; and poverty as a social scandal.

For example, one finds within texts of the Hebrew Bible both instructions to care for the poor and to show them compassion (Exod 22:22–24, 23:6, 23:10–11; Lev 19:9–10, 25:35–36; Deut 14:28–29, 15:7–10, 24:10–15; Prov 14:31, 17:5) and criticism of the poor alongside depictions of them as lazy (Prov 10:4, 13:4, 19:15, 20:4; Eccl 10:18). One also finds a reversing of the ancient world's general low status of the poor where the widow and orphan who are considered the most vulnerable are grouped with the Levites—the elite spiritual leaders of the people. Both groups are deemed to be important members of the community who are to be taken care of (Deut 14:28–29). Some texts associate material wealth with blessings from God (Gen 24:1; Deut 28:1–6; Eccl 5:18–20), while God demands that kings are not to amass fortunes on the principle that wealth in the hands of a ruler can lead to perversion of power (Deut 17:14–20). Thus, a robust examination of ancient Israel's views on wealth and poverty alongside Jesus's teachings on the subject uncovers the radicality of Jesus's thoughts. Jesus problematizes both wealth as a blessing and charity as the biblical solution to poverty, a solution that gives agency to the wealthy while leaving the poor subject to their whim.

Poverty as a Fact of Life

The view of poverty and wealth as a fact of life is prevalent in the wisdom writers. The book of Proverbs, for example, is set in the pre-exilic monarchical period when the relationship between the classes was relatively stable, with little indication of social unrest and an absence of a critique of the social order.[11] An absence of a radical critique of the social order may have more to do with the fact that the text served the needs of the elite, who "had little in common with the poorer peasants clinging desperately to their holdings or with the petty tradesman and artisans in the cities who suffered their own discontents and were evolving new values in their religious tradition."[12]

While just treatment of the poor is a mark of righteousness according to the wisdom writers, there is no exhibition of a consciousness that the wealth of the cities was obtained by exploitation of the peasant population, as the prophets would indicate. Proverbs does offer some sign of awareness and concern for the plight of the poor as a group (Prov 31:9, 20). However, the main concern here is to provide instructions and teach appropriate behavior for various human activities, including the proper attitude toward wealth and wisdom. While there is a command to acknowledge "the rights of the poor and needy" (v. 9) and an affirmation of one who "opens her hand to the poor and reaches out her hands to the needy" (v. 20), there is little attempt to elevate the collective poor, treat poverty as an undesirable existence, or call for a radical sharing to protest or address situations of inequity. Here, poverty is seen as an unfortunate fact of life that is permitted by God and an inherent element of the world order that must be accepted as such.

The rich and the poor have this in common:

the Lord is the maker of them all. (Prov 22:2)

The poor and the oppressor have this in common:

the Lord gives light to the eyes of both. (Prov 29:13)

The essential message is that although there exist social differences within humanity, all are creatures of God. Humans are seen as equal, but there is no condemnation or critical analysis of the social disparity among them.

Poverty as Retribution and Wealth as Blessing

The view of poverty as a form of retribution and wealth as a blessing aligns with the perspective that the world is just and orderly and asserts that people get what they deserve. Hence, one's economic status is seen as indicative of one's virtue, and therefore a sign of God's divine blessing. This understanding can be found in the book of Proverbs, which says that "in the house of the righteous there is much treasure, but trouble befalls the income of the wicked" (Prov 15:6), and it is echoed in the Psalms:

Happy are those who fear the Lord, who greatly delight in [God's] commandments. Their descendants will be mighty in the land; the

> *generation of the upright will be blessed. Wealth and riches are in their houses, and their righteousness endures forever.* (Ps 112:1–3)

Descriptions of God's blessings upon Old Testament patriarchs also reflect this view. Abraham is described as "very rich in livestock, in silver, and in gold" (Gen 13:2, 24:35). Isaac is described as one whom "The Lord blessed . . . and the man became rich; he prospered more and more until he became very wealthy" (Gen 26:12–13). Jacob "grew exceedingly rich, and had large flocks, and male and female servants and camels and donkeys" (Gen 30:43). The writer of Kings enthusiastically detailed the riches of Solomon[13] and described such riches as a gift of God.[14] Numerous other sayings echo wealth as a reflection of God's divine favor and poverty as divine retribution[15] and the result of wastefulness (Prov 21:20), laziness (Prov 6:6–11, 10:4–5), drunkenness, or the pursuit of pleasure (Prov 21:17).

However, the perspective of Job differs from the wisdom writers in the book of Proverbs. Rather, Job represents a challenge to the wisdom writers' thinking. Job's story can be seen as mocking the understanding within the wisdom tradition that life takes place within a well-ordered universe in which God made sure that people and nations got what they deserved. There is a strong sense in Job that the poor are poor because they are exploited.

In one of his speeches to Job, Zophar observes that since the rich have obtained their wealth through wrongdoing, it must be returned to the poor. The implication is that Job had gained his wealth unjustly and therefore was suffering (Job 20:10). In one passage, Job appears to wait for God's judgment against wicked injustices such as moving landmarks or boundary stones and seizing flocks (Job 24:2), mistreating orphans and widows and misusing pledges (Job 24:3–4), and abusing the poor and the needy (Job 24:4), who are made to live under unbearable conditions (Job 24:5–11). The impoverished and disenfranchised are abused and murdered, but God remains silent (Job 24:12–14). The concept of poverty is highly prophetic in character, aligning itself more with the understanding of such as found among the prophets.

The book of Job can also be seen as a foreshadowing to a new or nuanced theological understanding, if not reversal. Although Job defends his actions and gives examples of his just behavior (Job 29:12, 15–17, 31:18), he makes his treatment of the poor and disenfranchised the litmus test of his righteousness. "If I have withheld anything that the poor desired (Job 31:17), . . . or have eaten my morsel alone, and the orphan has not eaten from it (Job 31:17), . . . if I have seen anyone perish for lack of clothing, or a poor person without covering (Job 31:19), . . . then let my shoulder blade fall from my shoulder, and let my arm be broken from its socket" (Job 31:22). And although the book has been labeled as "the most intellectually demanding book of the Hebrew Bible" that leaves the reader with "no unequivocal message,"[16] its message about having concern for the disenfranchised and holding suspect the notion that wealth is the blessing of the righteous is quite clear.

In dialoguing with Zophar, Eliphaz, and his two other would-be comforters, Job insists until the end that he has done nothing to deserve his suffering. His friend Eliphaz turns to the retribution and blessing tradition to speak against Job. "Who that was innocent ever perished? Or where were the upright cut off?" (Job 4:7). Job, Eliphaz says, has no right to complain because Job's plight proves he has committed some wrongdoing. After all, it was a well-ordered moral universe.

However, the book of Job also challenges this prevailing view on several fronts. It debunks the thought that faithfulness brings God's blessing in the form of prosperity while faithlessness leads to exile and deprivation. It offers a new way of understanding the plight of the impoverished. The poor are continuously placed in the contexts of exploitation, oppression, and injustice, and there is a definite link between oppression and wealth. Moreover, God does not always come as liberator. Sometimes God appears as the God whom Hagar encountered in the wilderness—who sends her back to the oppressive household of Abram and Sarai.[17] God's justice is not always easily understood. Still, there is a strong sense that God is a defender of the poor and disenfranchised, a position that is strongly reminiscent of the prophetic writings.

A final redactor partially sabotaged the book's nuanced understanding of poverty and wealth, as well as its portrayal of the complexity of God with the depiction of God's power and ultimate deliverance.[18] The implication is that God is indeed the author of all things and that all that happens is just and purposeful. "Where were you when I laid the foundation of the earth?"

God asks Job rhetorically (Job 38:4). Job is told to keep silent because God is more powerful than Job. However, the criticism of this theological understanding, which not only ties the acquisition of wealth to God's blessings but also oversimplifies suffering, could not be so easily erased. The exposed cracks in the prevailing explanations for suffering, poverty, and wealth experiences remain.

Poverty as a Scandal

Poverty as a scandal became the prevalent attitude in prophetic circles as the prophets undertook the defense of those whom they saw as victims of the social crisis of their time. The prophets denounced all forms of oppression brought on by economic development, including the exacting of tribute and charging of extraordinary rents (Amos 4:1, 5:11–12; Isa 3:14–15), fraudulent business dealings (Amos 8:4–6; Hos 12:8), monopolizing of land (Mic 2:1–3; Ezek 22:29), selling of destitute debtors into slavery (Amos 2:8; 8:6), and unjust legal sentencing (Amos 5:12; Isa 10:1–2, 32:7; Jer 5:28, 22:16).[19] Unlike the wisdom writers, the prophets subjected the whole of Israel, including its political institutions and theological options, to a biting critique and they draw a definite connection between the poverty of the poor and the wealth of the rich.

Although there remained a widespread praise of riches, and complete surrender of one's property was considered taboo, social changes introduced by the formation of the state were subjected to the criticism of the prophets. As Old Testament scholar Rainer Albertz notes,

> *The creation of large estates, from the crown downwards, made holes in the old Israelite order and . . . forced aside the egalitarian ideal of the period before the state (Micah 2.1f). A prosperous stratum of large landowners, officials, military, and merchants had set themselves above the traditional small farmers, intent only on self-sufficiency (Micah 3.1–9; Isa. 1.23; 3.12.14), and far outstripped them with market-orientated surplus production. This creeping social development became critical . . . many small farmers . . . were forced to the brink by the tougher economic conditions. They were less and less in a position to cope with the*

> *normal risks of agricultural production from their own resources, and it became increasingly difficult for them to bear the usual burdens of state taxation and forced labour; they were compelled more and more frequently to resort to loans in order to get by . . . [and] driven to dependence upon [the expanding upper class] and became permanently impoverished.*[20]

The prophet Amos, in particular, offers insight into the plight of the poor in ancient Israel as those who are "at the mercy of the arbitrary expectations and demands of the rich."[21] Though he was from the Southern Kingdom, Amos was called to preach in the Northern Kingdom during a period of prosperity and when society was undergoing transition. Under kings Joash and Jeroboam II, the Northern Kingdom regained some of its previous territorial losses and was once again prosperous, as it had been under David and Solomon (2 Kgs 13:24–25, 14:25, 28). In spite of the widespread optimism regarding the Northern Kingdom as a result of its economic prosperity, Amos was pessimistic and critical about its future. His critique was not only directed at the lifestyle of the wealthy, but at how such wealth was accumulated—at the expense of the masses of destitute and impoverished members of the community.[22]

> *[The] means by which this wealth was gained—the unscrupulous exploitation of the masses by those in a position to oppress them—seemed to [Amos] impermissible, at least with the basic experience of Israel.*[23]

This basic experience told the nation that Yahweh not only scorns that which is mighty and strong, but he also takes his place at the side of those who are weak and thought of as insignificant in the social order, providing them with life's necessities.

The primary method that those in power used to promote their interests was manipulation of the law. This abuse, in turn, led to a corrupt administration of justice and left those who were the weakest—the widow, the orphan, the foreigner, and the poor—to become the most vulnerable to being exploited. One such exploitation was the confiscation of lands. This confiscation shattered adherence to Israel's tribal constitution with its implied democratic union of families, who "in principle [were] free and equal villagers with full civil rights" and for whom "the concept of inherited possession [of land] . . . was . . . allotted in equal measure to each clan and family and was never to be sold but passed on only through hereditary succession."[24] As a result of this practice, free Israelite citizens lost their status and became subjects with limited rights and compulsory labor and tax obligations, while their confiscated lands were used for bestowing gifts upon officials.[25]

Moreover, the monarchy not only meant the establishment of a new aristocracy who were initially recruited from among the educated elite of the Canaanites. It also created an environment in which the Canaanites' view of the acquisition of money and land would become the view of those Israelites who made it into this administrative upper class. The Canaanites, unlike the Israelites, regarded land as a commodity that could be freely transferred and they valued the pursuit of gain without qualifications. Furthermore, the monarchy's transition from the barter economy to a money economy made it increasingly difficult to pay debts, especially taxes that were accrued based on what one produced. As a result, debtors accrued exorbitant amounts of debt that became increasingly difficult to pay off.[26]

It is in this context that Amos preached his message, which portrayed God as "the God of the lowly, victims who were crushed without pity in the economic machinery of the Israel of that age."[27] Preaching that "It is not competitiveness and the ruthless pursuit of gain that should be taken as a model, but rather solidarity and the provision of adequate living conditions for all,"[28] Amos was the first to problematize the prevailing valuation of wealth and cry out on behalf of the poor. Such a call for justice and righteousness for the poor and needy, weak and wretched would be repeated by Isaiah and Micah.

Judaic Responses to Poverty and Wealth

Two main trajectories emerged in the Jewish community as it transitioned from a life of nomadic shepherding to farming, and ultimately to city dwelling, and as attitudes toward accepting wealth as desirable intensified: a more radical position found in the writings of the prophets and a "compromise" tradition.[29] The radical tradition, which understood poverty as a scandal, called for a critique of the acquisition of wealth and the behavior of the wealthy. The compromise tradition legitimized the possession of private property and wealth and continued to see such as a gift from God to the righteous, even as it stressed almsgiving and the care of weaker members of society. Both could point to the theology of the Deuteronomist for their rationale. For example, on the one hand, Deuteronomy called for a year of release of debts every seven years (Deut 15:1ff., 12ff.) and a year of Jubilee in the fiftieth year after seven release years in which property had been returned to its original owner (Lev 25:8ff.). Such a tradition of the redistribution of land and goods, which was obligatory for all, was to be done out of faithfulness to God, God's call for justice, and care for the poor:

> *The land shall not be sold in perpetuity, for the land is mine; with me you are but aliens and tenants . . . if anyone of your kin falls into difficulty and sells a piece of property, then the next of kin shall come and redeem what the relative has sold . . . if anyone of your kin fall into difficulty and become dependent on you, you shall support them; they shall live with you as though resident aliens. (Lev 25:23, 25, 35)*

On the other hand, the possession of private property was protected by the Decalogue (Exod 20:15, 17; Deut 5:19, 21) and the theology of the Deuteronomist historian is evident in the early wisdom sayings that portray riches as a sign of God's blessings (Prov 10:15, 13:11, 19:15), even as it calls for a right relationship with wealth (Prov 19:17) to personally avoid poverty.

The prophet Amos challenges what was emerging as a tradition that endorsed individuals amassing fortunes while ignoring the increasing extremes of wealth and want, privilege and powerlessness around them. His oracles against the nations of Judah and Israel (Amos 2:4–16) serve as an example of the more radical position that centers God's covenant with Israel regarding the ways in which they ought to relate to God and to each other. Amos not only denounces the prosperity of the Northern Kingdom; he also connects their wealth with acts of oppression. Amos pronounces God's judgment on the Israelites who, "sell the righteous for silver, and the needy for a pair of sandals" (2:6) and who "trample the head of the poor into the dust of the earth, and push the afflicted out of the way" (2:7a).

Jewish communities developed a system of caring for the poor that was arguably among the most unique in antiquity and extremely effective. The basis for their system of welfare was the third tithe, the tithe for the poor which was commanded in Deuteronomy 14:28–29 and 26:12.[30] Within the Hebrew Bible, no concept is as central and significant for all relationships as justice and righteousness. As theologian Peter Phan states:

> *Justice is the social principle that held the Hebrew social fabric together. It is fidelity to the demands of a relationship as established by the Law—the web of relationships between king and people, judge and complainants, family and tribe and kinsfolk, and community and the resident alien, the whole humanity of God.*[31]

Legislation on behalf of the poor was comprehensive and included, along with the tithe for the poor (set aside every third and sixth year of the seven-year sabbatical cycle), the Pe'ah (the corner of a field left unharvested for use by the poor), forgotten sheaves (any sheaf abandoned in a field and dedicated to the poor), first fruits, the festival offering, deeds of loving-kindness, and, at least by the second century CE, a fundraising system in which collectors went door to door collecting for the Poor Fund, which was then distributed.[32] The widow, orphan, and alien were to be supported (Exod 22:20–23), lending procedures for loans to the poor were specified and regulated (Exod 23:6–8), and a legal obligation to protect the disenfranchised was stipulated (Exod 23:6–8; Deut 24:17). However, with the establishment of the monarchy, as the acquisition of wealth became more prominent among the elite, the adherence to legislation on behalf of the poor became less of a practice. The prophets were committed to this tradition and to addressing their particular contexts with a radical call for justice.

The sayings of Jesus in the Gospels suggest that Jesus further radicalized this radical trajectory, calling for perpetual Jubilee, egalitarian human relationships, and a distinctive attitude toward poverty and wealth which we shall now explore.

Jesus's Valuation of Wealth and Poverty in the Gospel of Mark

The first hint of Jesus's valuation of wealth in the Gospel of Mark is given early in the text. Mark 1:16–20 narrates the call of four men who follow Jesus. After proclaiming God's realm has drawn near and is here,[33] Jesus begins gathering the new community, or rather, citizens of that realm. However, following Jesus is only the first step. Understanding and faithfulness in following are the more difficult tasks. Thus Mark 1:16–20 indicates more than just the compelling nature of Jesus's call of the first disciples. Situated within this "he saw, he called, they followed" formula, is the foreshadowing of the action that must accompany the following; namely, leaving one's old life behind and detaching oneself from all that would hinder one's vision of and ability to participate in a nonhierarchical, nonauthoritarian, egalitarian view of community. This required detachment from one's material possessions. As biblical scholar Emerson Powery notes,

> *Jesus' first activity, in Mark, was to seek followers [and] Rabbis rarely selected their own students. [This] radical social reorientation championed by Jesus' mission continued when he encouraged these young men to leave their family businesses, a disrespectful act in first century Jewish culture.*[34]

That the first disciples voluntarily "left their nets and followed him" (Mark 1:18) and "left their father Zebedee in the boat with hired men and followed him" (1:20) suggests those in similar positions could and should react similarly to Jesus's call.

Like the call of the first disciples, the Parable of the Sower (Mark 4:13–20) primarily demonstrates the need for Jesus's followers to listen to and be rooted in his every word to participate in the realm of God. However, it also speaks to what happens when one underestimates the power of external factors to "choke the word" (v. 19). As Powery points out,

> *In [Mark] 4:13–20 Jesus suggests that there are external factors—such as Satan (like "devouring birds"), troubles and persecutions*

> *(like the "scorching sun") and the "cares of the world," the "lure of wealth," or the "lust for other things" (like "thorns")—that distort the fruitful development of the logos ("words"; cf 2:2), the message of God's reign.*[35]

Thus, Jesus's enactment of the realm of God—gathering followers, performing healings and exorcisms that significantly alter a person's social status, eating with all sorts of people, and bringing liberation to the poor and wretched—also includes a brief but precise critique of wealth. Focusing on wealth acquisition interferes with being fruitful followers of Christ.

Within the instructions Jesus gives to the disciples as he commissions them (Mark 6:7–11) are stipulations about provisions to be made for the journey that suggest Jesus had little value for material possessions. The disciples are told to "take nothing . . . except staff; no bread, no bag, no money in their belts" (v. 8). Biblical scholar H. B. Swete has argued that the staff was allowed because it was the universal companion of the traveler.[36] New Testament scholar William Lane maintains that the staff reflected the shepherd's crook and symbol of office[37] and alluded to Exodus 12:11, which commands one to eat the Passover with "your loins girded, your sandals on your feet, and your staff in your hand."[38] Still, others have made various arguments about the sandals (to take or not to take) and the two tunics (to wear or not to wear). But the essential point is that excess was to be avoided and the renunciation of luxury was to be practiced. A shared egalitarianism of spiritual and material resources was to be observed in carrying out the mission. New Testament scholar John Dominic Crossan compares the Jesus movement to that of Greek Cynicism:

> *What it [the wallet/knapsack] symbolized for the Cynics [first-century Greek radical missionaries] was their complete self-sufficiency. They carried their homes with them. All they needed could be carried in a simple knapsack slung over their shoulders. Similarly, the staff. It represented their itinerant status, the fact that they had no fixed abode in any place; that they were always spiritually on the way elsewhere. The two items together underlined their itinerant self-sufficiency.*

> *The Jesus missionaries, in contrast, are told precisely to carry* no *knapsack and hold* no *staff in their hands . . . the idea of no-staff [Matt 10:10; Luke 9:3] and no-knapsack is symbolically correct for the Jesus missionaries. . . . Since commensality is not just a technique for support but a demonstration of message, they could not and should not dress to declare itinerant self-sufficiency but rather communal dependency. Itinerancy* and *dependency: heal, stay, move on.*
>
> *. . . what Jesus called the Kingdom of God . . . [is a] radical messages[s] that taught and acted, theorized and performed against social oppression, cultural materialism, and imperial domination . . .*[39]

If dependence upon and trust in God were to be embraced, so too was non-dependence upon and, in fact, devaluation of all that was previously thought to sustain one's life, including material possessions and wealth.

Jesus's sayings on cross-bearing and sacrifice (Mark 8:34–38) are also a source for understanding his teachings on wealth and poverty. The references to taking up a cross, losing one's life to gain one's life, and not being ashamed of Jesus shed light on the radical new relationship that Jesus calls his followers to have.[40] This relationship not only involves mutuality and reciprocity but also values the perspectives of the "least of these" and renounces unjust hierarchies of privilege and domination. The result is that the "first are last and the last are first" (Mark 10:31), or indistinguishable from each other. Elsewhere in the Gospel, the call to follow Jesus cites the same imperative. If one is to follow Jesus, one must sever ties with material possessions and even radically redefine who one's family is. While new life in Christ does not require martyrdom or persecution for all followers, it does require a devaluation of materiality, which governs the old world, and a revaluation of human relations, connectedness, and family.

An Invitation (and Refusal) to Radically Share

The story of the rich man's invitation and refusal to discipleship (Mark 10:17–31) is one of the most explicit about Jesus's valuation of wealth and poverty.[41] The first section of the story concludes with the command to "go, sell what you own, and give the money to the poor, and you will have treasure in heaven" (v. 21). The radicality of this command is not that it dictates giving to the poor or acquiring treasures of a different sort. These are not new teachings during Jesus's time. Rather, the radical sharing and new devaluation of wealth run counter to both the rabbinic teaching about treasured wealth and despised poverty and the Qumran teaching that directed particular Jews to give to those within their own community.[42] In addition, the command goes beyond merely portraying sympathy for the poor to inferring the notion that humanity's possessions bind one's heart and hinder one from both being a true follower of Christ and entering into the realm of God.

The fact that possessions are not to be destroyed but given away might lead one to conclude that there is little ethical importance to valuing wealth. However, identifying the poor as the recipients of wealth renunciation and redistribution indicates Jesus's radically different valuation of wealth and poverty. As Powery notes, "the rich man's question . . . confronts directly the relationship between financial status (wealth as a sign of God's blessing) and following Jesus."[43] Moreover, Mark's mention of the poor for the first time in conjunction with the challenge to sell and give shows that Jesus did not overlook economic injustice. Indeed, these references indicate that redistribution of goods to the least is a sign of one's repentance, belief in the "good news," and commitment to God's reign.

Jesus's understanding of wealth and its relationship to one's faith does not indicate that wealth is an extension of God's blessing to be acquired and held onto or that someone is to give only a portion of their wealth from their excess based on the person's own standards. Rather, Jesus's intention was to communicate a general prescription about discipleship that extended beyond this man's particular case.[44] In reciting the commandments "you shall not murder; you shall not commit adultery; you shall not steal" (v. 19), Jesus appears to be continuing with this generalization when he states that "you lack one thing; go sell what you own" (v. 21), especially considering the similarity of this statement and Mark 8:34.[45] In both instances, Jesus communicates that a person not only must embrace the general idea of following but also the act of selling and giving or the dispossession of one's earthly treasures and "the establishment of a new reality that requires the rethinking of old traditions."[46] For Jesus, the act of following cannot be divorced from selling and giving or participating in transformative boundary breaking and liberative moves like revaluing wealth and poverty.

Devouring Widows' Houses

Another Markan story that provides insight into Jesus's teachings about poverty and wealth is the story of the widow's offering (Mark 12:41–44). It reveals a "contrast between the outward meagerness and inward richness of the widow's service, and the outward pretension and inward barrenness of the Pharisees' religion."[47] The widow's coins each equated to just one-eightieth of a laborer's daily wage,[48] which was the smallest copper coin in circulation in Palestine at the time.[49] Yet the widow's gift surpasses the others' gifts because "all of them have contributed out of their abundance; but she out of her poverty."[50] The story continues to highlight that she gave everything that she had. In fact, she gave all she had to live on.

The story has been used to show the image of someone who is triply oppressed in the community—a female, a person who is economically destitute, and one without the legal protection of a male—as a model for discipleship. However, Jesus does not point to the woman giving all that she has to advocate a practice of giving to the point of impoverishment.[51] The story is not meant to sanction placing burdens on the poor to give until it hurts. Rather, Jesus is providing an example of how the scribes "devour widows' houses" (v. 40) by the ways in which the scribes' treasury consumes the resources of the poor.[52] It is a condemnation and a lament over a religious and social system that would have the most vulnerable surrender that which they need to survive.

Valuing Humanity over Costly Oil

The story of Jesus's anointing at Bethany by the woman with the costly oil (Mark 14:3–9) provides another look into Jesus's position on poverty and wealth. Jesus is not devaluing the redistribution of wealth. Nor is he valuing devotion to himself over caring for the poor. Rather, he is aligning himself with the poor and valuing the woman's great sacrifice. Jesus, in this story, is "the poor human par excellence" who is infinitely more valuable than this costly oil, not an object of devotion in opposition to the poor. The contrast Jesus sets up is not between the poor and himself. Valuing the costly oil over Jesus is like valuing the material goods of the empire over human life, human relations, human needs, and communal sharing. Jesus is challenging the community's value system and uncovers their idolatry.

This story also reveals a contrast between "always" and "not always." That Jesus's intention is not to be in opposition to the poor is even more obvious as the story is told in the book of Matthew (26:6–13), where it is preceded by explicit statements where Jesus identifies himself with the poor ("for I was hungry, and you gave me food . . .," Matt 25:35–45). Nor is his declaration that "you always have the poor with you" meant to imply the inevitable continued existence of poverty[53] or discourage caring for the poor, particularly since it is followed by "and you can show kindness to them whenever you wish" (Mark 14:7). Rather, Jesus is rebuking those who participated in self-righteously singling out and judging this woman when the ongoing presence of the poor is a judgment against them and the entire community.[54] Jesus is commending this woman for her giving ("she has done what she could," v. 8) just as he commended the widow for her gift in Mark 12:44 ("she out of her poverty gave everything she had"). In both cases, Jesus is exemplifying these women's actions as examples of radical sharing and wealth devaluation and redistribution. Their actions are concrete, practical steps to be taken by all would-be followers.

Lastly, it should be noted that not only does Jesus again use a woman to point the way to true discipleship, but also in this case, the woman's act is also a prophetic one. According to Dewey:

> *Anointing on the head is an act of great symbolic importance. To tend someone's feet, as in Luke and John, is the act of a social inferior—a slave or a woman. But a host might anoint a guest's head as a sign of rejoicing. To anoint is also to call a person to God's service, to consecrate him or her for a special task. Prophets and priests were anointed, but above all, prophets anointed those chosen to be king. So the unknown woman at Bethany was a prophet, fulfilling the prophetic function of choosing and empowering Jesus for his messianic role . . . [and] We can say . . . that Mark's head anointing version probably predates the foot anointing versions, since by the time men were writing the Gospels they were already minimizing women's roles.*[55]

In other words, what we have here is the in-breaking of the realm of God in human history and a foretaste of the reversal that is being ushered in. Women, who are deemed as other, and the last, become the first. The unnamed, unknown, and untitled offer powerful examples of the true nature of discipleship. The value of human relations far outweighs any economically and socially valued possessions.

Jesus's Valuation of Wealth and Poverty in the Gospel of Matthew

Some scholars argue that the book of Matthew constitutes a spiritualized and softer version of Jesus's demands about material redistribution and devaluation.[56] However, in the Gospel it is still the rich who have difficulty entering God's realm. While the book includes the command to give alms (Matt 6:3–4), which does not require wealth renunciation or redistribution, it also includes the parable of the treasure and pearl (13:44–46) in which the individuals sell all they have for the realm of God. If Matthew may be said to have spiritualized the first Beatitude ("Blessed are the poor *in spirit*" [5:3]), he may also be said to have added new material from independent sources, including the sayings about laying up treasure in heaven (6:19–21), serving two masters (6:24), and being anxious for nothing (6:25–34), which could have all been spiritualized, or omitted, if the intent was to soften the teachings.[57] In fact, while Matthew omits the story of the widow's offering, the disciples' call (4:18–22), the decree to would-be followers to deny oneself (16:24–27), the story of the rich man (19:16–30), and the woman's anointing of Jesus at Bethany (26:6–13) are all retained.

The spiritualization of the first Beatitude does not lessen the sting of Matthew 6:24 ("No one can serve two masters . . . you cannot serve God and wealth") or 19:23–24 ("Truly I tell you, it will be hard for a rich person to enter the kingdom of heaven . . . it is easier for a camel to go through the eye of a needle than for someone who is rich to enter the kingdom of God"). Rather, the message in Matthew is consistent with that found in Mark. No stigma is placed on poverty, no limit is placed on giving, and no easier way for the rich to enter the kingdom of heaven is offered. Wealth devaluation and redistribution are acts of true discipleship.[58]

In fact, Matthew 6:19–21 prohibits accumulating material possessions. These material treasures cannot provide the security or satisfaction that consistent faithful actions can bring. As New Testament scholar Thomas E. Schmidt notes:

> *Verse 19 makes a clear prohibition of accumulation of possessions: "treasures" must here refer to anything and everything put away out of anxiety for tomorrow (v.34). Not merely gold and jewels, but even spare food and clothing are in view . . . [thus] the dispossession of goods is the natural opposite and the only alternative to the accumulation of goods prohibited in v. 19.*[59]

Moreover, Schmidt notes, while verse 21 may have originally been a separate saying,

> *It fits well here both because of its backward-pointing reference to treasure and because of its more subtle forward-pointing reference to the heart—the spiritual organ of love/devotion/service (v.24) and anxiety/seeking (vv.25–34). To spiritualize the saying into a command to submit one's heart to God's sovereign rule is to reverse the order of treasure and heart. The hearts follows the treasure. . . . There is no more explicit statement in the NT of the integral relation between conduct with regard to possessions and right relation to God.*[60]

Jesus's command to lay up treasures in heaven is not a general reference to good works. It is a specific reference to wealth renunciation. The book of Matthew suggests that if treasure is the determinant of the heart and the heart follows the treasure, then in order to submit one's heart to God, one must seek God—God's love, God justice, and God's desire for communal wholeness—and divorce oneself from all other treasures.

There have been a number of attempts by scholars to spiritualize Matthew 6:22–24.[61] This story commends generosity and condemns greed.[62] The evil eye represents accumulation, which assumes or expresses greed, and Matthew recognizes the evil eye as the embodiment of stinginess.[63] Just as the heart follows what it treasures and service follows the choice of savior, so does the body follow the eye. One's conduct regarding material possessions determines her or his spiritual state. Attitude and action cannot be separated. Those who are generous and renounce wealth acquisition and all that goes along with it, including privilege and power, are the light of the world. Those who accumulate what the world values over human life and dignity—the idolatry of the empire—and do not embrace the radical way of being in the world that Jesus suggests have resigned themselves to darkness.

Matthew's story of the rich man (19:16–30) contains a number of changes from the Markan version that warrant attention. Biblical scholar Paul S. Minear contends that Matthew's addition of the words "if you want to be perfect" (v. 21) shows there is a level of acceptance of the man's behavior and a ranking of such from its present level to an even greater one.[64] But the words do not appear to denote an accepted hierarchy of behavior or a double standard, for they do not diminish the fact that the man's obedience to keeping the commandments still leaves him "lacking" (v. 20). Furthermore, the man's question, "What do I still lack?," along with the reference to treasures in heaven (v. 21) and the discussion of entrance to the kingdom (vv. 23–24), all make it clear that, just as in Mark's version, here too the question is what actions are to be taken to obtain eternal life, not a special ranking within the kingdom.

Blount makes an excellent observation that Matthew is focusing on "the kind of righteousness that he understands is necessary for entrance into the kingdom of heaven."[65]

> *Righteousness became the communal code word for Matthean ethics. . . . Righteousness, though, was defined and determined by proper interpretation of and thus, obedience to the Torah. Matthew demanded that such obedience be radical. And therein lies the problem. Matthew defined radicality oppositionally. Radical obedience of the law, [or] "better righteousness," meant doing the law in a way that was "better" than the way the scribes and Pharisees observed it (5:10). In other words, according to Matthew, the community that represented "formative Judaism" was observing the Jewish Torah improperly.*

> *The primary problem was the legalistic mutation of God's gift (the law). Concentrating only on its external demands, the scribes and Pharisees gleefully acknowledged the letter of the law, while they ignored the spirit of its original, God-directed intent. The end result: they had the cognitive capacity to teach the law but not the internal commitment to live it. . . . They did what was legally necessary, not what was kingdom required. It was this ostentatious, empty display of legal fidelity devoid of interior commitment that drew the Matthean Jesus' ire and subsequent charge of hypocrisy.*[66]

The Matthean Jesus proposes a "better righteousness" that demands responses to the law that derive from an internalized, radical, kingdom-driven ethical behavior. Indeed, Jesus's spiritualizing does not validate an interior commitment to God's realm that lacks transformative human activity. Instead, Jesus calls for followers to align their repentant responses to the approaching realm of God with a gratitude that motivates their behavior. Rather than a legalistic or cultic response, the required response to the sovereignty of God involves one's whole person and seeks human wholeness and transformation for all humanity. As biblical scholar Frank Matera notes, "to be wise is to *do* Jesus' words; that is, to produce the fruit of righteousness."[67] The goal is to exact better ethical behavior and create a new and distinct community because the things the righteous do are directly connected to the things they believe.

Jesus's Valuation of Wealth and Poverty in the Gospel of Luke

The Gospel of Luke also speaks to the spiritual dimensions of discipleship and salvation. It speaks as well to renouncing and redistributing wealth as an act of faith and demonstrating one's right relationship with God. There are those like New Testament scholar Thomas Schmidt who refute the view that Luke's Gospel is indeed "the Gospel of the poor," or that it urges solidarity with and advocacy on behalf of the world's underprivileged people.[68] However, whether the Lukan Jesus is speaking to issues as varied as the proper treatment of possessions, relationships with strangers, the need for prayer, the power of persistence, or the expectation of repentance, as Blount rightfully points out,

> *there is a link to the Jubilee theme that launched Jesus' fateful preaching tour. . . . Reversal is in the air. It is part of the fabric of kingdom life; it becomes the modeling mandate for the kind of life expected of kingdom followers.*[69]

The Magnificat (1:46–55, especially vv. 52–53) contains the first evidence of Luke's attention to overturning common expectations. Mary's hymn of praise proclaims a new order and warns those who hoard their power and possessions. It celebrates the way that God uplifts the lowly and those in need as evidenced by the way God acts in her life. Yet, the song also speaks to God's concern for all as it assures the poor and marginalized—all those who count for nothing in the world—that they more than count for something. It warns the proud, powerful, and rich who see the impoverished as humanly less than themselves that they are in danger of being scattered, dethroned, and sent away hungry (vv. 51–53). Thus, the hymn foreshadows Jesus's words and actions.

Mary's chosenness and poverty exemplify the Lukan Jesus's message of a reversal of humanity's cultural and socioeconomic conditions that does not merely switch people's roles within the same system of wealth, power, and privilege. Rather, Jesus speaks of a reversal of a world fashioned by unjust, inequitable practices that foster the maltreatment of the most powerless to a world that is reordered in justice, equity, and egalitarianism. It speaks not so much of God's preference for the poor and oppressed as it does God's equal concern for and attention to the liberation of the poor and disenfranchised alongside all of humanity. For instance, Mary's home of Nazareth is an insignificant, small rural town in Galilee. Her social, political, and economic status is quite low, and her pregnancy by someone other than her husband promises to lower her status even more. Even Mary and Joseph's presentation of the six-week-old Jesus in the temple for his purification illustrates their status. Mary and Joseph do not present the sacrifice of a lamb, the offering of people with ample resources. Instead, they bring the sacrifice that was allowed as a special concession for people with few resources—a pair of turtledoves or two young pigeons (Lev 12:8). Yet, an impoverished Mary is chosen to give birth to royalty (Luke 1:33).

God's reversal of the world order indicates not only a spiritual concern but socioreligious and socioeconomic concerns as well. New Testament scholar Joel Green notes that, in the Greco-Roman world, wealth and poverty were not exclusively matters of money, but elements of relationship. Thus, status and power were part of Luke's understanding of the poor. "Status honor is a measure of social standing that embraces wealth, but also other factors, including access to education, family heritage, ethnicity, vocation, religious purity, and gender."[70] Indeed, Luke's understanding of the poor includes the captive, blind, oppressed, hungry, weeping, excluded, reviled, maimed, lame, and leper (4:18, 6:20–25, 7:22, 14:13, 21, and 16:20–22). Yet, Luke also uses the term "poor" to refer to economic poverty (18:22 and 21:3).

Jesus's radical revaluation of poverty and wealth also alters historical fortunes as he associates with women, lepers, sinners, and those on the margins. In this Gospel, Jesus begins his public ministry by returning to his home in Nazareth where he rises to read Isaiah 61:1–2 in the temple (Luke 4:16–21). The proclamation explicitly groups the captives, blind, and oppressed under the rubric of poor whom Jesus has been sent to set free. Moreover, the insertion of this Jubilee thought is to be seen as representative of Jesus's preaching and teaching. However, Jubilee is not only about liberty; it also is about a liberation that extends to outsiders for all time. With Jesus's message to outsiders (4:23–24) and his assertion that even Elijah and Elisha were sent to outsiders when Israel was in need of salvation (4:25–27), Jesus shows concern for the deliverance of the oppressed and the transformation of the social order. In this new social order, food is provided for the hungry, and those oppressed by the arrogant, the rich, and the privileged are released. The spiritual realm is understood and embedded in the socioeconomic and political reality.

Luke's Sermon on the Plain (6:20–49) begins with four blessings. Addressing the causes of social, political, and economic oppression—poverty, hunger, sadness, and hatred—the Lukan Jesus retains his messianic declaration of bringing release and setting the captives free. Poverty and hunger are not character traits, but "literal social and political evils that will be overturned."[71] Such a reversal has implications for how would-be followers should live their lives. Entry into the realm of God requires a rigorous observance of Jesus's teachings, which include fostering egalitarian, nonexploitative, and nonauthoritarian relationships, connecting one's spiritual repentance with one's social repentance and imitating Jesus, and doing one's part in ways that will have concrete historical impact.

While Matthew's version of the first Beatitude proclaims "blessed are the poor in spirit" (Matt 5:3), the Lukan first Beatitude states "blessed are you who are poor" (Luke 6:20). Jesus is not saying that poverty itself is a blessing, but that those who endure poverty are no less beloved of God. In a world that equates human value or goodness with the valuation of one's property, belongings, or acquisitions, Jesus is not just calling for a radically different valuation of wealth and poverty, but also for a different valuation of humanity. This new valuation of humanity does not equate poor people with being cursed or elevate those who have over those who lack. All humanity is equally beloved in the eyes of God, and all must practice a commitment to and dependence upon God as they seek to create a more equitable society and world. In the same vein, the woes (Luke 6:24–26) that follow the blessings are directed at all hearers who would continue to perform conventionally, or contrary to Jesus's teachings. Those who hold onto their riches while others remain impoverished, those who experience fullness while others go hungry, and those who laugh while others mourn are all being warned. Marginalizing circumstances must not be ignored; power differentials must be eliminated, egalitarian relationships must be sought, and radical sharing instituted.

The Parable of the Rich Fool (12:13–21) is Jesus's response to "someone in the crowd" (v. 13) who wants Jesus to intercede in the division of an inheritance. Biblical scholar Alfed Plummer has suggested that its main point is simply that life consists of more than securing possessions.[72] Theologian John Navone suggests that its main point is that possessions will not bring security or save one from mortality.[73] But Jesus's response has much broader implications. First, his response suggests that there would be no dispute to bring before an arbitrator if it were not for human greed.[74] Second, the parable suggests that not only is one's life not secured by one's possessions, but it is by *not* storing up earthly riches that one receives abundantly from God. The parable teaches that the one who stores up riches as a blessing and fails to see the redistribution of such possessions as redemptive is one who is not in right relationship with God, humanity, or material possessions. In fact, a refusal to let go of one's possessions to bring about the wholeness of others indicates displaced values and priorities. The Parable's teachings continue into Luke 12:22–34, which emphasizes wealth devaluation and redistribution as the proper alternative to hoarding and worrying about one's material possessions because "where your treasure is, there your heart will be also" (v. 34).

The story of the Rich Man and Lazarus (Luke 16:19–31) also indicates Jesus's valuation of wealth and material redistribution. In the story, the Pharisees, "lovers of money," mocked Jesus for his illustration of the unjust steward whose shrewd act shows him to be one who allows himself to be governed by the world and not by God.[75] The rich man's condemnation comes from his not caring for Lazarus *and* not sharing his wealth. He is described as one who eats, drinks, and is merry (v. 19); as one who ignores the hungry (vv. 20–21); as one who has many goods (v.25); and as one who received comfort in life (v. 25). His privileged lifestyle, though exalted among humans, earns him condemnation, and he serves as a warning to those who fail to care for the poor and devalue and redistribute their wealth. Womanist biblical scholar Stephanie Crowder makes an excellent observation that,

> *The reader cannot help but ask whether the rich man is a "murderer" because he did nothing to help Lazarus in his destitute state. Just as significant is the question whether Jesus advocates that provisions for the needy only come in the afterlife.*[76]

Crowder correctly proposes that Luke is suggesting that one's actions on earth affect one's eternal status. There is, however, no instruction for how the dispossessed can impact their situation. The lesson is intended for those who create and support systems of inequity and domination. The proper alternatives to hoarding possessions are dispossession and distribution to the poor.

In the story of Zacchaeus (Luke 19:1–10), however, there is a lesson for all—the rich as well as the poor. As chief tax collector, Zacchaeus is not only a man of means. He also participates in the domination of the Roman Empire, which renders him a despised outsider among his people. Yet, Jesus declares, "Zacchaeus, hurry and come down; for I must stay at your house today" (v. 5). Zacchaeus quickly complies with Jesus's request without any prompting. Zacchaeus offers to redistribute half of his wealth to the poor and to make restitution to all whom he has cheated. In response to this, Jesus says, "Today salvation has come to this house, because he too is a son of Abraham" (v. 9). By demanding redistribution of one's personal possessions as a way to express one's obedience to and dependence on God, Jesus presented material redistribution as a required act of faith and showed wealth to be antithetical to salvation. His teachings also set radical new standards for whom and what are to be revered as blessed in the material world: all of humanity rather than the wealthy or the poor.

Part Two

MAPPING THE TRAJECTORY OF THE LEGACY OF A THEOLOGY OF PROSPERITY

3

THE VALUATION OF POVERTY AND WEALTH IN THE EARLY CHURCH

WE NOW TURN to an examination of particular sermons and writings of St. Augustine and John Calvin to understand and recognize the presence of mainline Christianity's early long-standing ambivalence toward Jesus's revolutionary revaluation of wealth renunciation and redistribution, beginning with St. Augustine of Hippo.

Augustine's Adoption of Constantinian Christianity

The tendency toward spiritualizing the notions of wealth and poverty may have begun during New Testament times, but Augustine and his adoption of Constantinian Christianity solidified it for Western theology. Jesus's edict that possession of abundant material goods be discarded was largely replaced by Augustine's spiritualized notion of wealth and poverty. Such a notion sanctions one's possession and acquisition of wealth as a blessing from God, albeit a blessing to be wary of. It calls for the renunciation of wealth in the spiritual rather than the material realm and infers that a discord between one's inner humility and outward existence is both acceptable and beyond humanity's realm of judgment.

During Augustine's lifetime, the Christian faith changed from being a banned religion within Rome to being tolerated and supported by the state. With Constantine's conversion to Christianity, his legalization of Christianity, and the imposition of Christianity as the religion of empire, the mutual support of state and church began to find expression in the church's accommodation of the state's needs. As Christianity gained status as an official religion, the church's image became more linked to the political authority of the state and its self-understanding underwent radical changes. As the emperor became the protector of the church,[1] new pressures were imposed that changed the church's structure, administration, and theological emphasis.[2]

If Rome fell, then the church would also fall. Such was the rationale with which the pragmatists contended.

As Constantinian Christianity[3] matured and flourished, Jesus's prophetic message of radical egalitarianism, love, and humility became increasingly corrupted and ultimately set aside for a more palatable one—one that appeared less dangerous and less subversive to the authority of the state. American philosopher Cornel West notes,

> *As the Christian church became increasingly corrupted by state power, religious rhetoric was often used to justify imperial aims and conceal the prophetic heritage of Christianity. Immediately after his conversion, Constantine targeted numerous Christian sects for annihilation—such as the Gnostics and other groups that questioned the books of the Old Testament—as he consolidated power by creating one imperial version of Christianity. . . . The corruption of a faith fundamentally based on tolerance and compassion by the strong arm of imperial authoritarianism invested Christianity with an insidious schizophrenia with which it has been battling ever since.*[4]

West points out that this marriage between church and state and its resulting schizophrenia within the Christian movement led to "so many of the church's violations of Christian love and justice—from the barbaric crusades against Jews and Muslims, to the horrors of the Inquisition . . . [to] the ugly bigotry against women, people of color, and gays and lesbians . . . [and the] dogmatic justification of slavery."[5] Constantinian Christianity sanctioned a Christian identity that was antithetical to Jesus's radical teachings and values, including Jesus's teachings on egalitarian relationships, radical sharing, wealth renunciation, and material redistribution. With only a few exceptions, the view that wealth and poverty are part of the natural order and that they are somehow connected to God's blessings became part of Christian theological understanding.

By the fourth century, the expansion that had characterized Augustine's Roman North Africa in the previous century had come to a halt. It left in its stead North African Roman cities surrounded by "shanty towns" populated by poor farmers who lived off the land and depended upon the rich who owned it for protection.[6] Ten years before Augustine's birth, Southern Numidia would witness a peasant revolt as a result of these farmers' harsh existence.[7] Yet Augustine would be shielded from such misery. His father would make sacrifices to give him the education he needed to become a schoolmaster and later a bishop.[8] As an educated African, Augustine became a part of that small class of men who, while not considered rich, had no direct contact with either the land or the ensuing misery and "bent backs" from trying to cultivate it.

For the masses of the Roman provinces of North Africa, however, economic conditions during these times were hard.[9] Thagaste may have served as a safe haven for rich refugees driven out of their Roman homes by the revolts and invasions such as that of the Goths,[10] but for its citizens of the lowest classes, neither the influx of these rich aristocrats nor the maintenance of the social status quo brought any relief. Nor did the official church appear to help the situation. Instead, as the impoverished continued in large part to suffer under the burden of substantial tax payments, they came to feel that the church possessed more than its share of goods and that the clergy were among their exploiters.[11]

They were partly right in their assessment. As the long decline of the Roman economy was continuing apace and productive activities were being progressively starved of capital, the population decreased, as did the mobility of labor. The burden of taxation in support of the Roman government increased, together with the degree of concentration of ownership of land in the hands of the already wealthy. And while taxation of the poor and the middle classes grew to an extortionate rate, the Catholic clergy continued to benefit from state support and increasing exemptions due to the concessions of Constantine and his successors who followed his suit.[12]

Constantine's legalization of Christianity with his Edict of Milan (313)[13] halted religious persecution for all Christians and even allowed a few to advance in the army and civil service. However, it paved the way for the prosperity of the Christian church and its leadership not only by returning church property, but by giving political power and economic concessions to priests and bishops in hopes that they would become reverent to the emperor and the empire.[14] Thus, state-sponsored Christianity brought the emergence of new forms of wealth, power, and state patronage among church leadership. The local Christian leader, who bore the Greek title *episcopus*, translated as "overseer" from Latin, and later into "bishop," and who had the ear of the emperor, became a powerful, wealthy, and authoritative figure to be reckoned with. Even a lowly priest, as Augustine professed to be,[15] experienced a life of abundance compared to the masses.[16] Classical scholar James O'Donnell notes:

> *Augustine accepted that not all good Christians would divest themselves of wealth, but he was careful to market himself by his behavior and dress and his studied lack of care for his appearance. He still worried, in his early forties, that the temptation of "worldly ambition" was the one that might most easily ensnare him as a bishop before his congregation. His thoughts in this vein are so consistent and so understandable that we might easily grant him the benefit of the doubt, while observing the persistence of the theme. But we should not let him draw us in too easily. By making the issue an internal one—how one handles the fact of eminence—Augustine distracts us from the genuine social achievement and trappings of his life.*[17]

Even the church's administrative structure was impacted by the infrastructure of the Roman Empire. The church's flow of demands and suggestions traveled up the hierarchy to the emperor and its series of laws was conveyed to the people through the emperor's officials. In fact, during the fourth century, the empire's structure of governance became the structural template for the church.[18]

One can understand why some Christians from the lower social strata would protest the established church as well as the existing socioeconomic order by sympathizing with those who spoke against the oppressive status quo. Among them was the heretic Pelagius, who, defining wealth as a superfluity of unnecessary possessions, argued:

> *The question whether [wealth] comes from God, who is the source of fairness and justice, I leave to your judgment. Evidently, God did create [it] along with everything else, not with the purpose that one*

> *should become prosperous through holding limitless riches, while another suffers excessive deprivation, but so that everyone should in equal proportion and equitably own what the author of fairness has provided. . . . Take away the rich man and you will find no pauper. No one should own more than is necessary, but everyone should have what they need. A few rich people are the reason why there are so many poor.*[19]

Augustine, however, had come to accept the notion that, while charity was expected of the Christian who had a right relationship with wealth, wealth and poverty were indeed part of God's order and wealth renunciation was an affront to God who had bestowed it.

Wealth, Poverty, and the Religious Life

Augustine's theology on the grace of God, which he elucidates in the heat of the Pelagian controversy, gives insight not only into his perception of human frailty and responsibility, but his teachings on the valuation of wealth, poverty, and the religious life. Until the Pelagian controversy, the doctrine of grace had not been a significant issue for the Christian church.[20] Pelagius, responding to what he saw as the moral laxity, "active cruelty, passive selfishness,"[21] and blatant unjust luxury of Christians in Rome, asserted that because humans had free will to act or not, those who chose to do evil and not keep all of God's commandments would be condemned to hell. Insisting that God would not have given his commandments had God not supplied all of humanity with the power to fulfill them, Pelagius argued that the possibility of avoiding sin or achieving perfection was within everyone's reach. God's grace was the redemption from sin by Christ, followed by Christ's life as the inspiration for, and example of, pursuing a perfect and just existence. Pelagianism assumed that one could, by one's own virtue, set oneself apart to live a virtuous life and not succumb to sin or selfish behavior. It was a reform movement developed in response to what some saw as the corruption of Christians during the Later Roman Empire.[22]

Pelagius's appeal for a radical change in the Christian's life and his call to embrace wealth renunciation on a grander scale set in motion the great debate over providential grace, original sin, and human free will—a debate that would ultimately lead to the decisive condemnation of Pelagianism as a system that, according to Augustine, exalted human effort over God's grace, and ultimately threatened the very existence of the Christian church and its ministry. While Pelagius argued that moral reform was necessary to change society,[23] Augustine saw any suggestion to reform society as heretical.[24] And while Pelagius maintained that the abuses of the wealthy were intolerable and the rich could not enter heaven without first renouncing their wealth, Augustine upheld that renouncing one's wealth was not only *not* necessary, but indeed an affront to God's ideal design of and intention for humanity.

Insisting upon the frailty of humans and the necessity of God's grace at every stage and turn of the Christian life from birth to death, Augustine opposed Pelagius's teachings vehemently. Human beings, Augustine said, did not have the necessary freedom to take the initial steps toward doing right. They were in possession of a will, but one that was corrupted and tainted by sin, which biased them toward evil and away from God. Only God's grace could counteract this bias, since humans had fallen from their original state with the fall of Adam and thus were now contaminated by sin from the very moment they were born. Only by God's unmerited and undeserved gift of grace could anyone have a fellowship with God.

Nor did Augustine embrace Pelagius's ideas on wealth and poverty. While he did concede that a few material things were necessary for everyone, such as food, clothing, and shelter, he also conceded that there were those select few for whom more was indeed required to sustain their life—the result of their acquired delicate tastes for certain comforts.[25] Still, one was encouraged to give to the poor that portion of one's wealth that was superfluous, since not giving to the needy what is superfluous is akin to fraud,[26] and since by doing so one was "[giving] the temporal and [receiving] the eternal; giv[ing] the earthly and receiv[ing] the heavenly."[27] However, determining what was to be considered superfluous was a fully private matter, between God and the individual.

For Augustine, the disparity between the rich and poor was not seen as either tragic or a social construction. Rather, he argued it was created by God to accomplish God's plan of salvation.

> *God made the poor to test the human in them, and made the rich to test them through the poor. God has done everything properly . . .*

> *and we must believe that it is good, even though we do not understand why it was done.*[28]

Preaching that "it is Christ, God of the prophets, who not only creates the rich by most graciously giving them goods, but also the poor by most justly withholding or taking away from them,"[29] Augustine maintained that God allows and indeed creates both wealth for the rich and poverty for the poor. This position, for Augustine, does not conflict with Jesus's teachings on wealth renunciation or the radicality of Jesus's command to "go, sell all you have and give to the poor" (Mark 10:21), especially since the command is not meant to be adhered to by all Christians. In fact, the command is not a command at all, but merely counsel for only those who wish to be perfect.[30]

Unlike Pelagius, Augustine seemed more impressed than disturbed by the wealth of his new rich neighbors. He was more committed to instructing the wealthy on the virtues of cultivating an inward (spiritual) humility than affecting the quality of life of the poor, as his letters 130 (to Proba) and 157 (to Hilary) suggest.[31] The economic imbalance between those who ruled over vast agricultural empires, like Proba, and those who were materially destitute, was not the issue at hand. In fact, while others, such as Pelagius, were making a plea for the just distribution of wealth, preaching that the poverty experienced by many was the direct result of wealth held by a few,[32] Augustine was speaking against radically changing the socioeconomic conditions of those on the lower social strata, since, to him, their condition was part of the natural order established by God.[33]

Letters and Sermons on Poverty and Wealth

Augustine's letter to Proba, an elderly widow of the richest man in the Roman Empire, is an excellent window into both his and the Western world's valuation of material possession, inequality, human responsibility, and the religious life. Influenced by a Neoplatonic understanding of the world as a hierarchical chain of creation, from the highest level of rationality and spirituality to the lowest level of materiality, Augustine could readily accept and proclaim a split between the haves and have-nots; between the spiritual existence where thoughts or attitudes reside and the outer realm in which the body finds itself.[34]

Augustine's letter to Proba was meant to be a response to her request for advice on prayer, that is, the significance of prayer for wealthy persons such as herself in light of being the heiress of a vast empire acquired by misappropriation.[35] Yet, while Augustine reveals in the first line of the letter that she is indeed to be prayerful, he provides her with much more than instructions on how or for what to pray. In fact, much of the letter provides a substantial amount of information on how wealthiness should be viewed in light of one's faith journey.

Augustine informs Proba that her salvation rests not so much on her proposed actions to alter her material existence and give away her riches to the poor, but on her attitude toward material possessions. He then informs Proba that her spiritual development requires inwardly despising her material possessions, not necessarily redistributing them, and praying without ceasing as a *desolate widow*. He assures her that while self-control is to be attempted and action is to be contemplated, her attitude is much more important than her actions in the sight of God. And only God, not the world, is to be her judge:

> *you are a widow of wealth and high rank, and the mother of a large family who are still with you and who still reverence you, but I want you to feel desolate . . . remember that you are desolate, however much you may abound in the good fortune of worldly wealth. . . . I say to you about pleasures: if pleasures abound, set not your heart upon them. . . . Many holy men and women have been on guard in every way against riches, as the very source of pleasures, and have cast them aside by distributing them to the poor. . . . [But] if you feel yourself bound by your duty to your family not to do this, you know what account you must give of them to God.*[36]

Thus, even if Proba's position of wealth remains unchanged, there is a place for her in the kingdom of God. Augustine tells her that while it is true that Scripture states "it is easier for a camel to pass through the eye of a needle than for a rich man to enter into the kingdom of heaven," Scripture also declares that the salvation of the wealthy is assured by "a marvelous and most merciful reassurance . . . that what is impossible for men is easy for God."[37]

Proba's task, Augustine says, is not to redistribute her riches, but to consider herself desolate, even as she enjoys her worldly status and wealth. It is her spiritual relationship to wealth that must be reconsidered.

Augustine spends a great deal of energy instructing Proba on how the wealthy are to be humble in their hearts before he begins his actual discussion on prayer. He also makes sure to inform her "do not rely too strongly on the fact they *[riches]* are not lacking to you, *[even though]* they minister to your satisfaction abundantly, *[even though]* they flow to you, so to speak, from a plentiful source of earthly happiness . . . all these things you must inwardly despise and reject."[38]

Thus, with such a spiritual detachment from the world, she is free to pray with true humility, being especially mindful of how she puts forth her supplications:

> *Pray, then as the widow praised by Christ, not yet seeing Him whose help you ask, and however wealthy you may be; pray like a poor woman, for you have not yet the true wealth of the world to come . . . you ought to look on yourself as desolate . . .*[39]

What are her prayers to consist of? Ultimately, she should pray, says Augustine, for true happiness—that is, to be a member of the household of God. Furthermore, she is told to pray for both those under her care and her enemies. Even prayers for "positions of rank and authority," for oneself and one's family, are not improper.[40] But never does Augustine instruct her, in either prayer or deed, to take on the responsibility of altering or accepting her role in maintaining the unjust socioeconomic status quo.

Augustine seems not only to sanction the continuation of the aristocratic lifestyle. He removes that lifestyle and the possession of excessive wealth from human reproof. While Proba is not released from seeking a spiritually pious existence, she is exempt from having to change her wealthy status or assist in any way in transforming the social economic order of her world. While she is told to pray without ceasing, at fixed times for the sake of discipline, for both neighbors and enemies, and for true contentment from God, she is left to decide for herself what other actions she should take as a practicing Christian.[41]

Augustine also wrote an extensive letter to a Sicilian named Hilary, who had written to Augustine asking about teachings that were being circulated around Syracuse. One of those teachings concerned whether a rich man who continued to hold onto his riches could enter the kingdom of God or whether he needed to sell all in order to be able to do so.[42] In his response to Hilary,[43] Augustine addresses several of his correspondent's theological concerns, including free will, the baptism of infants, and the issue of redistributing one's wealth.

Recognizing that Hilary's questions point to the influence of Pelagius's teachings, Augustine begins his response by refuting Pelagius's claims concerning free will, grace, original sin, and infant baptism. A major portion of his letter addresses Hilary's question about poverty and wealth. Augustine reminds his reader that possession of wealth is not problematic. Rather, he argues, it is one's attitude toward wealth that has to be checked. He makes the case that Abraham, Isaac, and Jacob all had wealth,[44] that it was wealthy Abraham who received poor Lazarus into the kingdom,[45] and that the rich man was condemned to hell not because he had wealth but because he showed no mercy toward the impoverished Lazarus.[46]

Augustine explains the ungodliness and sin of the rich man as essentially his pride, which directed him to trust in his riches and despise Lazarus.[47] He writes, "This was intended to show us that on the one hand it was not poverty in itself that was divinely honored, nor, on the other, riches that were condemned, but that the godliness of one and the ungodliness of the other had their own consequences . . ."[48] To make his point, Augustine holds up Abraham as a model of how a rich man should possess his riches; holding lightly onto them and thinking of them as having little worth in comparison with the commandments of God.[49]

In a similar manner, Augustine asserts that the correct interpretation of Matthew 19:21 does not lead one to conclude, as the Pelagian interpretation does, that Jesus instructed the rich man to sell his possessions without first making the distinction between doing what was needed to enter into eternal life—keeping God's commandments—and being perfect—selling all you have and following Jesus. Augustine argues that Christ did not tell the young man that if he desired to enter the kingdom of God he had to sell all he had, but rather that he had to keep all the commandments. Only if he wished to be perfect did he need to sell all he had, give to the poor, and follow Christ so he could have treasure in heaven. Augustine concludes:

> *the good teacher, nonetheless, distinguished the commandments of the law from the more excellent perfection. For he said . . .* If you wish to attain life, observe the commandments, *but here he says,* If you wish to be perfect, go, sell all that you have, *and so on. . . . Why, then, should we deny that rich people, though they lack that perfection, still attain life if they have kept the commandments and have given in order that it may be given them and have forgiven in order that it may be forgiven them?*[50]

Augustine interprets both Jesus's instructions to the rich man in Matthew 19:21 to "go, sell all your possessions and give the money to the poor"[51] and the Apostle Paul's instructions to Timothy to command the rich "not to be haughty, or to set their hopes on the uncertainty of riches, but rather on God who richly provides us with everything for our enjoyment"[52] as warnings to avoid against pridefulness and placing hope in the uncertainty of riches. It is not wealth itself that is problematic, but one's relationship to wealth. In fact, if viewed properly—not as an object that brings real enjoyment but as an instrument that can assist in the pursuit of such—earthly perishable wealth could be used to store up heavenly imperishable wealth.[53] Thus almsgiving, not renunciation, together with prayer and spiritual humility were to be used as antidotes to being wealthy. That such an emphasis could give rise to a number of problems for the economic behavior of rich Christians was insignificant.

In all his sermons on poverty and wealth, Augustine continues his emphasis on almsgiving, and more specifically, on giving what is not needed to sustain the lifestyle to which one has grown accustomed, and on providential inequality. The fact that such an emphasis gives rise to and sanctions inequitable social arrangements is not problematized. In a number of his sermons dealing with wealth, poverty, and almsgiving, Augustine also emphasizes his belief that the poor, whose existence was providential in that they provided the opportunity for almsgiving by the rich, could be used by the rich as stepping stones or instruments toward the goal of salvation. He explains in Sermon 60:

> *What are the poor to whom we give but bearers, our carriers, by whom we convey our goods from earth to heaven? Give then, thou art but giving to thy carrier, he carrieth what thou givest to heaven.*[54]

However, this did not mean that the rich were to redistribute all that God had given them. In fact, while Augustine understood the poor to be the porters who carry the treasures of the rich to heaven, those who were rich were made so as a way to test their faith:

> *Let the rich use what their infirmity has accustomed them to; but let them be sorry, that they are not able to do otherwise. For it would be better for them if they could. If then the poor man be not puffed up for his poverty, why shouldest thou for thine infirmity? Use then choice, and costly meats, because thou art accustomed, because thou canst not do otherwise, because if thou doest change thy custom, thou art made ill. I grant thee this, make use of superfluities, but give to the poor necessaries; make use of costly meats, but give the poor inexpensive food.*[55]

Again, just as wealth was seen as providential and an instrument that the rich could use to secure salvation, poverty was also seen as providential and conducive to salvation, but only for the poor:

> *Any of you then who are listening and are poor, don't seek to become rich. Listen to the apostle, not to me; see what he said: There is a great gain, he says, in piety with contentment. For we brought nothing into this world, and we cannot take anything out of it either; if we have food and clothing, let us be content with that. For those who wish to become—he didn't say, "who are," but "who wish to become"—those therefore who wish to become rich, fall into temptation, he says, and into a snare, and many foolish and harmful desires, . . . for avarice is the root of all evils, and some people by craving for it have gone astray from the faith . . . however, the apostle was not addressing those who are rich with these words, but those who are not, to warn them of wanting to be what they are not.*[56]

In spite of his concern for giving to the poor, when it came to discussing socioeconomic inequities within the social order Augustine reverted to his Roman legal upbringing. He could preach and teach that those wealthy enough to loan money should forfeit receiving payment or collecting any interest, but he counted it a great crime when the poor rebelled and destroyed the extortionate letters of credit by which the rich held them in bondage.[57] He could assert in his letters and sermons that, apart from their socioeconomic status, the poor and the rich were equal. Yet when the poor rebelled against "land-owners of honorable birth and gentlemanly breeding" he would call on the empire to restore order—an order in which the poor would be harshly treated.[58]

Wealth and Poverty in *The City of God*

Profound transition and political crisis characterized Augustine's era from the middle of the fourth century to the early fifth century. The sack of Rome in 410 by Alaric and the Christian Arian Visigoths provided the direct motivation for his writing *The City of God*, which has been regarded as his greatest work. Written as a rebuttal to the argument that Christianity, which usurped and condemned the worship of paganism, was responsible for bringing about the sack of Rome, Augustine would take thirteen years to complete this work. While *The City of God* is not intended to be a treatise, systematic or otherwise, of political thought, there are within it elements of Augustine's political and social thought, making it possible to extract a picture of his position on distributive justice, wealth, and poverty. The first five books were written with the Roman refugees in mind, who were lamenting their fate and blaming Christianity for the sack of Rome. In these opening books, Augustine set out to demonstrate that the Christian God alone prevails. Books 6 through 10 deal more specifically with Greek philosophy and assert that a "true philosopher is the lover of God."[59] In books 11 through 19, Augustine discusses his vision of human society and the doctrine of the two cities—the doctrine that not only sanctioned a dualistic notion of human existence, but also allowed for the continued practice of condoning economic inequality while spiritualizing wealth and poverty.

Augustine's doctrine of the two cities created a sharp separation between heaven and earth. In his statement, "the two cities were created by two kinds of love,"[60] the entire doctrine of *The City of God* is summarized. The selfless love of God was replaced in Adam and Eve by love of self. This love of self reached the point of contempt for God[61] and came to reveal itself in the first instance of pride and Adam and Eve's first disobedience. This error did not stem from something innate in the first humans, but from their response to a suggestion that came from outside. Thus, Augustine explains the origins of the two cities in the fall of the angels. The cities originated in the choice of the angels to serve and to not serve God. Pride, the notion that the self is supremely loveable, was the evil seed. This evil seed deposited in creation the possibility of human sin and manifested itself in Cain and Abel, the offspring of Adam and Eve.

Unlike the fallen angels, humanity was given a second chance through Christianity because humanity was not the original source of all the evil in creation. However, two separate societies were created with a boundary between them—a boundary that runs right through the earthly world:

> *This is assuredly the great difference that sunders the two cities of which we are speaking: the one is a community of devout men, the other a company of the irreligious, and each has its own angels attached to it. In one city, love of God has been given first place, in the other, love of self.*[62]

The material world, then, is disputed territory where the enemy holds sway for the moment. The followers of Christ, the citizens of the heavenly city, must live in this material world "as those on a pilgrimage"[63] or "alien sojourners,"[64] using the laws of the city to shelter themselves, while always planning and preparing to leave that city behind and return home. For the citizens of this material world, or earthly city, the earth seems (wrongly) to be home, and they treat it as such, abandoning their claim to citizenship above.

Augustine's articulation of these two separate worlds—worlds that are intertwined and entangled,[65] but do not touch one another in ways that foster true liberation and justice on the earthly plain—sanctioned the understanding that fallen humanity existed on a corporeal plane. It also sanctioned the notion that real religion was mainly concerned with and, indeed, impacted one's spiritual existence. It solidified the notion of an intractable separation between the bodily and spiritual domains, and that humanity's capacity to work toward seeking justice on earth is futile. In fact, for Augustine, focusing any attention on the social instead of spiritual realm for the sake of liberation on the corporeal plane is inconsequential. Such a separation of the material and temporal realities would not only come to support the disenfranchisement of the body, sexuality, and women in mainstream Western cultures. It would also perpetuate an ambivalent attitude toward Jesus's teachings on poverty, wealth, and material redistribution, making room for the beginnings of a legacy of a theology of prosperity to dominate Christian thinking.

Augustine's views on humanity's ability to invoke a just and equitable society arise from his views that moral debilitations of the human soul impede acting justly. Human beings are just insofar as they are able to know and love God, the supreme good and source of justice. However, their ability to know and love God is impeded by ignorance and weakness—two permanently debilitating effects of original sin on the soul.

Still, according to Augustine, the Christian community is to live in search of the true peace, justice, and liberation of the heavenly Jerusalem while avoiding any illusions about the transient world in which it finds itself. Such an illusion-less existence requires a detachment of the Christian church from the secular world. While secular governments attempt to seek justice and create lasting peace in a world destined to know only trouble and struggle until the last days, the Christian church is to exist on a subversive plane that does not necessarily impact these conditions. However, she—that is, the Christian church—is to "make use of the peace of Babylon,"[66] or rather, take advantage of all of the limited and partial justice and peace that human society has to offer without ever settling for it. She is to use the peace of Babylon, not work to bring it about or enjoy it, without ever taking her focus off the ultimate goal.

The vision of human society of which *The City of God* speaks is bleak. There is no imagining a better human condition. While Christianity offers humanity a hope, there is no changing the stark, damning realities of this present earthly existence. Only at the close of human history with the inception of the last things—death, judgment, heaven, and hell—will true change be realized. Until then, such will be the world of fallen humanity: good will remain inextricably mixed with the bad; the struggle between the two societies will continue to take place in the hearts of humans as a result of their fallenness; and the imperfect "visible" church, essential though dispensable, will continue to include good and evil while serving as a channel of grace and a guide to the true city.

Given his theological outlook and allegiance to the social and economic order of his status-laden Roman world, it may be unreasonable to expect that Augustine would have viewed the relationship between spirituality and wealth any differently. Whatever one thinks was the ultimate reason for Augustine not arguing for the renunciation and redistribution of wealth as an act of spiritual growth, history suggests that his position had a profound effect on the reluctance of later theologians to seriously explore wealth, deprivation, and material redistribution in theological terms. One such theologian was John Calvin, the chief founder and consolidator of the Reformed Church of France and French Switzerland, who not only left the imprint of his thoughts upon all other Reformed churches in Europe; his influence has also shaped theological thought from the time of the Reformation to the present day.

John Calvin and Poverty in the Middle Ages

Poverty as a concern is not a topic that most people think of or connect with the Protestant Reformation. Yet, Reformers did think about the biblical notion of poverty, including the position that the poor occupied in the teachings of Jesus and in the church. The Reformation had no one standard interpretation of poverty, and each Reformer's approach to the topic depended upon the conflicts he encountered and the role he played in the Reform movement. Yet, all of the Reformers, including John Calvin, were in agreement that poverty as it was understood in the Roman Church needed re-visioning. The concept of poverty in the Middle Ages was constantly in flux and inextricably bound to the doctrine of salvation. Poverty had not only become the means by which one lived a devout Christian life. It also became widely defined by humility of spirit and not by indigence. For instance, the practice of poverty among the Benedictine monks during the early monastic movement involved showing one's humility of spirit by leaving one's knightly class, family, weapons, and position of power. Thus, a poor person could be described as either one who has nothing and wishes for nothing or one who has much but behaves as if he or she has nothing. In the same manner, a rich person could be described as one who has wealth and therefore is inflated, or as one who has no wealth but wishes that he or she did.[67] That is to say, for these Benedictine monks and followers of the later Benedictine renewal movement, "The test of poverty would be a state of mind and not an inventory of worldly goods. By arguing this way Benedictines [and the Church], could be financially wealthy and still consider themselves as the poor of God."[68]

For instance, the interpretation of "the poor" in such biblical references as Luke 14:13–14 and 14:21 began to include the clergy.[69] The notion that the poor were in some sense favored by God and that God promised to hear their prayers and forgive them and those for whom they prayed—a notion that was first held by at least some of the early church fathers—became less associated with the involuntary poor and more with the voluntary poor. The consequences of this were threefold.

First, as the title "the poor in Christ" became more associated with the monks, and the voluntarily poor who left material possessions and social status for the sake of religious vows became known as "the poor in spirit" or "worthy poor," those who were indigent or poor by no fault of their own grew to be despised.[70] And as the Middle Ages progressed, the truly hungry and impoverished came to be seen as inferior in this economy of salvation. Second, the social significance of this resulted in the blasphemous acceptance of the state of involuntary poverty in society,[71] which not only "obscured the realities of misery," but even proliferated and sustained them.[72] Third, the monks and those who took vows of poverty were said to be more spiritually perfect than those who had not. This divided the church by implementing two levels of spirituality. The higher level of spirituality was reserved for those who took vows of poverty, while the lower level was occupied by everyone else who had not, and these were said to be distanced from God's favor. This meant that, because the church had the responsibility of receiving and dispersing alms, and the monks were deemed "the worthy poor" and seen as more spiritually perfect than the laity, a wealthy person's intended alms for the poor fell heavily into the hands and coffers of the clergy.[73] Thus, the church usurped not only the revenues intended for the poor, but their spiritual role as well.

During the high to late Middle Ages, some of these ideas were challenged. Religious orders like the Franciscans, led by Francis of Assisi, gave away their material goods to the poor as they preached a message of penance and called others to collect alms only for the poor and their own immediate needs. Francis offered an interpretation of biblical poverty that included a stronger ethic of simplicity and physical moderation. He argued that biblical poverty called for living a life of spiritual humility and practicing renunciation of wealth to limit material inequity. He also attempted to apply a corrective to ecclesial improprieties by laboring beside the poor and preaching that "the poor and the afflicted were valued for their intrinsic human and spiritual worth, and not as mere instruments for the salvation of the wealthy."[74] However, by the end of the thirteenth century, the Franciscans' practice of poverty had lost its effective edge due to the group's own internal battles over requiring wealth renunciation. Later interpretations of Francis's views and the poverty of the Franciscans would become "a more spiritual ideal than a literal one, an attitude of the heart and mind and not an actual physical state."[75]

As the Middle Ages began to decline and the population of the poor swelled, new and more hostile attitudes toward, as well as denigrating words to describe, the poor began to surface. By the second half of the fourteenth century, the disparity between the culture's glorification of religious poverty and the squalid realities of the poor was undeniable.[76] Even with increasing inequity in a developing money economy, the proliferation of heretical groups that challenged the papacy to divest of all its wealth, and the increasing discontent among the poor, the church resisted reforming its spiritualized understanding of poverty or including a stronger ethic of simplicity and physical moderation. It continued instead to neglect the physically poor while it grew in its own wealth and power, holding on to its spiritualized understanding of poverty as "poverty of spirit" and its development of the merit system of salvation. Early Reformers, such as Martin Luther who influenced Calvin's theology, spiritualized the biblical notion of poverty and wealth, stripping it of any socioeconomic significance and tying it to God's providence.[77] Luther disregarded the misery and oppression suffered by entire populations, as evidenced by his exposition on poverty preceding the Peasants' War.[78] Though Luther would later rail against the princes for their neglect of the poor, he would continue to stress that the responsibility for changing the conditions of the poor rested largely with the secular government.[79] Luther's refusal to see the eradication of poverty as a theological mandate and his rejection of socioeconomic interpretations of the biblical notion of poverty[80] became a standard for Calvin.

The Reformation and the Church

By the sixteenth century, the great wealth of the church could be seen everywhere. Vast landholdings and ornate cathedrals embellished with gold and silver were found in every major city across Western Europe. Bishops lived in lavish palace-like homes and enjoyed the privileges and the power of royalty. The grandeur of the church appeared as a stark contrast to the dauntingly impoverished realities of the poor. Urban communities had already begun to turn away from medieval Catholicism toward the evangelical Reformation views that had begun to circulate from the Reformer Martin Luther's Germany throughout Central Europe.[81] Religious struggles ensued, and Protestantism moved westward as Luther's version of the Reformation, which Calvin inherited, made inroads throughout Europe.

In the small city of Geneva, to which Calvin believed God had called him, the tensions which resulted in the adoption of the Reformation did not arise from a division between social classes but from political strains over whether to support Savoy or the Swiss Confederacy.[82] However, economic motivations were not totally out of the picture. In fact, Geneva's merchants were the ones who initially constituted the more zealous supporters of a Swiss alliance because their prosperity rested almost exclusively on the continued participation of Swiss and German merchants. They, along with other artisans who could be called the embryonic middle class of Geneva and the new nobility who had come from their ranks, sought to align themselves with the Swiss as a way to be free from both a Savoyard dynasty that could assure neither their commercial prosperity nor their military security, and from bishops whom they saw as merely actors on behalf of that dynasty.[83] It is doubtful if Calvin could have asserted as much influence as he did over the people if he had not had the support of the city's business sector. Calvin's ability to maintain a marriage of convenience between the city's economic and religious sectors, and his allowing the economy to develop unhindered, enabled him to maintain his control over this embryonic middle class. And as the new middle class grew, so did the adoption of Calvin's ideas.

The Swiss city of Bern converted to the Reformation in 1528 under the leadership of the early Swiss Reformer Ulrich Zwingli, and this helped to push Geneva in the same direction. In addition, the ability of its citizens to successfully sustain a political revolt against the duke and oust their bishop, with the help of Bern, made Geneva a ripe place in which to develop and propagate evangelical views. And although he certainly had no monopoly on bringing about these events, it was John Calvin who gave an entirely new expression to this change. Indeed, his publication, *The Institutes*, was used to foster a religious program of reform that was radically bent toward worldly action.

Calvin's thoughts on how to deal with economic disparity and other problems was based on his understanding of God in relation to God's humanity and God's world. For Calvin, both the nature of God as creator/ruler of all, and humanity as God's fallen creation whose sole purpose is to recognize the sovereignty of God in all things and act according to God's word, called for not just a reformed church but a reformed world, solely founded and ordered on the Word of God. This meant that both humanity's social and religious well-being were to be concerns of the church.

Every person was to know and accept his or her place in society without question. Begging was banned. Charity was expected. Gambling, drinking, and going to taverns, dressing in what was considered an immodest fashion, and extravagant living were regulated and were cause for fines, imprisonment, and banishment.[84] Women could be arrested for "arranging hair to an immoral height."[85] Parents were required to give their children names from the Old Testament.[86] Even entertainments such as music and plays were limited to those of a religious nature.[87] A system of visitation was established in which an elder would visit homes and question the occupants about every phase of their life, while Thursdays were reserved for bringing the accused before the Consistory, which would hear cases and determine the punishment. Offenses related to sexual misconduct were punished with exile or drowning, while adultery and blasphemy were punished with death.[88]

Calvin's twenty-year influence over Geneva's social, business, and ecclesiastical matters, which amounted to a near dictatorship, was not without its benefits to at least some of the disenfranchised. Although Calvin did not create the Genevan General Hospital, his Reformation teachings had a profound impact on the later developments of this all-purpose institution, established to provide for the social welfare of persons whose own resources could not meet their needs.[89] He insisted that deacons should be a separate lay ministry, with a particular set of functions and responsibilities that included caring for the poor and acting as the General Hospital's procurers (who gathered alms) and *hospitalliers* (who distributed those alms).[90] He also helped to maintain, and may have even helped to create, the Bourse française, a cash fund established to assist refugees who wanted to settle in Geneva.[91] His education policy provided elementary school children and orphans with free education in the city schools.[92] He secured the appointment of a physician to attend to the poor and instituted a sort of health service.[93] And, in an effort to curtail unemployment among his fellow French refugees, he persuaded the council to open a silk factory.[94]

Thus, Calvin's reformed ministry became pervasive. His professed reformed understanding of God and humanity not only greatly impacted the religious life, but the social welfare of Geneva's citizens as well. Still, his assertion that "God wills . . . proportion and equality among us, that is, each man is to provide for the needy according to the extent of his means so that no man has too much, and no man has too little,"[95] did not alter his belief that one's present condition, like all of human destiny, is assigned or predestined by God. Nor did it lead him to abandon the prevailing thoughts on wealth and poverty. Instead, like other Reformers, Calvin differed from his opponents only in the degree and extent, but not in the principle of privileging wealth.

Theological Perception on Wealth and Poverty

There is a paucity of material about Calvin's writing on the possession, acquisition, and redistribution of wealth.[96] However, his personal letters on wealth acquisition and redistribution,[97] statements made in several of his commentaries,[98] several passing remarks in his *Institutes*, and some brief references in his theological treaties, provide more than enough information for understanding Calvin's valuation of wealth and poverty. Calvin's involvement and belief in advancing a money economy based on industrial production and acquisition is evident. Not only did he believe that industrial production based upon a money economy was a necessary factor for the development of an advanced society. He approved of the acquisition of greater profits that could be accumulated through trade rather than the old agrarian professions. He saw these greater profits as a reward for greater diligence and greater risks. Although he did prohibit certain types of businesses in Geneva, it is generally agreed that Calvin was in favor of those that he thought promoted economic progress. He lobbied for establishing a cloth and velvet industry in Geneva, which, with the help of state funds, developed into a major industry. Later, when competition from Lyon forced this textile business to close, Calvin suggested manufacturing watches.

Some scholars have argued that Calvin did not regard worldly prosperity as a reward for, or a consequence of, a godly life.[99] At first glance, given Calvin's ambivalence toward wealth, his economics ethics may indeed appear complex and not easy to discern.[100] But even in his uneasiness and ambivalence, Calvin showed a clear and definite, though complex, position on worldly prosperity.

He not only upheld the right of individuals to possess property, but he allowed for lending money at interest, characterizing it as rent paid on capital. And while he attacked the aristocracy, including French aristocrats who were exiled in Geneva, for their stance on doing manual labor (something they considered to be beneath them),[101] he embraced "a kind of bourgeois realism that he thought authorized by Scripture,"[102] which called for a less radical interpretation of Jesus's teachings on wealth acquisition and allowed for inequality along social and economic lines. In other words, while Calvin argued that the poor are better off morally and in other respects than the rich—for they are more likely to be happier with their lives, friendlier, and more hospitable[103]—he accepted and defended social hierarchy in practice and attributed to God the appointment of "princes, aristocrats, nobles and all other ranks of magistrates and rulers." He defended honor, rank, and wealth which was "not at all to be condemned," and he argued "it is even a great blasphemy against God to disapprove of riches, implying that a man who possesses them is thereby wholly corrupted. For where do riches come from, if not from God?"[104] Thus, material inequality was inevitable, and not necessarily undesirable.

We should give, Calvin argued, but not without prudence. We should lend without hoping to receive back; but one is not prohibited from charging interest, for Jesus's commandments about giving are about being spontaneous.[105] Calvin not only chose to break with the church's nearly fifteen-hundred-year tradition of prohibiting usurious lending,[106] he also dismissed the Old Testament's literal and clear prohibition of charging interest (Exod 22:25; Lev 25:35–37; Deut 23:19–20; Ps 15:5; Prov 28:8; Ezek 18:8, 13, 17), which was unanimously forbidden in the Judeo-Christian tradition from at least 1000 BCE until the Protestant Reformation, as an accommodation to the specific needs of primitive Jewish society.[107]

A more likely explanation for the prohibition of charging interest among the Hebrews, which Calvin ignored, was their concept of brotherhood or kinship. This concept, which according to several authors was "presupposed as a matter of course" in the Hebrew biblical text laws regarding usury,[108] called for a display of familial love and care within the extended Hebrew communal family that saw usury as problematic.

Hebrews' concept of brotherhood and kinship was lived out among the Hebrew people in at least two ways. First, the Hebrews' concept of brotherhood and kinship directed them to care for the poor among them and to see the practice of usury as prohibitive since it led to "the unbrotherly act" of making a profit off the need of a financially distressed family member. Second, this concept helped to foster a sense of collective social liability and responsibility among them. This collective consciousness not only heightened the Hebrews' sense of communal well-being. It also led them to view allowing a person to go into debt, regardless of their economic status, as putting the entire community into financial jeopardy.[109]

Not only did Calvin view the Hebrew Bible's prohibition of interest as antiquated and relevant only to the specific needs of primitive Jewish society. He also viewed the historical arguments found in the writings of the church fathers against lending with interest—and, more specifically their use of Luke 6:35—as a misinterpretation of the New Testament text, which, he claimed, actually called not for a rejection of usury but an inclusion of love in all financial transactions, including usury.[110] He writes:

> *This utterance has been wrongly attached [by the church fathers] to usury, as though Christ were only forbidding His own to lend capital for interest. Clearly, from the earlier part of his speech it has a wider*

> *application. Once Christ had explained how the godless behave, in loving their friends and helping those from whom they expect some payback, and to lend to their own kind in order to get as much from them again, He adds how much He asks of His followers, namely, to love their enemies. . . . So we see that the phrase, "hoping for nothing again," is wrongly taken as a reference to interest, added to the principle, for Christ is urging them only to services that are spontaneous, and saying that mercenary actions win no favor in God's sight. . . . Now whether a Christian may from time make some profit on a loan, I have already shown that Christ only wished that the faithful in lending should go further than the profane . . .*[111]

Interpretation of Poverty and Wealth in Scripture

Calvin's commentaries on certain biblical passages also show his defense of wealth acquisition. Rejecting a literal interpretation of Christ's advice to the rich young man to sell all his possessions and give to the poor, Calvin interpreted Christ's advice to the young man as a way of forcing him to recognize his "concealed vice," which was greed:

> *So the reply of Christ [to the young man], which follows was suited to the man's disposition. . . . Christ does not demand anything beyond the commandments of the law, but . . . Christ employed other words for detecting the hidden disease of avarice. I confess that we are nowhere commanded in the law to* sell all; *but as the design of the law is to bring men to self-denial . . . it expressly condemns covetousness . . .*[112]

And Calvin defended wealth as a gift from God:

> *To keep what God has put in our power, provided that, by maintaining ourselves and our family in a sober and frugal manner, we bestow some portion on the poor, is a greater virtue than to squander [sell] all.*[113]

He further explains in his commentary that it was not the actual possession of wealth, but the relationship one had to it that concerned Jesus:

> *Christ warns them . . . how dangerous and deadly a plague avarice is . . . he made the entrance into the kingdom of heaven so difficult for the rich, because it is an evil . . . common to all to trust in their riches . . . this doctrine is highly useful to all; to the rich, that being warned of their danger, . . . may be on their guard; to the poor, that, satisfied with their lot . . . may not so eagerly desire what would bring [them] more damage than gain.*[114]

Focusing on the young man's question regarding what could he *do* to enter eternal life, and his rejoinder to Jesus that he has kept all the commandments, Calvin argues, "because the question was concerned with works" Jesus "refers him to the law,"[115] not as a way to teach that by keeping the law one may merit eternal life, but to show that eternal life is not to be merited by works and that "no [hu]man will ever be able to reach" its standard.[116] For Calvin, pride and vain confidence leads the man to respond that he has kept all the precepts of the law, and it is, according to Calvin, his blindness to this fact that leads Jesus to "employ other words for detecting the hidden disease of avarice."[117] Thus, Jesus is teaching here, according to Calvin, not wealth renunciation or redistribution. He is instructing his followers to "bear the cross" so that they themselves can "be prepared for hunger and poverty,"[118] if and when necessary. Calvin asserts,

> *For though the law nowhere obliges us to "sell all," yet as it represses all sinful desires, and teaches us to bear the cross, as it bids us be prepared for hunger and poverty, the young man is very far from keeping it fully, so long as he is attached to his riches, and burns with covetousness. And He says that one thing wanting, because He does not need to preach to him about fornication and murder, but to point out a particular disease, as if He were laying his finger on the sore.*[119]

Calvin sees poverty and bearing the cross as having the potential to become a vehicle of divine grace and blessing because poverty strips away self-confidence and false security while the experience of bearing the cross brings about knowledge of self. Poverty and afflictions promote self-doubt and vulnerability. They reveal humanity's *spiritual poverty* and inability to change. For Calvin, such truth should not only foster a sense of humility that allows the Holy Spirit to work in the human heart; but it is *poverty of spirit* that drives believers to depend upon the mercy of God and seek God's grace, which in turn provides a knowledge of God's divine glory and brings believers into communion with God. Poverty and afflictions, then, serve as a kind of revelatory vehicle of who God is, if the person *willingly* bears the cross as a way of following Christ and conforming to Christ's example.

Yet, in speaking to the role or place of poverty in the Christian life, Calvin comments that Matthew 5:3 expresses Christ's intention "more clearly"[120] and that "Luke (6:20) gives nothing more than a simple metaphor" that does not go far in explaining that in both texts Christ is pronouncing "those to be happy who, chastened and subdued by afflictions, submit themselves wholly to God, and, with *inward humility*, betake themselves to him for protection."[121] Thus, the message in both texts can be said to be a reference to those who are poor in spirit, who bear their afflictions or adversity patiently, and who put their hope in the heavenly life to come. Even Luke's pronouncement of a curse upon the rich is meant only for those "who are so completely occupied with their worldly possessions, that they forget the life to come."[122]

Those who do not redistribute their possessions are not excluded from the kingdom, provided they are not "lifted up by confidence in the blessings of the present life," including prosperity, and "they do not become snares for themselves, or fix their hope on the earth, so as to shut against them the kingdom of heaven."[123]

Neither did Calvin's thoughts concerning Christ's humble origins[124] lead him to see economic injustice as anything other than God's providence.[125] Even following Jesus's teachings on giving one's coat to someone who already had one's cloak was seen as mainly commendable for showing patience; and doing so did not bar one from arguing a case against such actions. And just as lending without hope of receiving was commendable but did not prohibit charging interest, selling all you have is "not to be applied too exactly."[126] And while he did, however, recognize what he called the "insatiable desire for possessions" as a "major plague,"[127] the acquisition of material wealth was indeed a blessing, one that carried with it the responsibility of aiding those less fortunate according to one's conscience.

Calvin did suggest that there was a greater likelihood for the poor to be numbered among the elect, remarking that although "by its nature wealth does not prevent us from following God . . . human nature is so depraved, it is almost certain that those who are well off will choke on their riches."[128] He also stressed that the poor, the special brethren of Christ,[129] consisted both of the deserving (the sick, disabled, widowed, and orphaned) to whom the wealthy were to give, and the undeserving (the strong and yet lazy). The task of the rich, in their giving, was not to give to both, but to discern between the two and give to the deserving. Thus, for Calvin, both kindness and harsh discipline were part of the actual Christian practice of almsgiving, and the message of giving to those who deserved and withholding from or punishing those who did not merely reflected the complex nature of his perception of the poor as Christ's special brethren and as guilty sinners. Thus, there had to be both deserving and undeserving poor to explain this dichotomy. Those considered the sick, disabled, widowed, and orphaned were separated from those considered strong and lazy. By the visible signs of their will, the poor were classified as either sheep or goats, and it was the task of the rich, that is, the governing elites, to interpret these signs.

In his exegesis of Matthew 25:35 and 36, Calvin's primary focus is on correcting what he sees as incorrect interpretations of these verses. He argues that the text does not teach that doing good works, such as giving to the poor, ensures eternal life:

> *We do not deny that a reward is promised to good works, but maintain that it is a reward of grace, because it depends on adoption . . . we must therefore hold these two principles first, that believers are called to the possession of the kingdom of heaven, so far as relates to good works, not because they deserve them through the righteousness of works, or because their own minds prompted them to obtain that righteousness, but because God justifies those whom [God] previously elected. Secondly, although by the guidance of the Spirit they aim at the practice of righteousness, yet as they never fulfill the law of God, no reward is due to them, but the term "reward" is applied to that which is bestowed by grace.*[130]

While giving to the poor is to be viewed as giving to God, doing so has no meritorious value for salvation for the giver. God rewards those whom God justifies by God's grace. Furthermore, Calvin makes a distinction between the faithful worship of God and doing good works. Calvin contends that, while charitable acts toward the poor are important, they are less important than "hearing the Word . . . observing the Holy Supper, and . . . bearing the cross, and prayer, and chastity."[131] In other words, there is, for Calvin, a hierarchical order to worshipping and pleasing God in which these are "more important than charity . . . and in like manner, faith and supplication . . . more valuable than alms . . ."[132]

Calvin was particularly against redistribution of wealth, which he saw as plundering the rich in order to deal humanely with the poor.[133] While he professed that economic life was to be controlled by the principle of stewardship, he saw poverty, wealth, and private property as fundamental to a social order created and ordained by God, vigorously defending the latter two and binding all three to the providence of God. And in so doing, he seemed to sanction the existence of economic inequality.

It was, for Calvin, "a great blasphemy against God to disapprove of riches . . . for where do riches come from, if not from God?"[134] According to Calvin, material inequality is not only inevitable, it is desirable because God's providence brings such about. And money, representing these goods, is the means that God uses to give humanity what is necessary to support its existence. Thus, God puts wealth at the disposal of certain persons so that they may use it to live their lives, run the society for which they are responsible, and use God's abundance properly.

Thus, while Calvin warned against the dangers of coveting material possessions, his teachings allowed money and material wealth to take on not just a utilitarian function, but a spiritual mission, especially in light of his claim in his sermon on Deuteronomy 8:14–20 that,

> *as a general principle . . . riches come not at all to men through their own virtue, nor wisdom, nor toil, but only by the blessing of God. . . . Though others are rich before they are born, and their fathers have acquired great possessions . . . this is not by accident, but the providence of God . . .*

and his assertion that,

> *The poor . . . serve as a positive function in God's overall scheme of things . . . they serve as a type of barometer of the faith and charity of the Christian community . . . God sends us the poor as his receivers. And although the alms are given to mortal creatures, yet God accepts and approves them and puts them to one's account, as if we had placed in his hands that which we give to the poor.*[135]

In his commentary on Paul's teachings on II Corinthians, Calvin's ambivalence toward wealth, poverty, and Jesus's radical egalitarian teachings comes through loud and clear. He begins by acknowledging Paul's praise of the Macedonian churches, who, though extremely poor, voluntarily gave to those in need:

> *The Macedonians . . . making no account of themselves, and almost losing sight of themselves, concerned themselves . . . [with] providing for others . . . beyond their ability . . . from their slender means.*[136]

He continues by warning the wealthy that it is their duty to aid the poor:

> *Those who have riches, whether inherited or won by their own industry and labor, are to remember that what is left over is meant not for intemperance or luxury but for relieving the needs of the brethren . . .*[137]

And he invokes Christ as the model for radical giving and generosity:

> *Christ* was rich, *because he was God, under whose power and authority all things are . . . even in our human nature, which he put on, as the Apostle bears witness, he was the* heir of all things. . . . *He nevertheless* became poor, *because he refrained from possessing. . . . We see, what destitution . . . awaited him immediately on his coming from his mother's womb. We hear*

> *what he says himself [in Luke 9:58], "The foxes have holes, and the birds of the air have nests: the Son of man hath not where to lay his head." Hence he has consecrated poverty in his own person, that believers may no longer regard it with horror. By his* poverty *he has* enriched *us all for this purpose—that we may not feel it hard to take from our abundance what we may lay out upon our brethren.*[138]

Yet, neither his recognition of the need to give to the poor, his stress upon Christ's humble origins, nor his understanding of Christ as the ultimate example for giving led him to abandon his stance on material redistribution, as he goes on to say, "indeed . . . we are not bound to such an equality as would make it wrong for the rich to live more elegantly than the poor."[139] For, according to Calvin, it is quite natural for the poor to eat "coarse bread and a scanty diet," while the rich live "more abundantly, according to their circumstances," as long as they (the rich) do not fail to give what they do not use to the poor.[140]

While it may be argued that the Scriptures were the original source for the ideas that Calvin expressed in his theological writings, Calvin also drew upon previous theologians from among the generation of reformers whom he followed, and from the early church fathers. Scholars have long since noted that St. Augustine was among those from whom Calvin drew heavily.[141] The unique and constant influence of St. Augustine upon Calvin is undeniable.[142]

Even as he rejected Augustine's (and the church's long-standing) condemnation of lending money at interest, he would remain influenced by and indebted to Augustine, further perpetuating ambiguous thinking about material possession and acquisition.[143]

Institutes of the Christian Religion

As historian of Christianity François Wendel notes, the whole of Calvin's theological thought can be found in his publication, *Institutes of the Christian Religion*. The *Institutes*, initially designed and published in 1536 as a catechism of six chapters, was written in direct response to Francis I's persecutions of French Protestants.[144] By its final edition in 1559, it had been expanded to a treatise of eighty chapters. The *Institutes* at once presented a system of doctrine that dissented from the medieval understanding of the Christian life and established Calvin as a frontrunner among the literary champions of the evangelical faith. An exposition of the Christian religion in general, a vindication of the evangelical faith in particular, and an apologetic aimed at defending Protestant believers against persecution, the *Institutes* is considered by some scholars to be the most systematic presentation of the Christian life that the Reformation produced.[145]

The *Institutes* shows that central to Calvin's theology is the absolute transcendence and total "otherness" of God in relation to a fallen humanity. Calvin's conception of God was one of ruler and king of the universe. Nothing and no one exists in any state outside of the realm of God's will. While God's rightful place in the universe is creator of all, sovereign ruler of all, and redeemer of whom God elects, humanity's rightful place in the universe is as God's creation, subject to and radically dependent upon God's will and God's grace for salvation. Indeed, one's ability to truly understand oneself is contingent upon one's ability to understand the infinite distance and distinction between oneself and God. Thus, for Calvin, coming to grips with humanity's utter dependence upon God and the role of God as creator and redeemer is the first step in coming to grips with oneself and one's place in the world.

But not only is a person's knowledge of her/himself seen as, first of all, inseparably connected to her/his knowledge of God as creator (and redeemer) and, second, controlled by God.[146] Even our ability to move beyond our rudimentary knowledge of God as creator (that is, beyond what Calvin calls our "natural knowledge" which is distorted by human sin) to a more complete knowledge of God as redeemer, as revealed through Scripture and mediated through Christ, is providential.[147] Humanity, enfeebled by sin, can only rise to its true intended state of being not through worldly wisdom or self-reliance, but by God's undeserved grace. Yet human beings do have a responsibility to obey God; a God who knows and wills what is best for God's creatures; who designed creation in an orderly and utilitarian fashion; who made humanity the most excellent example of God's works and the most privileged of all creation;[148] who distributed to humanity both poverty and riches; and who fashioned all else in creation to serve this humanity.

The scholar Albert Hyma argues that Calvin "said nothing of the slightest importance about economic theories . . . in his most famous work, *The Institutes of the Christian Religion*."[149] However, there is significant evidence of Calvin's ambivalent thoughts on wealth and poverty in this work. On one hand, Calvin strictly warns that the proper Christian stance is not to amass wealth or,

> *greedily to strive after riches and honors—whether relying upon our own dexterity of wit or our own diligence, or depending upon the favor of men, or having confidence in vainly imagined fortune—but [for us] always to look to the Lord so that by his guidance we may be led to whatever lot he has provided.*[150]

On the other hand, similar to what he wrote in his commentaries and sermons, Calvin argues:

> *We must consider that what every man possesses has not come to him by mere chance, but by the distribution of the supreme Lord of all. For this reason, we cannot by evil devices deprive anyone of his possessions without fraudulently setting aside God's dispensation.*[151]

In fact, he sees it as mockery to strive after wealth *and* call upon God for one's daily bread:

> *[For] those who, not content with daily bread but panting after countless things with unbridled desire, or sated with their abundance, carefree in their piled-up riches, supplicate God with this prayer are but mocking him.*[152]

Material inequality was, for Calvin, inevitable, and not necessarily undesirable. Although he argued that all were called to recognize themselves as "a debtor to his neighbors [who] ought to, in exercising kindness toward them, set no other limit than the end of his resources,"[153] he also maintained that the prosperous might well enjoy the benefits of their wealth, as long as they *identified* with the poor, who were co-members in the body of Christ and who were even God's favored children. It was holding to "the rule of love" and "mutual affection," and maintaining the conviction that "I cannot separate myself from those" who are in need and "to whom God has knit me," that was of the utmost importance.

Thus, neither material inequality nor hierarchy and subordination were seen as problematic, but as divinely ordained precepts. The first condition (material inequality) provided the opportunity to practice selflessness and conquer one's attachments to worldly possessions while better adapting to Christ's teachings on self-sacrifice. The second (hierarchical socioeconomic roles) reflected the different functions of the Christian faithful, metaphorical members of the body of Christ, and thus provided for an appropriate social order. One could even distance oneself from Geneva's poor-relief system, as Calvin did, since one was encouraged to participate in face-to-face charity, like the deacons who took up collections during the service of the Lord's Supper for the poor among them.[154]

4

THE LEGACY OF A THEOLOGY OF PROSPERITY ON AMERICAN SOIL

NEARLY TWO CENTURIES after Calvin's theology helped to further a set of social teachings that upheld an ambivalent attitude toward wealth and poverty in the Western Christian tradition, that same attitude remained largely unchanged. Two theologians who tried to counter this legacy with radical new perspectives on the acquisition and redistribution of wealth were John Wesley and Walter Rauschenbusch. The responses of Rauschenbusch and Wesley to the problem of poverty and wealth led both theologians to reinterpret the notions of "kingdom" and "salvation" in the face of the inadequate formulations they inherited.[1] They both endeavored to forge a social soteriology in which the gap between Christianity and social action is bridged and to widen the scope of salvation to include the social good. They both provided a critique of wealth and poverty with regard to the impact of each upon the community and allowed for Western Christianity's provisional opening for rethinking poverty, wealth acquisition, renunciation, and redistribution.

Wesley's Methodist teachings would be carried onto American soil by those he would hand pick and send. His theology of stewardship, with its threefold injunction to "gain all you can; save all you can; give all you can," prioritized almsgiving to the poor and would have a profound impact on American Protestants' attitudes toward individual wealth, poverty, and redistribution of material possessions. However, Wesley's teachings did little to alter the prevailing ambivalent attitude toward wealth accumulation. This ambivalent attitude toward Jesus's teachings on wealth, poverty, and material redistribution moved across the American theological landscape[2] buttressed by the Puritan work ethic, a contempt for the poor, a view of the poor's existence as punishment for their sins,[3] and a Darwinian understanding of socioeconomic enterprise and human evolution. Among the Christians in this "New World" who, like Wesley, attempted to bring a critique to this legacy[4] was the leading social gospel theologian, Walter Rauschenbusch.

A product of German middle-class Protestantism of a late-Calvinist, Radical Reformation bent, Rauschenbusch's inherited conservative Christian thinking was radically transformed by his experience as a pastor of the Second German Baptist Church in New York's Hell's Kitchen—the underside of what was then America's largest city. His new acquaintance with poverty led him to conclude that the suffering he encountered among the poor on a daily basis had human causes. For Rauschenbusch, poverty was not the result of God's providence but a result of an economic system that earned feasts for some at the price of starvation for others. He reinterpreted the classical theological categories of "the kingdom of God" and "salvation" that he inherited, and he argued that seeking the kingdom of God and salvation required an analysis of the social order.

Rauschenbusch's argument for a revaluation of wealth, poverty, and material acquisition and his disparagement of those who minimized the contemporary significance of Jesus's teachings on wealth, poverty, and material possession would also fail to seriously hinder the prevalence of what I call a "legacy of a theology of prosperity." Still, his formulation of a theology that at once calls for the church's involvement in redeeming humanity's corporate life and incorporating a sociohistorical interpretive focus on redemption and the kingdom of God is instructive for countering both an ambivalence toward Jesus's teachings and theologies of prosperity. While theologians of a religiously inclusive nature might rightfully argue against Rauschenbusch's perception of progress and his desire to "Christianize the social order and all aspects of the social life,"[5] he was one of the few religious thinkers to problematize rendering social aid without any intention of reconstituting the social community. Thus, uncovering his important but often overlooked thoughts about poverty and wealth can help us to construct a theology that advances a communal vision for abundant living.

John Wesley and His Influence on the Legacy

John Wesley was born into a family that could boast two generations of ministers and was deeply influenced by the religious and political conflicts of seventeenth-century England.[6] Both of Wesley's parents had been born into Calvinist families but had rebelled against the Church of England. They would later migrate into High Church Anglicanism after marriage, taking with them their heritage of dissent, methodical religious exercises, strict morals, and belief in the spiritual as well as social value of discipline.[7] These would come to have a deep influence upon Wesley.

Wesley graduated from Oxford University and became a priest in the Church of England in 1728, but it would be several years before his work as an itinerant preacher began. From 1729 to 1735, he remained at Oxford as a teacher, where he involved himself in a religious society initiated by his brother that combined social service with strong religious commitment.[8] After an unsuccessful mission to Georgia, a colony in America, to Christianize and evangelize the population, he returned to England and established more religious societies focused on reforming Christianity into a religion that emphasized strict piety and Christ-like sharing.

Though unhappy with the Church of England's failure to act as the moral catalyst of society and address religious laxity and the social condition of the poor, Wesley's desire was not to establish a new church. Rather, his goal was to challenge the existing one. His development of religious societies into a system, as well as his use of lay preachers and officers within them, was the result of the movement's growth.[9] However, because his sermons contained strict religious, economic, and ethical instructions that called the faithful to imitate Christ-like sharing, he was unwelcome in many of the Church of England's pulpits. As a result, he resigned himself to preach chiefly in these ever-growing societies. In 1739, his friend George Whitefield, who had been preaching in Bristol to coal miners, invited Wesley to join him in "open-air field preaching,"[10] and thus began Wesley's itinerant preaching ministry to and on behalf of the poor—a ministry that would span the remaining fifty years of his life.

Wesley defended what his opponents called his "enthusiastic preaching," and the crowds' enthusiastic response to him, by saying that he was simply teaching the truth according to both Scripture and the Church of England. He argued that his preaching outside the established church allowed him to take the message to where the people were. And though he would continue to regard his societies as part of the Church of England, his teachings promoted considerable controversy because of what he termed the *doctrine of Christian perfection*,[11] and his insistence that, in this life, the born-again Christian could have the mind of Christ and come to a state where the love of God, or perfect love, reigned in every aspect of one's living—including one's love and care for others.

Wesley went on to argue that since Christ's teachings delineated one's spiritual and social responsibilities, including one's responsibilities toward a brother and sister, there was no getting around it—one was to live among, and give all one could, to those in need, especially the poor. Thus, for Wesley, the holistic nature of salvation as modeled by Christ necessitates connecting the reality of sanctification to active ministry or stewardship to those in need. This meant actively responding to Jesus's teachings on wealth redistribution.

Wesley's Socioeconomic Context

The evangelical revival of the eighteenth century was not a monopoly of Wesley's. There were a number of efforts at the onset of the century to initiate a more involved and less lethargic religious life, including one initiated by Wesley's father, Samuel Wesley. Religious societies were introduced in London and elsewhere to allow for prayer, Scripture reading, frequent communion, aiding the poor, soldiers, and others, and encouraging preaching. But these were local efforts and limited in influence. The evangelical revival did not swell into a mighty tide until John Wesley, along with his brother Charles and George Whitefield, came onto the scene.

Perhaps Wesley stands out because of the broad influence of the "Wesleyan movement," and his unyielding insistence upon responsibility to God for the goods and gifts of creation. Perhaps it is because of what has been considered the extreme nature of his divergent teachings on wealth and poverty.

Wesley's work—work that would ultimately influence Christianity on American soil—can also be viewed in the context of the development of a philanthropic impulse in eighteenth-century England. Both inside and outside the church, enterprises of humanitarian service spread. This was a huge changeover from the old position based on class distinction and almsgiving to one that would have dramatic implications for the impending new world being ushered in with the Industrial Revolution.

By modern standards, eighteenth-century England had little government, most of which was exercised locally through parish vestries and town corporations. The national government was not only limited, but was also non-intervening in its attitudes, anxious to avoid unpopularity. The House of Commons essentially represented men of property (women could not own property) and was controlled by aristocratic patrons. Thus, the aristocracy dominated eighteenth-century England. They had power and were influential in determining government policies and laws, and the decisions of the monarchy. The monarchs during the eighteenth century were indifferent to the general public.[12] The monarchy and the aristocracy were concerned with riches, power, and social prestige. They took great advantage of Great Britain's expansion and its leading place in the world's economy with little or no concern for the internal social and economic conditions of the general population.

The indifference, opportunism, and almost complete lack of compassion for those who were poor manifested in the curtailing of the Poor Laws, which stated minimum wages for apprentices, servants, and laborers, as well as other requirements to protect the well-being of workers. This law, and others intended to protect the poor, were abused, and several reforms to the Poor Laws did more to punish the poor than help them.[13] Both the aristocracy and the government viewed the poor as scapegoats for the ills of society. Both believed that the administration of the Poor Laws was making the poor less responsible for their poverty and increasing rather than decreasing their numbers. And both, therefore, were in favor of reforming the Poor Laws to create standards to which the poor, who were seen as responsible for poverty's restraint on the economic growth of the empire, had to adhere in order to receive assistance.[14]

Eighteenth-century England saw tremendous change, including an increase in the production of goods, capital investment, individual enterprise, and the number of factory workers. Great Britain's conquest of India, and India's production and exportation of wood and cotton, gave the British a monopoly on the production and trade of these two items. Landowners changed the use of their lands from agriculture to the production of wood, which required less labor and fewer workers. A new theory of economics developed as well, evidenced by Adam Smith's publication, *Inquiry into the Nature and Causes of the Wealth of Nations*. This theory opposed a government-controlled economy and called for greater freedom in economic matters. It argued that an enlightened self-interest would benefit both the well-being of the individual and society.[15] Yet its implementation marginalized farm laborers by replacing them with machines and displaced others from their rural lands. It initiated economic practices that sanctioned forcing women and children into the workforce under deplorable conditions. Furthermore, it reinforced the understanding that material inequality as well as hierarchy and subordination were part of the natural order of society.

This dehumanizing trend brought on by the Industrial Revolution and the migration from England's countryside into its cities not only initiated squalid living conditions, sprawling dirty factories, and exploitative labor in the name of free enterprise. It also increased philanthropy in England, which was bolstered by an increase of wealth among the upper classes and the survival experience of the previous century, during which the plague had taken the lives of thousands.[16]

But despite such philanthropic efforts, the masses and the poorest of the poor were not reached by the benevolence of the wealthy. For, although charity and philanthropy were growing during the eighteenth century, such endeavors were also becoming more organized and institutionalized. These institutionalized charities established standards to identify the "deserving poor" and discourage begging.[17] They followed the example of the Poor Laws, the main goals of which were to limit the number of recipients who would receive help, determine who were the "deserving poor," and reduce society's responsibility for all others in need. Thus, the economy of eighteenth-century England was marked by contrast and contradiction. The vast economic growth and new theories that purported economic freedom and equal opportunity for all strongly favored the upper and middle classes, leaving the lower classes poor and in a state of servitude and hopelessness.

The new economic theories, the administration of the Poor Laws, and the increase in philanthropic endeavors did not bring significant relief to the poor. Nor did they spark a radical response from the eighteenth-century Anglican Church, the established Church of England.[18] The priests were strongly allied with the aristocracy and were, as was the Anglican Church, dependent upon the aristocracy for subsistence and on Parliament and the monarchy for official recognition. They showed little interest in the poor, and their ideologies became almost indistinguishable from their rich patrons.

Even the Anglican bishops, who were political appointees and who sought social prestige and political power, followed the footsteps of the rich.[19]

Thus, the prevailing economic theory and positive view of prosperity and self-interest, adopted by the wealthy, the politically powerful, *and* the Church of England, left little room for a serious critique of the existing valuation of poverty and wealth and predicament of the poor. There was no institutionalized response to the social condition of the masses from the church, and though it supported the few local pastors who provided assistance to their parishioners on their own, the church would remain a silent bystander and supporter of material inequality.

Against this backdrop, Wesley would not only actively care for the poor but also offer a critique of the church's position and its silence. His critique was informed by his conviction that a pursuit of holiness and one's spiritual formation was intricately tied to one's engagement in ministry to and with the poor and his writings are filled with references to this conviction.[20] His teachings on wealth, poverty, and material redistribution represented an ethical critique of the social problems he encountered in eighteenth-century England. He attempted to address the condition of the nonpropertied masses who were becoming increasingly disenfranchised economically, politically, and religiously by preaching against wealth accumulation and advancing a doctrine of stewardship, as his sermons on wealth, the use of money, and stewardship all illustrate.

Early American Methodism

Wesley's mission to the American colony of Georgia as an employee of the Society for the Propagation of the Gospel in Foreign Parts was the ground on which he tried to employ his teachings. His instruction was to serve as the parish priest for Georgia's settlers and to convert the area's Chickasaw Native Americans. However, Wesley had another goal in mind. His mission, as he saw it, was to practice his model of holiness and reinstate Primitive Christianity. He sought to imitate the practices of Christ and the early church by experimenting with what would become the essential ingredients of his religious movement: intensive prayer meetings, precise sacramental observances, confession, penance, ascetical discipline, hymn singing, preaching outdoors, employing lay itinerants, and ministering to the poor and outcast.

Wesley would spend less than two years on American soil. However, before he left the colony in late 1737, he published the first Methodist psalm book and began formulating his own peculiar brand of theology, one that would stress a believer's free will, the availability of salvation to all, and the tangibility of religious conversion. His teachings were spread across American terrain, first by George Whitefield, though with a Calvinist bent, and later by Wesley's hand-picked itinerant preachers who were more closely aligned with his own teachings. While Georgia proved to be fertile ground for much of Wesley's teachings, what did not take root in full measure was his valuation of poverty and wealth redistribution and his directives on meeting the needs of one's neighbors through self-denial and sharing; what he called works of mercy. Indeed, Wesley's argument that the act of retaining one's wealth instead of sharing it with the poor was an indication of a decline in one's spiritual growth[21] would be contested time and again by his American religious converts, even as they held to his other teachings.

Sermons on Riches

Wesley's audience was primarily the working poor, and "after [his] soul searching conversation with Whitefield, he overcame his commitment to 'decency and order' and began preaching in the streets and the fields . . ."[22] His task as he understood it was to take the Gospel to poor multitudes to "convince the masses of his time that there was at hand news from God, . . . that the news was good,"[23] which made possible Christian perfection and which called the faithful to social holiness through a zealousness in good works.[24] Though he consorted mostly with those who owned very little and who could never be certain of their financial future, Wesley preached widely and became so well known that his personal income eventually reached £1,400 per year—equivalent today to £397,000 or more than $495,000 (US). Yet he chose to live on £30 while giving the rest away, to embody what he was advocating for those to whom he preached.

The heart and substance of Wesley's teachings on Christian faith can be found in his sermons. Of the 151 sermons he left behind in print,[25] 10 percent of these treat the subject of wealth and poverty at great length.[26] Of this 10 percent, five are exclusively devoted to the topic of wealth and poverty, and four of these provide an excellent understanding of his thoughts on acquiring wealth and addressing the needs of the poor.

Sermon 108: "On Riches"

In his sermon "On Riches,"[27] which concludes his second series of sermons published in 1788, Wesley articulates both his thoughts on the perils of wealth and his definition of who he considered to be the wealthy. For Wesley, the possession of wealth was dangerous because of the ways wealth hindered the rich from "have[ing] the mind that was in Christ," and "walk[ing] as Christ walked: Such are the hindrances to holiness, as well as the temptations to sin, . . . which surround him on every side."[28] And who, for Wesley, are the rich? Using Matthew 19:24 to assert his argument that, "It is easier for a camel to go through the eye of a needle," than it is to have riches and not trust in them,[29] Wesley defines the rich as "not only a man that has immense treasures, . . . that has heaped up gold as dust, and silver as the sand of the sea; but anyone that possesses more than the necessaries and conveniences of life . . . that has food and raiment sufficient for himself and his family, and something left over."[30] And here, as in earlier sermons,[31] he attempts to make the case for how the acquisition of wealth is damaging even to the most exemplary Christian.

It is here also that Wesley shows a different interpretation of this text than Calvin. Wesley does not diminish Jesus's reproof of wealth. Neither does he particularize Jesus's saying to only the one rich man in the text. Nor does Wesley believe, as does Calvin, that it is one's trust in, or relationship with, wealth that one must be on guard against. Wesley understands that it is wealth itself that Jesus finds destructive to a person's ability to live holy:

> *It has indeed been supposed, he [Jesus] partly retracts what he had said concerning the difficulty of rich men's being saved, by what is added in the tenth chapter of St. Mark. For after he had said, (verse 23,) "How hardly shall they that have riches enter into the kingdom of God!" when "the disciples were astonished at his words, Jesus answered again," and said unto them, "How hard is it for them that trust in riches to enter into the kingdom of God!" (Verse 24.) . . . Our Lord did not mean hereby to retract what he had said before. So far from it, . . . he immediately confirms it by that awful declaration, "It is easier for a camel to go through the eye of a needle, than for a rich man to enter into the kingdom of God." . . . Both of these sentences . . . assert the very same thing.*

> *The meaning then of our Lord's assertion is this,—that it is absolutely impossible, unless by that power to which all things are possible, that a rich man should be a Christian. . . . Such are the hindrances to holiness. . . . The root of all religion is faith, without which it is impossible to please God. Now, whether you take this in its general acceptation, for an "evidence of things not seen," of the invisible and the eternal world, of God and the things of God, how natural a tendency have riches to darken this evidence, to prevent your attention to God and the things of God, and to things invisible and eternal! And if you take it in another sense, for a confidence; what a tendency have riches to destroy this. . . . Or if you take faith, in the proper Christian sense, as a divine confidence in a pardoning God; what a deadly, what an almost insuperable, hindrance to this faith are riches!*[32]

Wealth destroys one's sense of humility, has the ability to halt the development of, and even diminish, one's faith or one's "divine confidence in a pardoning God," and causes "trust, either for happiness or defense, in them [riches], not 'in the living God!'"[33]

The acquisition and storing up of wealth, Wesley argues, leads to the inevitable downfall of the Christian because it also destroys patience and produces vices and passions that are:

> *Contrary to the love of our neighbor: Contempt, for instance, particularly of inferiors, than which nothing is more contrary to love—Resentment of any real or supposed offense; perhaps even revenge, although God claims this as his own peculiar prerogative—At least anger; for it immediately rises in the mind of a rich man, "What! To use me thus! Nay, but he shall soon know better: I am able to do myself justice!"*[34]

It produces not only an increase in pride, but a reduction in one's ability to love one's neighbor as oneself, as well as an increase in an inability to see one's faults and imperfections. It leads to forgetfulness of God and a kind of practical atheism.[35] Ultimately, as one uses it to seek gratification and happiness from the world, it leads to idolatry, and loving the creature instead of the Creator: "But how many species of idolatry is every rich man exposed! What continual and almost insuperable temptations is he under to 'love the world!' and that in all its branches—the desire of the flesh, the desire of the eyes, and the pride of life."[36] Wesley would continue his stern advice in other sermons on this topic.

Sermon 87: "The Danger of Riches"

The straightforward message in this sermon is that pursuing riches hauled people into hell. Preaching from I Timothy 6:9 ("They that will be rich fall into temptation and a snare, and into many foolish and hurtful desires, which drown men in destruction and perdition"), Wesley maintains this is not just true for a select few, but for anyone who would seek material possessions "above the plain necessaries, or at most conveniences, of life":

> *The Apostle does not here speak of gaining riches unjustly, but of quite another thing: His words are to be taken in their plain obvious sense, without any restriction or qualification whatsoever. St. Paul does not say, "They that will be rich* by evil means, *by theft, robbery, oppression, or extortion; they that will be rich by fraud or dishonest art"; but simply, "they that will be rich": These, allowing, supposing the means they use to be ever so innocent, "fall into temptation and a snare, and into many foolish and hurtful desires, which drown men in destruction and perdition."*[37]

Property was to be shared, according to God, the proprietor of all. Those who pursue money, or the things that money could buy, are denying God's will. Indeed, by increasing their wealth, they become lax and prideful:

> *You cannot deny yourself the poor pleasure of a little sleep, or of a soft bed. . . . Indeed, you "cannot go out so early in the morning; besides it is dark, nay, cold, perhaps rainy too. . . ." You did not say so when you were a poor man. You then regarded none of these things. . . . You are but the shadow of what you were! What have riches done for you?*[38]

And such pride and sloth leads one to distance oneself from the poor. One ceases from identifying with them and ministering to their needs:

> *Do you fear spoiling your silk coat? Or is there another lion in the way? Are you afraid of catching vermin? And are you not afraid lest the roaring lion should catch you? Are you not afraid of Him that had said, "inasmuch as ye have not done it unto the least of these, ye have not done it unto me?"*[39]

Wesley does not confine himself to an exposition of the text in this sermon but uses his own life story as an example to make his point. Here, his point takes a slight turn; for riches are *not* to be totally avoided, but gained, saved, and ultimately given away:

> *Permit me to speak as freely of myself as I would of another man . . . I* gain all I can *(namely, by writing) without hurting either my soul or body. I* save all I can, *not willingly wasting anything, not a sheet of paper, not a cup of water. I do not lay out anything, not a shilling, unless as a sacrifice to God. Yet by* giving all I can, *I am effectually secured from "laying up treasures upon earth." Yea, and I am secured from either desiring or endeavoring, it as long as I give all I can. And that I do this, I call all that know me, both friends and foes, to testify.*[40]

Wesley presents a somewhat accommodationist response to acquiring wealth. One is justified in having possessions as long as, if one gains all, one saves all, and gives all that one can:

> *Two-and-forty years ago, having a desire to furnish poor people with cheaper, shorter, and plainer books than any I had seen, I wrote many small tracts, generally a penny a-piece; and afterwards several larger. Some of these had such a sale as I never thought of; and, by this means, I unawares became rich. But I never desired or endeavored after it. And now that it is come upon me unawares, I lay up no treasures upon earth: I lay up nothing at all. . . . I cannot help leaving my books behind me whenever God calls me hence;*

> *but, in every other respect, my own hands will be my executors . . . let you that are rich, be even as I am.*[41]

While Wesley continues to profess the import of escaping the snares of wealth, he gives space, albeit limited, to the notion that material prosperity is the gift of divine providence. It is not to be tossed in the sea, since it is "what God hath given us . . .," but "an excellent talent [to be] employed much to the glory of God."[42] While he set a rigorous personal example himself of living simply, his self-contradiction regarding gaining all one could of what he now termed this "gift" from God, and an "excellent talent," essentially hindered his attempts to effectively counter the prevailing legacy of a theology of prosperity and ambivalence toward Jesus's teachings on wealth renunciation.

Sermon 126: "On the Danger of Increasing Riches"

In this, one of his last sermons, published in 1790, referring to Matthew 19:24 and centering his message around Psalm 62:10 ("If riches increase, set not thine heart upon them"), Wesley takes the opportunity to, once again, define who are considered rich:

> *But a man may be rich that has not a hundred a year, nor even one thousand pounds in cash. Whosoever has food to eat, and raiment to put on, with something over, is rich. Whoever has the necessaries and conveniences of life for himself and his family, and a little to spare for them that have not, is properly a rich man . . .*[43]

Again, Wesley reiterates, "none can have riches without being greatly endangered by them," and that "much greater is the danger of increasing them!"[44] Not only is having riches a danger for those who inherit their wealth, Wesley maintains. It is an even greater snare "for those who acquire them by their skill and industry." Therefore, he warns, if one's wealth increases, "set not thine heart upon them."

But here, Wesley appears to employ a qualifier to his previous definition. Though his intention may be to merely avoid "forming a hasty judgment concerning the fortune of others,"[45] his inclusion of qualifiers weakens both his definition of wealth and the litmus test for how one is to live, and act, as a follower of Christ:

> *A person may have more than necessaries and conveniences for his family, and yet not be rich. For he may be in debt; and his debts may amount to more than he is worth. But if this be the case, he is not a rich man, how much money soever he has in his hands. Yea, a man of business may be afraid that this is the real condition of his affairs, whether it be or no; and then he cannot be so charitable as he would, for fear of being unjust. . . . Those especially that trade to a very large amount; for their affairs are frequently so entangled, that it is not possible to determine, with any exactness, how much they are worth, or, indeed, whether they are worth anything or nothing. Should we not make a fair allowance for them?*[46]

And here also, he reverses what appears to have been his previous uncompromising attitude toward wealth and the acquisition of such when he claims, "It is true, riches, and the increase of them, are the gift of God. Yet great care is to be taken, that what is intended for a blessing, do not turn into a curse."[47] These self-contradictions and qualifications can be observed in his earlier sermons on the subject; qualifications that appear to acquiesce to both an ambivalence toward wealth renunciation and the prevailing legacy of a theology of prosperity, even if they do not diminish his emphasis on the necessity of giving to the poor.

Sermon 50: "The Use of Money"

It is here that Wesley sets forth his famed formula of "gain all you can, save all you can, give all you can," a formula he does not recant. The sermon is an exposition of Jesus's parable of the Unjust Steward (Luke 16:1–8). Wesley attempts to point out that the "children of this world are wiser in their generation than the children of light" (Luke 16:8) when it comes to the use of money (the mammon of unrighteousness). And he continues by explaining that the Scripture's point is that they are not truly the wiser, for, he says, "those who seek no other portion than this world" are "one and all, the [biggest] fools, the most egregious madmen under heaven."[48] They are, he notes, more consistent in their corrupt behavior, truer to their principles, and steadier in pursuing what they value and their ultimate goals "than the children of light," who are the followers and disciples of Jesus Christ.

But Wesley does not continue in this line of thinking. Moving away from Christ's rhetoric of reversal (the first shall be last), Wesley explains that Christians can learn how to give a better rendering of their stewardship by observing the unjust steward, who decides to turn to lying and thievery instead of becoming a common day laborer ("I cannot dig," v. 3) or begging in order to sustain himself. It appears that Wesley misses the connection between the unjust steward's claim that such a decision will allow him to be welcomed into "the homes of his master's debtors" (whose debts he has, for a fee of course, dishonestly reduced [vv. 5–7]) and Jesus's critical observation that following the dishonest manager's actions will indeed get one welcomed *into the homes of those whose homes are indeed not eternal* (but, Jesus infers, *not into the true eternal home—heaven*). Instead, Wesley interprets Jesus's response to be a commendation of the steward's actions, and thus he proffers:

> *"Make yourselves friends," by wise, timely precaution, "of the mammon of unrighteousness . . ." by doing all possible good, particularly to the children of God; "that, when ye fail,"—when ye return to dust, when ye have no more place under the sun,—those of them who are gone before "may receive you," may welcome you, into the "everlasting habitations."*[49]

For, according to Wesley, here is:

> *An excellent branch of Christian wisdom . . . inculcated by our Lord on all his followers, namely, the right use of money a subject largely spoken of, after their manner, by men of the world; but not sufficiently considered by those whom God hath chosen out of the world. These, generally, do not consider, as the importance of the subject requires, the use of this excellent talent. Neither do they understand how to employ it to the greatest advantage; the introduction of which into the world is one admirable instance of the wise and gracious providence of God.*[50]

There is no direct comment on the unjust steward's behavior. Instead, his focus is on the employment of money "to [one's] greatest advantage; the introduction of which into the world is one admirable instance of the wise and gracious providence of God."[51] While "poets, orators, and philosophers, in almost all ages and nations, [have] rail[ed] at this, as the grand corrupter of the world, the bane of virtue, the pest of human society," what they all purport is "mere empty rant" and "without any solid reason"[52] . . . for, according to Wesley, it is:

> *"The love of money," [that] "is the root of all evil"; but not the thing itself. The fault does not lie in the money, but in them that use it. It may be used ill: and what may not? . . . It is of unspeakable service to all civilized nations, in all the common affairs of life: It is a most compendious instrument of transacting all manner of business, and (if we use it according to Christian wisdom) of doing all manner of good. It is true, were man in a state of innocence, or were all men "filled with the Holy Ghost," so that, like the infant Church at Jerusalem, "no man counted anything he had his own," but "distribution was made to everyone as he had need," the use of it would be superseded. . . . But, in the present state of mankind, it is an excellent gift of God, answering the noblest ends . . . it is food for the hungry, drink for the thirsty, raiment for the naked: It gives to the traveler and the stranger where to lay his head. By it we may [replace] . . . a husband to the widow, and . . . a father to the fatherless. We may be a defense for the oppressed, a means of health to the sick, . . . ease to them that are in pain; . . . eyes to the blind, . . . feet to the lame; yea, a lifter up from the gates of death!*[53]

What Wesley is advocating for is not wealth renunciation or a radical redistribution of such, but a right relationship with money, and he connects having such a relationship with having a right relationship with God. In line with his predecessors Calvin and Augustine, he embraces the notion that money is "an excellent gift" from God. Those who are no longer good or innocent enough to participate in the radical redistribution of material goods, as did those in the early Christian church, are to be faithful stewards of this "mammon of unrighteousness."

Instructing his readers on faithful stewardship, Wesley provides three rules for proper use of money by Christians. The first rule is "gain all you can."[54] By claiming that it is the duty of the Christian to gain all one can gain, though one is to do so without paying too dear a price for it,[55] Wesley allows for wealth accumulation and its continued attachment to both God's providence and blessing. But, unlike Augustine and Calvin, while Wesley does more than require a proper relationship with wealth, he provides a twist to his predecessors' theological thinking and ultimately makes stewardship central to the Christian faith by presenting a straightforward critique of accumulating wealth without the intention of distributing a portion of it. And he is careful to delineate what Christians ought not to do in seeking riches:

> 1. We ought not to gain money at the expense of life, nor (which is in effect the same thing) at the expense of our health . . . no gain whatsoever should induce us to enter into, or to continue in, any employ, which is of such a kind . . . as to impair our constitution.
> 2. We are, Secondly, to gain all we can without hurting our mind any more than our body. . . . We must preserve, at all events, the spirit of a healthful mind. Therefore, we may not engage or continue in any sinful trade [or] any that is contrary to the law of God . . .
> 3. We are . . . Thirdly, to gain all we can without hurting our neighbor. . . . We cannot, if we love everyone as ourselves, hurt anyone *in his substance*. We cannot devour the increase of his lands, and perhaps the lands and houses themselves, by gaming . . . overgrown bills . . . or . . . requiring or taking such interest . . . as the laws of our country forbid . . . [and] we are not allowed to "do evil that good may come." None can gain by swallowing up his neighbor's substance, without gaining the damnation of hell!
> 4. Neither may we gain by hurting our neighbor *in his body*. Therefore, we may not sell anything [that] tends to impair health.[56]

Furthermore, his instruction to "gain all you can" is given with the command that one must do so using "by honest industry," not wasting any time, using wisdom, doing everything as well as possible, and pursuing gain "with [all] thy might."[57]

Once one has gained all one can in this manner, the next rule is to "save all you can."[58] This, Wesley argues, one must do without giving any consideration to wasting it on "desires of the flesh" or any kind of pleasure, but especially "the pleasures of tasting" including not only drink that is intoxicating but any "elegant epicurism," that is, any costly food which, although it "doesn't seem to be harmful to body or impair the mind," should be avoided because of its considerable and unnecessary expense.[59] Here, again, Wesley departs from the teachings of Augustine and Calvin as he instructs his listeners that it is indeed wrong for any Christian to spend on luxuries simply because she or he can afford to do so.[60] All Christians should avoid delicate foods and variety and "be content with what plain nature requires. . . . Cut off all this expense!"[61] For Wesley, no part of "so precious a talent" (money) should be used on any expense that is superfluous, including not just expensive diets but expensive clothing, furniture, books, or anything that "please [the] taste or other senses" and provoke others to "applaud thy elegance in taste," while also causing "a stronger attachment to these pleasures which perish in the using"[62] and costing one's soul while gaining one human admiration and pride.

Nor should the Christian waste money on her or his children any more than on herself or himself, for doing so is merely buying them "more pride or lust, more vanity, or foolish and hurtful desires" and "increase[ing] their temptations and snares."[63] Leave the bulk of your estate to the child who knows its value and who would "put it to its true use," and to all the others give just enough to allow them to live in the manner in which they are accustomed. And if there is not one among your children who know the value of money, then, Wesley says, give to each that which would sustain them and "bestow all the rest in such a manner as . . . would [do the] most for the glory of God."[64]

Thus, for Wesley, as for Calvin, material wealth has not just a utilitarian function, but also a spiritual mission. However, while for Calvin the spiritual mission is complete when one has achieved identification with the poor in spirit and conquered one's attachment to worldly possessions, for Wesley the mission is not complete until one has altered one's lifestyle and followed all three rules, the last of which is to "Give all you can." The Christian is not to imagine that she or he has done anything by just gaining all and saving all one could if she or he stops there. There is a greater end to one's stewardship than gaining and saving: "If . . . you would indeed 'make yourselves friends of the mammon of unrighteousness,' add the Third rule to the two preceding. Having, First, gained all you can, and, Secondly saved all you can, Then 'give all you can.'"[65] If one desires to follow God's direction and be a faithful and wise steward (give all one has to God), one must, after first providing for oneself, then provide for the needs of one's family. And one must also, if there is surplus, then give to those of the household of faith. And if there is still surplus, one must continue to give "as you have the opportunity, [to] do good to all . . ."[66] In this way, Wesley suggests, one "render[s] unto God the things that are God's."

What is lacking from Wesley's argument is a rationale for gaining all one can. There is neither justification of such thinking in the text used nor in any other texts of the Gospels. Indeed, one does not need to gain all one can if one is to provide for only the necessities of life for oneself and one's household and give the surplus away to others who are in need. Earning what one needs to provide for oneself and family and give to others does not produce riches. And who cannot justify the amount one lays up as a necessity for caring for oneself and family? Wesley's lack of rationale for this threefold rule is odd, especially in light of his claim that an increase in riches naturally leads to a decline in holiness. Furthermore, his ambivalent rhetoric about wealth being both a blessing from God and simultaneously a bane to one's Christian walk is self-contradicting. Did Wesley mean to maintain that God blesses humans with that which naturally causes them harm, and ultimately perdition? Was he merely trying to soften the blow for those who would have a difficult time shifting their relationship to and practice of wealth accumulation?

While Wesley's early sermons on wealth, such as this one, gave license to acquire wealth, the Christian was to do more than identify with the poor in spirit, as Calvin and Augustine insisted. One is, according to Wesley, to live a simple life, devoid of all luxury or extravagance. And even though one is to acquire and save all one can, one is to also give all one can. Wesley, like Augustine and Calvin, does not doubt that it is the individual Christian's decision to judge, according to their conscience, what she or he must do. Still, while he did not directly challenge the idea of material acquisition or the idea of wealth and poverty being divinely ordained precepts, Wesley did pose a challenge to acquiring material goods without an intentional focus on giving.

Wesley's threefold rule and conclusion that doing good with money and redistributing it would provide one a place in heaven deviated from the prevailing teachings around wealth acquisition. Moreover, his conclusions and famed formula for giving did much to inform the practice of stewardship not only for Methodists but also for others in Western Christianity. It did not, however, challenge the notion of the blessedness of wealth, and ultimately compromised his appeals for understanding material acquisition as antithetical to the teachings of Jesus. His formula would fail to produce the social holiness he was aiming for. Wesley would come to think of his project and Methodism as a failure, based on the rules he established to initiate exemplary Christian behavior that was aligned with Jesus's teachings. Still, he would continue to preach his threefold rules, which became a standard in his sermons.

Walter Rauschenbusch and Countering the Legacy with a Social Christianity

As Western Christianity's prevailing ambivalent attitude toward wealth accumulation moved across the American theological landscape,[67] it was buttressed by the Puritan work ethic, a basic contempt for the impoverished, and a view of their state of existence as punishment for one's sins,[68] along with a Darwinian understanding of socioeconomic enterprise and human evolution. A number of Christians in this "New World" would also attempt to bring a critique to this legacy.[69] Among them was the leading social gospel theologian Walter Rauschenbusch.

Transformed by his experience as pastor of Second German Baptist Church in New York's Hell's Kitchen neighborhood, Rauschenbusch abandoned his inherited conservative Christian thinking that saw poverty as a product of the providence of God and concluded that poverty did indeed result from human causes. Working among the poor in what was then America's largest city, Rauschenbusch would come to maintain that the poverty he encountered was not the result of God's providence, but an economic system that afforded luxurious living for some citizens at the expense of others. While Wesley introduced a doctrine of individual stewardship that prioritized almsgiving without connecting wealth, poverty, and the social–political order, Rauschenbusch maintained that it is problematic to render any social aid to the poor without reconstituting the social community and its institutions. His distinctive interweaving of the kingdom of God with an analysis of the social order represented a key shift from a focus on personal redemption to one that involved a sociohistorical interpretive focus on the kingdom of God. Wedding the vision and spirit of Christ to a progressive understanding of being concerned with redeeming the corporate life of humanity, Rauschenbusch connected living according to such an understanding with one's salvation.

Using the Lord's Prayer in Matthew 6:10 as foundational to the gospel, Rauschenbusch would assert that Christianity's central concern is the kingdom of God on earth, emphasizing God's kingdom as an earthly pursuit rather than the heavenly one achieved through spiritual salvation. After all, "the men who were baptized by John [the Baptist] were not looking forward to death and to salvation after death, but to the coming of the Kingdom of God and of His Messiah."[70] "The kingdom of God is humanity organized according to the will of God,"[71] the messianic theocracy as refashioned by Jesus and applied to the twentieth century. Salvation, the "voluntary socializing of the soul,"[72] a "social process"[73] or "force"[74] is the essential concern of the kingdom. "Heaven and earth are to be parts of the same realm."[75] Thus Christianizing all aspects of the social sphere, or rather acting to turn around the manifest injustices found in all social systems, including the economic system, was for Rauschenbusch approximating the kingdom-ideal constitutive of Christianity.

While the evangelical call to live the divine life had certainly gotten its grip on the individual soul through piety, revivalism, and millennialism, it had little to say about society's massive problems, including the tenement life of New York's poor. Rauschenbusch lamented that the church "has nothing to say about the justice of holding land idle in crowded cities, of appropriating the unearned increment in land values, of paying wages fixed by the hunger of the laborers and taking the surplus of their output as 'profits,' or of cornering the market in the necessaries of life."[76] His concern was for the corporate life of humanity and the corporate nature and responsibility of Christianity. His understanding of the inadequacy of the individualistic ethics of the nineteenth century to respond to the social ills of his time was the product of, as church historian Robert T. Handy concludes, Rauschenbusch's confrontation with the conditions of the poor working people who made up his church and its surrounding community rather than an outgrowth of his religious heritage. It was in light of the pressing social problems he encountered that he sought to relate the old evangelical passion with a growing passion for social action.[77] His own statement about his developing concern for social reform supports this conclusion:

> *It came from outside. It came through personal contact with poverty, and when I saw how men toiled all their life long, hard, toilsome lives, and at the end had almost nothing to show for it; how strong men begged for work and could not get in hard times; how little children died—oh, the children's funerals! They gripped my heart.*[78]

Rauschenbusch's Socioeconomic Context

Born on October 4, 1861, in Rochester, New York, Rauschenbusch, the son of a Lutheran pastor who arrived in the United States as a missionary,[79] was raised to value his German identity.[80] His education, a significant portion of which took place in Germany, and his pastorate at the Second German Baptist Church in New York City[81] reflect this commitment. He would leave the pastorate to teach in the German department of the Rochester Theological Seminary as professor of New Testament in the same position that his father had once occupied. In 1902, when the German department of the seminary was established as an independent institution, Rauschenbusch stayed with the seminary and took a position in the English division as professor of church history. He would hold that position until his death. He also would remain connected with the German Baptists, maintaining his membership in one of Rochester's German Baptist congregations and remaining active in the conference throughout his life.[82]

While "the legacy of pietism in Rauschenbusch created a series of crucial perspectives and formal attitudes which never left him,"[83] it would prove inadequate while pastoring as he came face to face with the harsh social and economic realities of the members of his congregation. During those eleven years (1886 to 1897), Rauschenbusch pastored on the edge of New York's Hell's Kitchen,[84] the concrete context for his work and the ground from which grew his passionate concern for the poor. It is in this context that his theological vision found in *Christianity and the Social Crisis* first crystallized.[85] The writings he published during his tenure at Rochester secured his influence as a theological spokesperson for the social gospel movement. His publication *A Theology for the Social Gospel* provides a foundational interpretation of Christian theology in social gospel terms. His text *Christianity and the Social Crisis* critiques the relative indifference of Christians to the moral and political issues raised by the extreme inequalities of wealth and poverty. Others would use his work to further the social gospel teachings and the praxis of a social Christianity.

In speaking of the half century after the Civil War, urban historian Raymond Mohl asserts that it was "the rise of the industrial city, perhaps more than any other feature . . .[that] characterized the social and economic development of the period."[86] Though urbanization exemplified the entire industrial era, it was during this period that the industrial city became a major factor in the American scene, with the 1880s witnessing a virtual urban explosion.[87] The growing concentration of populations within cities was, as one social scientist of the period stated, "the most remarkable social phenomenon of the present century."[88] It is during this period that the nation shifted from a predominantly rural to a predominantly urban population. While the nation's total population almost tripled, the number of urban dwellers across the country increased almost ninefold.

For instance, in New York City, the thirty years between 1860 and 1890 saw the population increase from 813,669 to 1,515,301.[89] While a similar growth pattern appeared in other cities, especially in the northeastern and north central states, New York City reflected the changes caused by rapid urbanization more dramatically than any other. Among the various ethnic groups, the Irish and the German were the largest. Until approximately 1880, the Irish dominated. After that time, however, the Germans displaced them as the dominant minority with nearly 400,000 German immigrants living in New York City.[90]

The rapid urbanization, along with the underlying industrial capitalism, which was one of its primary causes, triggered unprecedented changes in both the economic and social spheres and significantly affected city life. In essence, these redefined the urban social order. As cities became centers for the arts, sciences, business, and industry, they also developed as "breeding grounds of poverty, misery, vice and crime," and dramatized the extraordinary increasing gulf between classes in America.[91] While the new order presented the possibility of unbounded growth and almost unimaginable opportunity for some, more often than not the promise of the industrial city remained an illusory dream for most. It lured the farmer and the immigrant and became the dwelling place of humans struggling against heavy odds for a better life. American historian and urbanologist Lewis Mumford observed that, while industrialism and its accompanying urbanization supplied "the main creative force of the nineteenth century," it also "produced the most degraded urban environment the world had yet seen."[92] Grinding poverty, political corruption, social disorder, alcohol abuse, immigration, problems in the areas of housing, jobs, industrial relations, schooling, social welfare, and public health were all interconnected, were exacerbated by the rapid growth of the city, and contributed to unprecedented levels of social disorder.[93]

The demand for housing caused by the exploding population led architects and builders to provide two new types of residential dwellings: the apartment house for the upper classes and the tenement house for the workers, immigrants, and the poor. It was the tenement house that became both the symbol of all that was wrong in the new industrial cities and home to the poorest of the city's people. It reflected the most unjust industrial relations and "provided excellent investment opportunities for landlords, at the expense of despair and disease for residents."[94]

The typical form of the tenement house emerged in New York City. The standard lot was one hundred feet deep by twenty-five feet wide. Generally, all but ten feet at the back of the lot was used for the construction of the building, which, because of the shape of the lot, tended to be narrow and deep. Usually, from four to six stories in height, each floor consisted of four separate apartments with some form of central hallway providing entrance to each. Frequently built on adjacent lots with adjoining or even common walls, interior rooms had no windows until the Tenement Reform Law of 1879. While this law imposed certain minimum standards for light and ventilation, it only alleviated the worst of the problems.[95]

William T. Elsing, a city missionary, described living in New York's tenement-housing in this manner:

> *An ordinary tenement-house contains five stories and a basement, four families usually occupying a floor. The halls in nearly all the*

> *houses are more or less dark, even during the brightest part of the day. In winter, just before the gas lighted, dungeon darkness reigns. When groping my way in the passages I usually imitate the steam craft in a thick fog and give a danger-signal when I hear someone else approaching; but even when all is silent, I proceed with caution, for more than once I have stumbled against a baby who was quietly sitting in the dark hall or on the stairs.*[96]

By 1890, three-fourths of the city's 1.5 million people[97] inhabited tenements,[98] the overwhelming majority of whom were immigrants, many from Southern and Eastern Europe. It was in such tenements that a majority of the members of the Second Church, the church Rauschenbusch came to pastor, made their homes. In a correspondence, Rauschenbusch notes, "The congregation consists of about 130 members. . . . Almost all of them live on the West Side in the large tenement houses where often twenty-five families live in one building."[99]

Adding to this housing situation were the recurring cycles of boom and depression that created highly unstable economic conditions and uneven employment for the majority. Between 1870 and 1900, the economy went through three periods of prolonged economic depression, the "great social volcanoes of 1877, 1886, and 1894."[100] Each of these periods were marked by strikes, labor conflicts, and riots. Unemployment soared to unheard levels as one-fourth of the city's labor force went without jobs, and nationwide unemployment would later peak at three million between 1877 and 1878. By 1878, an estimated one-half of the nation's labor force was either wholly or partially unemployed. The panic of 1893 ushered in the century's last period of prolonged depression, marked to a much greater degree than the earlier ones by bank and business failures.

Even households with multiple income sources—that is, those families whose income was from the father, mother, children, and gifts—lacked enough to consistently sustain themselves and were "constantly on the verge of dependence."[101] The individuals and families without work on a frequent or consistent basis were in even more dire straits. Citing one study, Rauschenbusch stated: "About four million persons are dependent on public relief in the United States; that an equal number are destitute but bear their misery in silence; and that ten million have an income insufficient to maintain them even in a state of physical efficiency even to do their work."[102]

It was also during this progressive era of American history that the gulf between the rich and poor rapidly widened. One 1896 study found that:

> *Less than half the families in America are property-less; nevertheless, seven-eighths of the families hold but one-eighth of the national wealth, while one percent of the families hold more than the remaining ninety-nine. . . . One-eighth of the families in America receive more than half of the aggregate income, the richest one percent receives a larger income than the poorest fifty percent. In fact, this small class of wealthy property owners receives from property alone as large an income as half of our people receive from property and labor.*[103]

Unions were the main vehicles that workers could use to fight for better employment conditions and wage scales.[104] Thus workers sought reform by organizing, bargaining, protesting, and advocating for legislative reform. However, each endeavor to make a change was resisted by both business and the state.[105] Income rates were linked to the fortunes of labor–capital dynamics, and thus the unequal bargaining position of workers in the face of an employer's resistance to unions limited workers' ability to maintain and achieve a true living wage. The aims of management were simple: to deny any connection between earnings and productivity and to resist increasing wages in a period of rapidly rising productivity. These objectives were achieved by such tactics as unilateral wage reductions, the adoption of a common labor rate, and the hiring of unemployed immigrants willing to work for very little.[106]

The transition from individual enterprise to corporate business power[107] is roughly coextensive with industrialization and urbanization, and the Rauschenbusch years were on the cusp of both. Historians have described this transition as a passage from proprietary capitalism to the first stage of corporate capitalism and liberalism,[108] and from competitive to monopoly and corporate capitalism. Essentially, small business, which generally operated in response to the market, was superseded by big business, which acted upon the market in either an oligopolistic or monopolistic way.[109] Both the expansion and absorption of small manufacturers in the consumer goods industry into larger units of production businesses and the shift to a concentration of industries created a situation of "intensified pressures . . . upon the workers to increase production [and capital gain] at relatively lowered costs."[110]

Noteworthy here is the fact that while Rauschenbusch and other white social gospel leaders focused their attention on the working class as the benefactors of the social gospel movement, they excluded African Americans who endured violence, racist treatment, and discrimination in the housing and labor markets. African Americans had no protection under a racist and sexist legal structure. Included in this group were not only Black men but also Black women, such as domestics toiling in hostile work environments and more affluent Black women who bore the responsibility of garnering public approval for African Americans whose status was deemed as less than human and whose compromised safety in the public sphere was the norm. According to newspaper reporter and social reformer Jacob Riis, the discrimination and higher rents that poor African Americans endured were not only the result of landlords charging exorbitant rent prices. It was also due to the desires of immigrant groups to stay away from Blacks and the real estate agents who promoted housing discrimination with the principle, "once a colored house, always a colored house."[111] Rauschenbusch would use his pulpit to speak to the issues and problems faced by the poor immigrant working class, confronting the church leaders and affluent in society who tended to blame the poor for most of their problems.[112] He would remain silent on the plight of Blacks whose economic struggles were compounded by racial discrimination and racialized violence.

Rauschenbusch's Theological Context

Both a product and critic of the religious and theological milieu of the late nineteenth century in America,[113] Rauschenbusch contended that attention to "the least of these" was a necessary component of Christianity. Using the phrase derived from Matthew 25:40 to describe who he saw as society's marginalized, he argued for a theology that would elevate the working class to an equal social standing. He was not, however, the only theologian to challenge the traditional theological approaches of his day. The social gospel movement was on the rise in Protestant churches and on the verge of gaining credibility in the theological world. Liberal Protestantism[114]—of which the social gospel was both a kind of species and a challenge to its hegemonic long-cherished orthodoxy—was already dominant in intellectual circles.

Other voices from diverse contexts who also challenged the economic and political status quo of laborers in the newly formed industrial America included: Washington Gladden of the First Congregational Church in Springfield, Massachusetts; Josiah Strong, author and church pastor in Topeka, Kansas; Richard Theodore Ely, professor of economics at the University of Wisconsin; and Charles Monroe Sheldon, a theologian, Congregational minister, racial reform advocate, and author of the international bestselling novel, *In His Steps: What Would Jesus Do?*, which helped to catapult the social gospel movement into the mainstem. However, with the exception of Charles Sheldon, both Rauschenbusch and his white social gospeler contemporaries failed to address in any consistent manner racial oppression or the terrorism of lynching. Their message of social reform almost exclusively focused on the social and economic disenfranchisement of poor white immigrants. Rauschenbusch, often silent on the subject of race and the persecution of Blacks in America, would come to confess no moral authority on the issue of race in the United States.

Though it is hard to argue against the fact that Rauschenbusch made far-reaching contributions to the theological enterprise by asserting a social Christianity that focused on transforming the structures of society to foster equality, freedom, and just communities, it is also hard to ignore his exhibited blindness regarding white supremacy and the dehumanizing social and economic disenfranchisement and persecution of African Americans. In fact, while Strong argued that Anglo-Saxons were the chosen people, that America was the chosen place for the coming kingdom of God on earth, and that therefore America's Christians had an obligation to spread their high ideals to the rest of the world, few white social gospel advocates countered Strong's argument. Fewer still were interested in or willing to add racial equality to their agenda. In fact, the most definitive statement that outlined the teachings of the social gospel, the Social Creed of the Churches (adopted in 1908 by the Federal Council of Churches) avoided any explicit commentary on race. In *Breaking White Supremacy: Martin Luther King Jr. and the Black Social Gospel*, social ethicist Gary Dorrien notes Rauschenbusch's "painfully belated attempts to address racial justice . . . [and that he] later confessed that he had been silent about racism, because it seemed overwhelmingly tragic to him."[115]

It would take America's Black social gospelers to initiate a social Christianity that addressed the disenfranchising social, political, and economic conditions endured by America's late-nineteenth- and early-twentieth-century Black communities. Among them were Reverdy Cassius Ransom and Richard Robert Wright Jr., two preeminent African American Episcopal (AME) clergymen in Chicago, as well as the Black club women, Nannie Helen Burroughs, Josephine Ruffin, Mary Church Terrell, Frances Ellen Watkins Harper, and Ida B. Wells Barnett.[116] While Ransom and Wright stressed racial uplifting both to neutralize the public perception of African Americans as socially inept and improve their socioeconomic status, Black club women, who functioned similarly to their ordained male clergy counterparts as religious reformers committed to confronting racism and improving socioeconomic conditions of Blacks, also highlighted the evils of sexual oppression against Black women, lynching, and anti-suffrage. Notwithstanding their reliance on class status and class politics to advance a theology aligned with the aims of the social gospel, their understanding of social Christianity and religious activism fostered a nuanced view of God and Christianity that further challenged the theology espoused by most white religious leaders.[117] For these social gospelers, employing the social gospel message meant addressing the dehumanizing and staggering levels of poverty, unemployment, poor education, and racial and gender injustice to which Black people were constantly subjected.

These women and men were not only the embodiment of a forgotten, yet nation-altering chapter in both Western Christianity and American race relations. They were also at the center of the deep theological shifts which initiated a social Christianity that endorsed communal salvation and a practical theology that connected spiritual and earthly salvation to the problem of economic and racial inequity.

While Rauschenbusch's views on racism were tragically typical of his white social gospel contemporaries, he became the prevailing social gospel theologian. His argument for a theology that reinterpreted the categories of "the kingdom of God" and "salvation" along social lines and his challenge to an economic system that earned feasts for some at the price of starvation for others represent a distinctive contribution to the theological ethics of transformation, or social Christianity. His work must be understood as a response to both the traditional Protestant faith that he found inadequate for addressing the poverty and injustice of nineteenth-century America and to liberal Protestantism, which he thought deficient when it came to social ethics.

As Charles Hopkins notes, "[t]he prevailing institutionalized faith of American Protestantism was the supernaturalistic religion of the bible."[118] More specifically:

> *The characteristic religion of mid-nineteenth century America comprised a well-articulated body of doctrines and doctrinaires effectively insulated against the corrosive forces of the new science and of social unrest by an otherworldly dualism that resulted in a smug preoccupation with the salvation and perfection of the individual.*[119]

Salvation—an essentially private, soul-saving affair whose center of gravity is the afterlife—is God's absolute gift of redemption in Jesus Christ, given to heal the rift between God and humanity caused by original sin and personal sin. It is at once the destiny of the elect and the conclusion to a dangerous journey from sin and its temptations to salvation,[120] made effective through the substitutionary atonement of Christ. Thus, atonement was a central feature of the Protestant orthodoxy that Rauschenbusch had been taught in seminary,[121] as was the dominant understanding of dispensationalism, "a type of religious thought that divides God's dealings with the world into certain 'times' or 'dispensations,' each characterized by unique duties and responsibilities,"[122] where the Parousia would either inaugurate or conclude a thousand-year period that was expected to be a cataclysmic, apocalyptic period preceding the final judgment.[123] While the theory of atonement dates back at least to Anselm, dispensationalism originated and flourished in Great Britain and the United States in the latter half of the nineteenth century.[124]

Not only did atonement, dispensationalism, and millenarianism tend to locate salvation in a heavenly future, it also saw the kingdom of God—the "fundamental principle of Protestantism"[125] that grounds and expresses the whole constellation of faith through the sovereignty of God, the love of

Christ, and the advent of redemption[126]—as a future hope and a predominantly interior spiritual experience. An individual was led to seek salvation through a personal experience of conversion, regeneration, or rebirth, and often, during this period, through attending revivals. As a young minister, Rauschenbusch himself attended a revival led by Dwight Moody where he "[gave] himself to God unreservedly."[127]

Perhaps the most important element of the theological and religious setting in which Rauschenbusch was located was pietism. A reform movement that originated within Lutheranism in the seventeenth century, pietism sought to encourage personal surrender and heartfelt devotion to the love of Christ. It quickly spread to other parts of Europe and to Calvinist America. While the German pietism Rauschenbusch received from his Lutheran-born father "strove from its inception for a transformed world order in which the rule of Christ extended to every realm of life,"[128] the pietistic impulse as a whole in the late nineteenth century tended to reinforce personal devotion, prayer, and individual salvation, and not concern for the social order.[129]

The conversionist pattern of religious experience also tilted away from the social order, as did Revivalism, which tended to emphasize the looming afterlife along with the traditional atonement theory,[130] and gave up on the social order and the poor.[131] Nor was its success directly linked to the present advancement of the kingdom.[132] Social morality, at best a by-product of "real Christianity," was rapidly becoming even less of a concern in the era's latest forms of evangelism.[133] Salvation and the kingdom of God were seen as future goals, insofar as they touched one only internally. Thus, responding to the social problems in the here and now would require a new theology capable of speaking prophetically and transformatively.

Rauschenbusch's religiosity and work would be at once continuous and discontinuous with his religious heritage and upbringing.[134] Despite the transformative dimensions of Calvinism, these dimensions left social ethics impoverished. While Rauschenbusch inherited the Calvinist notion that the human order must be made to conform to the will of God, the focal points of conventional theological thought—the afterlife, the apocalyptic, the interior life, substitutionary atonement, and individual salvation—decidedly held no concern for the social order. The era was instead typified by "orthodoxy's pietistic view of life and its almost medieval belief in the present existence as a period of testing, along with its conception of heaven as a reward for individual virtue or suffering."[135]

Quest for a New Theology

Rauschenbusch's concern for the social order led him to call for a new theology, which would provoke social transformation. He maintained that theology, if it is to be faithful to the biblical message, must address social problems. However, for Rauschenbusch, the prevailing orthodox Protestant theological understandings were ill-equipped to do so. Thus, his theological vision required a new theology: a theology for the social gospel.

Critics of Rauschenbusch have frequently accused him of confusing, and ultimately equating, faith in God with faith in a democratic and Christian America, and embracing a model of engagement in which nearly all critical distance is forfeited.[136] And because Rauschenbusch's search for a new theology capable of supporting social reform sounds, at least on the surface, like a utilitarian theology it is not difficult to sympathize with his critics. However, Rauschenbusch's religious vision authorized not only a constructive participation in, but also critical engagement of, the American socioeconomic and political milieu. Rauschenbusch put forth a kingdom of God concept that both served as a bridge to involvement and an ultimate perspective over and against the American socioeconomic and political order. For Rauschenbusch, the kingdom of God serves as a religious loyalty that takes priority over institutional and ideological loyalties, and that ultimately provides principles of criticism.

Rauschenbusch's economic and political critique begins with his frustration with the church and its theological tenets.[137] The problem, according to Rauschenbusch, was that there existed a gap between the church and the problems associated with the social crisis of late industrialism.

> *The ordinary religious conception seemed to cover only some part of [life]. "Christ died for a sinner. He can be saved again by justification. He can be regenerated. After that, he can be sanctified. Finally, he will die and go to heaven." Yes, but where does the social question come in? Where does the matter come in of saving the world? That does not seem to have any place there, does it? And*

> *that was the real difficulty in my thought all the time—how to find a place, under the old religious conceptions, for this great task of changing the world and making it righteous; making it habitable; making it merciful; making it brotherly. Somehow, I knew in my soul that that was God's work. Nobody could wrest that from me. Jesus Christ had spoken too plainly to my soul about that. I know that he was on the side of righteousness, and on the side of his poor brother. But where could I get it in my old Christianity—with my old religion?*[138]

He later recalled that his denomination had discouraged his interest in social reform:

> *This is one of the saddest things I have to say, but I cannot get it out of my mind. The church held down the social interest in me. It contradicted it; it opposed it; it held it down as far as it could; and when it was a question about giving me a position or preferment, the fact that I was interested in the workingman was actually against me—not for me. They did not say: "Now here is a young man who loves the working man, and has some thoughts about him—let us put him into a theological professorship." No! "The fact is, this young man thinks like the workingman, but works against improvement too much, therefore, he ought not to be a theological professor." That is the way they looked at me.*[139]

Rauschenbusch would later write that the "chief purpose of the Christian Church in the past has been the salvation of individuals."[140] Moreover, salvation was restricted to a transcendent realm beyond historical existence. "The Christian Church in the past has taught us to do our work with our eyes fixed on another world and a life to come."[141] The eternal well-being of the individual dominated the church's teaching so thoroughly that the church proved incapable of providing guidance for addressing the conditions of the urban poor. In *Christianizing the Social Order*, he describes the incongruity between the moral demands of the day and the limits of the inherited theological tradition:

> *Here is the problem for all religious minds: we need a great faith to serve as a spiritual basis for the tremendous social task before us, and the working creed of our religion, in the form in which it has come down to us, has none. Its theology is silent or stammers where we most need a ringing and dogmatic message. It has no adequate answer to the fundamental moral questions of our day. It has manifestly furnished no sufficient religious motives to bring the unregenerate portions of our social order under the control of the Christian law. Its hymns . . . rituals . . . prayers . . . its books of devotion, are so devoid of social thought that the most thrilling passions of our generation lie in us half stifled for lack of religious utterance. The whole scheme of religion which tradition has handed down to us was not devised for such ends as we now have in hand and is inadequate to them. We need a new foundation for Christian thought.*[142]

Rauschenbusch was well aware of the attempts that had already been made to discover this new foundation. He maintained that the new foundation was not actually new but a return to the essence of Christianity or rather a return to the originating moment of Jesus of Nazareth. That is to say, to understand life, and especially Jesus's teachings, required understanding Jesus not as an abstract figure but as a human being with a cultural and religious background. Such an understanding required an examination of Jesus's religious heritage found in the Hebrew Bible.

Rauschenbusch applauded what he saw as previous investigations that uncovered neglected resources: "the Christian law of love," "the doctrine of stewardship," "the Golden Rule," and "following Jesus in daily conduct."[143] He concluded, however, that while all of these resources were valuable for personal morality, they failed to offer guidance for ordering laws, institutions, and groups:

> *These are truly religious ideas, drawn from the teaching of Jesus himself, and very effective in sweetening and ennobling our personal relations. But they set up no ideal of human society, demand no transformation of social institutions, create no collective enthusiasms, and furnish no doctrinal basis for public morality.*[144]

Though he found these attempts inadequate for transforming the social order, he applauded their historical interest in Jesus and offered his own interpretation of the essence of Christianity that was centered on Jesus and the kingdom of God.

For Rauschenbusch, the Christian essence begins in the prophetic tradition of biblical Israel. Because the "beating heart" of the Hebrew Bible is the prophetic movement, understanding the prophets becomes crucial for understanding the teachings of Jesus and Jesus as a historical person. In his attempt to "lay bare those large and permanent characteristics which are common to" the prophets,[145] Rauschenbusch concludes that in the context of the ancient Near East, the prophets were religious innovators who shifted from the priestly religious understanding that relied on "the ceremonial method of placating [God], securing [God's] gifts and ascertaining [God's] wishes" to a prophetic religion characterized by its concern for morality.[146] Placing morality at the center of the religious life of Israel, the prophets insisted that the God of Israel was a God of righteousness, that "religious morality [was] the only thing God cares about,"[147] and the priestly emphasis on ceremonial observance and religious ritual was a hindrance to the true worship of the God of righteousness. True worship, in fact, consists of righteous living rather than proper observance—a message the prophets not only preached, but "backed . . . by active participation in public action and discussion."[148]

Thus, for Rauschenbusch, God's righteousness was concerned not simply with private virtues but with the social order, and the prophetic ethic was not a private morality of the home but a public morality on which national life was founded. In fact, for Rauschenbusch, the prophets condemned injustice and oppression, and called for just institutions and moral actions. Furthermore, the prophetic tradition understood pursuing God's will for the social order begins with sympathizing with and being on the side of the oppressed. Their passion for and pursuit of social righteousness often took the form of defending the poor against the wealthy. For Rauschenbusch, they envisioned God as one who sided with the oppressed and the vulnerable against those who exploit them, and not one who merely empathized or even shared suffering.[149] Although they were denounced by the powerful, the prophets had remained hopeful. They believed that God would restore the nation of Israel and they taught that this restoration would take place on the "day of Jehovah" as a sudden and dramatic day of deliverance. Deliverance would come as a social revolution in which God would overthrow the oppressors of the people, whether those oppressors were foreign rulers or fellow Israelites.[150]

Acknowledging that the prophetic movement, as well as the messages of the prophets, evolved with the changing circumstances in which the prophets conceived their messages,[151] Rauschenbusch agreed with those who claimed that Israel's exile to Babylon was the primary turning point in the history of the prophetic movement. As a result of the despair generated from being in exile, Rauschenbusch explains, the prophets' social hopes faded, and individualistic and utopian elements came to characterize the prophetic message. Apocalyptic themes came to dominate. "The sunlight of the prophetic hope gave way to the limelight of the apocalyptic visions of later Judaism."[152] Thus, identifying the pre-exilic prophets as the high point of the prophetic movement, Rauschenbusch sees later revisions of the earlier prophetic message as corruptions. Though these corruptions could be understood to some extent as appropriate given their context, they were limited in their ability to exact ethical obedience and address social injustice.

John the Baptist, for Rauschenbusch, reinstates the classical tradition of the prophets with his appearance, conduct, and message.

> *He wore their austere garb; he shared their utter fearlessness, their ringing directness of speech, their consciousness of speaking an inward message of God. The substance of his message was also the same. It was the old prophetic demand for ethical obedience.*[153]

John's moral vision was focused on ending oppression and establishing social justice as indicated in the Gospel of Luke where he instructs "tax-gatherers and soldiers" to "stop being parasites and to live on their honest earnings."[154] This vision becomes incorporated in the social aims of Jesus. "Moreover, in joining hands with John, Jesus clasped hands with the succession of the prophets with whom he classified John."[155] Because Rauschenbusch believed that Jesus linked John closely to himself,[156] John plays a key role in Rauschenbusch's interpretation of the historical Jesus and serves as a link between the "prophetic type of religion" and Jesus, who "appropriated its essential spirit."[157]

It is interesting to note that, while Rauschenbusch observes a "revolutionary consciousness in Jesus"[158] that called for exalting the lowly and bringing down the proud, he maintains that,

> *Jesus was not a social reformer of the modern type. . . . Sociology and political economy was just as far outside of his range of thought as organic chemistry or the geography of America. . . . He saw the evil in the life of men and their sufferings, but he approached these facts purely from the moral, and not from the economic or historical point of view.*[159]

For Rauschenbusch, this does not mean that Jesus preached a God of the status quo. His purpose, which was more profound, encompassing, and inspiring than that of contemporary advocates of social reform, called for loyalty to the kingdom of God, which surpassed any economic or political reform. The love of Jesus and the establishment of God's kingdom of right relations was the "dominant purpose of Jesus' life."[160] Jesus lived and died striving to make God's kingdom a social reality in the life of humans. He fought for God's reign against those who resisted its initiation. He condemned those who placed religious ceremony above justice. He believed that God's reign was one of right relations rather than right ceremony. He refused to follow nationalistic teachings that pitted Jew and Gentile against each other and instead practiced a radical hospitality that cut across social boundaries and welcomed the meek and lowly with love and gentleness.

Thus, Jesus's revised conception of the kingdom of God was an evolving social movement grounded in love or solidarity that was already emerging and visible in the form of right relations between people. The movement was not entirely encased in the future. The movement also welcomed all and not just a particular nation or group. In Jesus's concept of the kingdom Rauschenbusch believed he had discovered the essence of Christianity and the heart of the new theology necessary to faithfully respond to the modern social crisis. By establishing a link between Jesus and the classical prophetic tradition with its vision of God as primarily concerned with social relations rather than ritual observance, Rauschenbusch located a rich metaphor to not only challenge privatistic religious beliefs and behaviors but also the prevailing attitudes on poverty and the acquisition, renunciation, and redistribution of wealth.

Rauschenbusch maintained that "Jesus did not fear riches merely as a narcotic" that poisoned the soul, but as a hindrance to "create[ing] a true human society" and as a "divisive force in actual life" that "wedges society apart in horizontal strata between which real fellow-feeling is paralyzed . . . [and] lifts individuals out of the wholesome dependence on their fellows and equally out of the full sense of responsibility to them."[161]

Use of Scripture

Rauschenbusch made extensive appeals to Scripture to support his theological understanding, moral assessments, and prescriptive recommendations regarding the social order. However, he confined his treatment of the Hebrew Scriptures to the prophetic literature and emphasized the Gospels over other forms of New Testament literature with a concentration on the teachings of Jesus. For Rauschenbusch, one understands Scripture only when one understands Jesus Christ. Jesus is the message and the meaning of Scripture, and Christianity "is not the religion of a book but of a man."[162] Thus, the narratives of Jesus's life and his teachings have a preeminent authority. This preeminence, in essence, authorizes the Gospels as particularly pertinent data. Jesus is the hinge upon which the testaments turn. Before Jesus, everything was in development toward him. After Jesus, everything was a developing interpretation of him.

In *The Social Principles of Jesus*, Rauschenbusch's most concentrated biblical work, he explores Jesus's teachings as "an attempt to formulate in simple propositions the fundamental convictions of Jesus about the social and ethical relations and duties of men . . . challenge[ing] college men and women to face the social convictions of Jesus and to make their own adjustments."[163] Remarking on Jesus's teachings of "the great reversal" in Luke 6:20–26, he states:

> *In these Beatitudes, as Luke reports them, Jesus clearly takes sides with the lowly. He says God and future are not on the side of the*

> *rich, the satiated, the devotees of pleasure, the people who take the popular side on everything. Ultimately the verdict will be for those who are now poor and underfed, who carry the heavy end of things, and who have to stand for the unpopular side. In the report of the Beatitudes given by Matthew (5:3–12) the terms are less social and more spiritual, and the contrast between the upper and lower classes is not marked; but even there the promise of the great reversal of things is to the humble and peaceable folk, the hard hit and unpopular; they are to inherit the earth, and also God's kingdom. . . . Would it make Jesus a wiser teacher and nobler figure if he had reversed his sympathies?*[164]

And speaking of Jesus's solidarity with the poor, Rauschenbusch maintains:

> *No one can turn from a frank reading of the Gospels without realizing that Jesus had a deep fellow-feeling . . . for the mass of the poorer people of his country, the peasants, the fisherman, the artisans . . . he felt the sacredness of life even in its humble and hard worn forms, . . . he could not be at ease while the people were "skinned and prostrate," . . . So, he cast his lot with the people consciously . . . slept in their homes, healed their diseases, ate their bread, and shared his own with them. . . . His feeling was one of love and trust . . . [and] He saw them over against "the rich."*[165]

> *Not only did Jesus take sides with the poor and was not impartial between the two, but he also judged that "there was something disquieting and dangerous about the spiritual qualities of 'the rich,' and something lovable and hopeful about the qualities of the common [hu]man."*[166]

For Rauschenbusch, the acquisition and storing of wealth hinders the higher goal of acquiring "spiritual facilities, memories and relations" and "often becomes a passion . . . which leaves little energy for higher pursuits."[167] Indeed the acquisition of wealth was so dangerous and divisive that "Jesus felt the antagonism of private wealth and the Kingdom of God so keenly . . . he set God and Mammon over against each other and warned us that we must choose between the two (Matt. 6:19–24)."[168] In his exposition of Jesus's parable of the rich man and Lazarus (Luke 16:19–31), Rauschenbusch poses the question, "Why does Jesus send the rich man to hell as if it were a matter of course?" He concludes that though "no crimes or vice are alleged," perhaps "[i]t must be that a life given over to sumptuous living and indifference to want and misery of a fellow [hu]man at the doorstep seemed to Jesus a deeply immoral and sinful life [because] wealth divides. . . . It creates semi-human relations between social classes, so that a small dole seems to be a full discharge of obligations toward the poor, and [hu]manly independence and virtue may be resented as offensive."[169] Rauschenbusch not only allows Jesus's critique of wealth acquisition to stand, but he suggests that such a response is applicable beyond the specific situation of which Jesus was speaking:

> *This demand has been understood either as a test or a cure. Some think that it was merely a test; if he had consented to give up his wealth, it would not have been necessary to give it up. Some think it was a cure for the love of money, which was really needed in this exceptional case. On either supposition, the advice concerned merely this young man's soul; it was medicine to be swallowed by him for his own good alone. But Jesus immediately rises from this concrete case to the general assertion that it is hard for any rich man to enter the kingdom of God, harder than for a camel to wedge through the eye of a needle.*[170]

Rauschenbusch cautions that while "the solution for this 'hard saying' has been sought in the remark quoted only in Mark (10:24): 'How hard it is for them that *trust* in riches to enter the kingdom,' which allows one to safely acquire and hold on to riches, so long as one does not trust in them, in actuality, 'The solution lies in another direction.'"[171] The other direction, according to Rauschenbusch, is generated by Jesus's concern not merely for the young man's salvation in the life to come, but with his suitability for "the righteous society on earth which [Jesus] was initiating."[172] That righteous society was the kingdom of God. Furthermore, "the true humanity" required human relations based on justice, equality, and love.[173] Thus, concludes Rauschenbusch, since the kingdom of God requires such "wholesome human relations" and since "it is exceedingly hard for a rich man to be in normal human relations to others, as many . . . has discovered who has honestly tried . . . an act of renunciation in some form" is indeed required![174]

In his exposition of Jesus's parable of the Unjust Steward (Luke 16:1–8), Rauschenbusch interprets the parable not as a lesson in having right relationship with money or better stewardship as Wesley does. The parable is, rather, an admonishment to the rich and all who were listening to, as Rauschenbusch puts it, "get a plank ready for the coming deluge."[175] He remarked that "this is one of the wittiest stories in the Bible and must be read with some sense of humor." What is humorous about it? Rauschenbusch asserts that Jesus is not so much approving of financial trickery as he is at once commenting on the trickster's mindset who at least had sense enough to attempt to prepare for a new social situation and encouraging those "who hold dishonest money of the present era" to "use the brief term of power left to them before the Messianic era begins . . . [to] do kindness to the children of the kingdom [so] they may hope by their gratitude to get some sort of borrowed shelter when the situation is reversed and the pious poor are on top."[176]

For Rauschenbusch, if one understands the Scriptures as a response to the social question and if the Scriptures are understood in relation to their historical setting, then the Scriptures are properly understood. Then their purpose and direction—that is, their message—can be discerned. And that message, of course, is that the kingdom of God includes a righteous social order with right human relations, which encompass love, justice, equality, the abolition of inequitable economic and sociopolitical conditions and institutions, and even the renunciation of acquiring wealth and property that is not "saved to raise and educate children or achieve some social good."[177]

Part Three

A WOMANIST WAY FORWARD

5

WOMANIST SOURCES FOR A REDEMPTIVE RESPONSE

I AM PROPOSING a womanist, constructive response to counter the prevailing legacy of a theology of prosperity—a legacy that valorizes hierarchical distinctions, trivializes Jesus's teachings on wealth redistribution, and holds the Black Church captive to the dominant messages of material prosperity and American consumerism. This womanist response offers a way forward for the Black community to resist perpetuating the prevailing legacy of a theology of prosperity and ambivalence toward Jesus's teachings on wealth, poverty, and material redistribution. It perceives and promotes a radically new vision for God's people—a vision that includes equitable human relations and communal asset building, sharing, and thriving. This way forward, informed by the works of womanist theologians Kelly Brown Douglas, Delores S. Williams, and Keri Day, as well as womanist ethicist Katie Geneva Cannon and others, lays the foundation for a theology of communal plenty. This womanist way forward is also informed by my great-grandmother's response that "we have plenty"—the response she would offer whenever my sisters and I asked if we could invite someone to dinner. A womanist way forward sees the act of sharing and redistributing available resources—so that no one is lacking—as a sacred act that is in line with Jesus's teachings.

Today's prosperity theologies not only equate God's redemption with personal wealth accumulation. These theologies also fail to emphasize the liberation of the oppressed from structural and social domination as part of the salvation Jesus offers. Neither do prosperity theologies address, in any significant way, the multiple oppressions of women, children, and men, especially those considered the poorest of the poor, or "the *least* of the least" within the Black community. Drawing on womanist and proto-womanist[1] theological and biblical interpretation, sociopolitical analysis of wholeness, activism, and other praxiological approaches to fostering communal flourishing, I offer a way forward that I believe can better align the Black Church's theologies and practices with the teachings and practices of Jesus.

While Douglas does not explicitly address questions concerning poverty, wealth, or economic inequity, or capitalism, beginning with her work is critical. Douglas displays a keen awareness of the socioeconomic and class issues that impinge upon the lives of Black women, and she challenges the Black Church to oppose not just racism, but the multiplicity of oppressions faced by the least of the least within the Black community. Her argument that any theology that fosters wholeness and liberation must be accountable to the poorest of Black women points to the role that economics as a source plays in her theology.

Her womanist approach to theological and biblical interpretation, engagement of a sociopolitical analysis of wholeness, her religio-cultural analysis of the Black Church, and her use of both a hermeneutics of suspicion and a hermeneutics of appropriation provide an entry point for analyzing the impact of theologies of prosperity on the Black Christian faith community in general and Black women's lives in particular. Her development of a womanist Christology and analysis of the impact of a Platonized Christian tradition upon the nature of Black Christianity are also instructive.

Williams's groundbreaking work not only takes seriously the suffering and resistance of oppressed Black women but also lays the foundation for developing a theology that envisions and promotes communal flourishing and fullness of life. Williams, one of the founders of the womanist theological enterprise, challenges the Black Church's patriarchal theological presuppositions and the inadequacy of certain paradigms while placing a more nuanced emphasis on quality-of-life issues in order to address Black women's and the entire Black community's struggle to survive and "develop a positive, productive quality of life in the face of death."[2] Williams is the first womanist theologian to outline some survival strategies that poor Black women have employed to facilitate the well-being and at times flourishing of Black communities and she suggests some strategies for Black churches concerned with fostering the wholeness and well-being of the entire congregation.

Day is one of the few womanist scholars of religion to examine how American capitalism produces and sustains structural inequalities and disenfranchisement for poor Black women. She provides an analysis of how

Black churches have failed to respond to poor Black women's collective social and material deprivation, as well as the Black Church's potential to become an agent of change that fosters poor Black women's thriving. In *Unfinished Business*,[3] Day interrogates America's democratic project as a land of liberty, equality, and opportunity for all. She examines questions of how theology and faith influence the Black Church's response to American economic as well as political issues and how theology, faith, religious language, and beliefs can influence and even constrict the Black Church's ability to function as an institution that fosters liberation for the entire Black community. Day further summarizes why an examination of class alongside race is critical in constructing opportunities for communal thriving, offering a structural analysis of the material and social deprivation of poor Black women as a by-product of the structural inequities in the American economy.

Kelly Brown Douglas: A Christology from Below

Douglas is among the first generation of womanist scholars who made a seismic contribution to the theological field in general and the liberation theological camp in particular, generating novel academic discussions about the religious history of Black women. Unearthing the hidden voices and experiences of marginalized Black women while highlighting the themes, norms, traditions, and methodological strategies that inform womanist theology, she, along with founding womanist scholars, drew attention to the context that gave rise to womanist theological reflections as a distinct academic theology.[4] Central to the womanist project has been the task of connecting the biblical witness of Jesus with Black women's experiences to discuss God's transformative role in Black women's lives while exploring and offering understandings of Jesus and his salvific significance for the least of the people. Delineating Black women's egalitarian Christology, Douglas articulates how such a Christology has been operative in Black women's lives, nurturing their commitment to transcend the oppressive tendencies and structures of their churches and society.

Formulating a "Christology from below" that focuses more consistently on the empowering deeds of Jesus and his earthly ministry, Douglas asks whether affirming the blackness of Christ, which embraces the blackness of Black people and fosters in them a sense of self-esteem and pride in being children of God, is adequate enough to root out from Black religion and culture that which is not liberating and sustaining for the Black community.[5] She not only notes that "Black people oppress each other, and that racism is not the only barrier to Black freedom,"[6] Douglas also engages the challenge of making the good news of and about Jesus relevant to all elements of the Black community—a community that was forged, and that continues to forge ahead, in crisis.

The Black Christ and Prosperity Theologies

Exploring the roots of the Black Christ and Christ's significance for African American women, in *The Black Christ* (1994) Douglas cites the historical precedents formed during the slave period regarding the Black Christ and the importance of the Black Christ during the Civil Rights and Black Power movements. She then gives a sociopolitical and religio-cultural analysis of the blackness of Christ from a womanist perspective. Douglas notes that it is in slave religion that the earliest warrants for the Black Christ are found, and she contends that the concept here had less to do with Jesus's presumed biological race and more to do with those with whom he identified during his lifetime—the poor, marginalized, and despised.

The slaves ascertained the Black Christ's good intentions toward them in the stories portraying the liberating God of the Hebrew Bible and the ministry of Jesus, whose ministry of feeding, healing, and affirming the marginalized and oppressed resonated deeply with them. The enslaved Africans focused on Jesus's liberating ministry, while their white enslavers stressed the incarnation of God in the "white Christ" and imposed the hermeneutics of sacrifice on the enslaved Africans. Indeed, the theologies and life practices of the latter rendered Jesus's earthly ministry of little importance and insignificant to salvation. Salvation was seen as "automatic" after conversion, which countered Jesus's liberating actions on behalf of the poor as "a standard for Christian actions."[7] Later, nationalist offerings of the Black Christ would focus on the recognition or re-imaging of God/Jesus as biologically Black.

Douglas explains the emergence of the "Black Christ" in African American nationalist thought as a precursor to the development of a constructive womanist Christology. She cites Robert Alexander Young as one of the earliest to argue for the blackness of God, AME Bishop Henry McNeal Turner as the first to identify the need for Blacks to image God in their likeness, and Marcus Garvey as one of the first to affirm blackness as a biological characteristic of the historical Jesus.[8] She then notes that, despite these early attempts to articulate the significance of God/Christ in relationship to blackness, the Black Christ did not emerge as a formal category for theological reflection in liberation theology circles until Black Power met with Black theology. Black male theologians, particularly Albert Cleage, James Cone, and J. Deotis Roberts, in an attempt to contemporize the relevance of the gospel for oppressed Blacks, asked the question: "Who is Jesus Christ for us today?" And though their responses varied, they emphasized Jesus's suffering and self-proclaimed mission of liberating the oppressed[9] as that which characterized the essence of his identity. This led them to conclude that "Christ is Black."

It is these historical understandings of the Black Christ that Douglas challenges. She notes that racism is not the only challenge that theologians must consider. They must also consider sexism, heterosexism, and classism. They must, in other words, deal with the fact that "the 'haves' in the Black community—the middle class—often look down upon the 'have-nots'—the poor [and] too often harbor a sense of resentment toward the poor."[10] Such thinking, bolstered by a "pull yourself up by your own bootstraps" mindset, hinders a spirit of cooperation and the collective efforts needed to challenge and help those who remain trapped in the vicious cycle of poverty. This type of thinking also leaves Black people divided against themselves.

In response to this, Douglas employs Black women's experience and a "hermeneutic of suspicion"; that is, a hermeneutic that reflects the preferred perspective and moral agency of the least of the "least of these." Such a hermeneutic holds suspect anything that diminishes or terrorizes those who are othered and thought of as the outsider. It allows one to not only challenge the dominant Euro-American theologies that have sanctioned the multidimensional oppression of African Americans, but to interrogate the one-dimensional analysis of Black theology and the Black Christ. Noting that emphasis on the metaphysical nature of Christ, or Christ's divine incarnation, rather than his liberating ministry "makes what it means to be Christ inaccessible to ordinary Christians" and gives "little reason to strive to be an example of Christ in the world,"[11] Douglas maintains that such an emphasis makes Christ "someone to be worshipped, believed in, but not followed or imitated."[12] However, the reality of Christ for the Black community is not only one of sustainer and liberator but prophet as well, "sustain[ing] and deliver[ing] it from the multidimensional oppression that besets it," *and* "challenging the Black faith community to rid itself of anything that divides it against itself and to renounce any way in which it oppresses others."[13] That is, God's vision for a just world calls God's people to rid themselves of anything that sustains unjust hierarchies of privilege and domination. This, Douglas maintains, the Black Church and womanist theologians must do, if either are to take seriously Jesus's ministry and confront those aspects of the Christian faith that are lethal for the Black community. Furthermore, Douglas's emphasis on the life and ministry of Jesus in effecting salvation suggests that it is Jesus's prophetic teaching and healing activity that are not only the liberative import of the Gospel for African Americans, but key components of salvation. What Jesus did and taught becomes the basis for what it means for him to be Christ.

Thus, for Douglas, it is crucial, even before identifying the physical characteristics of Jesus Christ, to understand the image of the Black Christ as an analytical identification and utilization tool that engages the Black community and provokes in it a sense of economic, physical, and psychological well-being while informing its religio-cultural norms and practices. She poses the questions, "what does the Black Christ say to those Blacks who were, to some extent, 'integrated' into White racist political-economic structures, as a result of the Civil Rights and Black Power movements, and who vigilantly protect their positions within those structures, even at the expense of other Black people? How does the Black Christ challenge those Black people who look down on other Black people who have not 'made it' in White racist America?"[14]

Douglas notes that identifying Christ as Black does not ensure an understanding of Christ's ministry as a model for radical egalitarian living that promotes an inclusive Black faith community, and I would add, an inclusive larger world. Nor does it impel Black people to analyze and free themselves from the ideologies, systems, structures, and practices that imprison and perpetuate sociocultural stratification and oppression. While the Black Christ allowed the Black community to consider oppression as it has been articulated in a Black male/heterosexist perspective which was grounded in a social analysis focused on race, calling Christ "black" did not challenge either the Black Church or larger Black community to examine the ways in which it perpetuates oppression and supports inequity along gendered and economic lines.

Not only does a Black Christ theology fall short in fostering a deeper understanding and critical analysis of the ways in which the Black Church perpetuates the oppression of "*the least* of the least," but calling Christ "Black" does not lead one to examine or emphasize the radical teachings of Christ. Douglas contends that this may be the case because the Black Christ image has failed to address the multidimensional oppression of Black women and the pastoral concerns of the entire Black faith community.[15]

I concur with Douglas's argument. The Black Christ image has not provoked a critical analysis of the religio-cultural traditions and practices of the Black Christian faith community that continue to oppress the most marginalized within it. Nor has it led Black churches to embrace the radical teachings of Christ at the practical level. Not only has the Black Church's failure to engage Jesus's radical teachings hindered its analysis of oppressive traditions and practices within the Black faith community, but such a failure has also led to the Black Church's unwitting adoption and perpetuation of the legacy of a theology of prosperity, as well as Western Christianity's prevailing ambivalence toward wealth accumulation and redistribution. That is to say, although the African American religious experience has been and continues to be informed by both theological orientations and political sensibilities that can be traced back to their enslaved foreparents, it also continues to embrace and be informed by historic oppressive Western Christian religious traditions and theological underpinnings that have not been fully interrogated. This includes Western Christianity's legacy of a theology of prosperity.

Douglas's sociopolitical analysis "urges Black people, but especially Black women, to confront the ways in which societal oppression has left them less than whole humans beings—spiritually, emotionally, psychologically and so forth."[16] Douglas focuses on the actions of Jesus, that is, his work on behalf of, and his inclusion of, the least respected in society, to offer a womanist Christology that highlights what Jesus did as the basis for what it means for him to be Christ working for the wholeness of his community, and what it means to be a disciple of Christ, working toward attaining wholeness both inside and outside of one's community. Jesus, for Douglas, is not just sustainer and liberator as portrayed in Black theology. Jesus is also prophet, "challenging the Black community to rid itself of anything that divides it against itself and to renounce any way in which it oppresses others."[17] Working for wholeness is the standard by which Douglas evaluates Christ and Christ's followers. Thus, African American Christians must not only identify with Jesus. They must also imitate Jesus's prophetic role of challenging oppression, inequity, and unjust norms and systems within and without the community in their struggle to attain wholeness.

Platonized Christianity and the Black Church

It is Douglas's discussion of the nature of Black Christian ecclesiology and its adoption of a Platonized Christian tradition that can help us further understand how such a legacy has been adopted by and influential upon the Black faith community. In *What's Faith Got to Do with It? Black Bodies/Christian Souls*, Douglas discusses the problem with Platonized Christianity and its impact on contemporary Black Christian faith. Here Douglas specifically deals with how Platonized Christian tradition has fostered ambivalence in African Americans toward their own bodies and experiences.

Tracing the roots of a "heretical" tradition of an oppressive Christianity, Douglas contends that while African American Christians appropriated the liberating, prophetic aspects of Christianity, they also appropriated a Platonized theology that holds anti-Christ qualities and perpetuates ambivalence toward Black bodies and Black life experiences. By Platonized Christianity, Douglas is referring to the Christian tradition that resulted from the integration of Platonic and Stoic thought with Christian theology. This dualistic and antagonistic understanding was extended to the human person:

> *[As the] Platonic belief in the world of forms (that is, the immaterial/true world) as being different* and *superior to the world of senses (that is, the material/earthly world) combined in Christian thought with the Stoic ethic defined by apatheia [ascetic control of the sensual appetites] . . . a significant strand of Christian thought*

> *adopted a theology that esteemed the immaterial, or divine, world (what came to be viewed as the world of reason, spirit, and soul) while it renounced the material, or human, world (considered the world of passion, flesh, and body). This particular Christian tradition routinely divinized the soul and demonized the body.*[18]

This Platonized worldview provided the definitive dualistic paradigm that is built into the very fiber of Western worldviews. It is responsible for the dualistic paradigm that not only privileges the soul or spirit over the body, but also whiteness over blackness, male over female, heterosexual over homosexual, and rich over poor. Its projected dualistic divisions between people readily accommodate white patriarchal privilege, undergirded by white supremacist ideologies and the devaluation and brutalization of Black bodies. It is a paradigm that serves as a "theological shelter for social, political, and ecclesiastical discrimination and inequality."[19] In such a paradigm, one's sovereignty is diminished to the degree that one lacks any one valued human characteristic. If, for instance, Douglas argues, one is both white and male, one is afforded the highest level of political, social, economic, and ecclesiastical privilege and dominance. If one is white and female, the claim to gender privilege, or rather maleness, is diminished, but the right to racial privilege (whiteness) is maintained. To be a Black male signifies "racialized" male privilege, where one is able to exercise sovereignty over Black women, while to be Black and female signifies virtually no claim to privileges in a white patriarchal society, including the Black Church.

This dualistic understanding of opposites can be seen elsewhere, even in our understanding of Jesus. Devaluing difference and paradox, even the paradoxical nature of a fully human and fully divine Christ has led to the devaluation of Jesus's existential reality and earthly ministry. Such privileging of his ontological reality and atonement over his earthly ministry sanctions as well the degradation of what the incarnation establishes as sacred—namely, the human body and the sacredness of equal and just human relations.

And, as Douglas argues, while it may be easy to dismiss this inherently heretical Platonized theology from Black faith tradition on a conceptual level, it is not so easy to do on a practical level. Expunging it from the Black faith community at the concrete/practical level requires not only exposing its existence but unearthing the detrimental value of those beliefs and practices perpetuated by this Platonized theology that create dehumanizing conditions for the Black community, particularly for Black women and nonheterosexuals. Regarding the unholy alliance between Platonized theological thinking and the Black faith tradition, Douglas states:

> *Platonized theological thinking is anathema to the black faith tradition. It generates contingent beliefs and subsequent practices that contradict the core theological themes of black faith and thus contravenes spiritual, communal, and interpersonal harmony within the black community. For this reason, it must be unabashedly renounced. There is virtually no possibility for a reliable faith tradition that is at once platonized and black.*[20]

Thus, bolstered by a Platonized dualistic theological worldview that disregards and devalues marginalized realities and the Black community's harmony, the legacy of theologies of prosperity, with their ambivalence toward wealth accumulation, unconcern for inequity, and acceptance of unjust relations, has led many African American Christians, to deny racism, accept white privilege, perpetuate sexism, tolerate an unjust economic system, and elevate self-gratification and self-interest at the expense of communal health, wholeness, and responsibility.

Platonized Christianity and Theologies of Prosperity

I extend Douglas's argument here concerning this unholy alliance. A Platonized tradition within Western Christianity has supported and indeed continues to support the legacy of a theology of prosperity, elevating Jesus's incarnation over his earthly ministry and fostering an ambivalence toward Jesus's teachings as a model for living. Platonized theological thinking privileges the individual over the communal. It emphasizes a spiritualized otherworldly mindset over concern for and support of disenfranchised communities. It prioritizes the pursuit of the "high life"—more money, power, and privilege—over pursuit of the "good life," that is to say, a life that prioritizes fostering a just, nonhierarchical world with egalitarian human relations. Downplayed are historical as well as contemporary atrocities initiated by racialized and gendered exceptionalism, self-centered wealth accumulation, and the idolatry of building fortunes on the backs of others. So too is the history of selling, maiming, raping, and killing Black women, men, and children for the sake of accumulating wealth and power. The insane claim that there is a declining significance of race in America, along with a decline in systemic and institutionalized racial inequality, is not consistently challenged. That the profit motive has increasingly become a driving force in the Black community and nearly everything is viewed and ultimately valued in accordance with how or how much it can enrich and empower goes unquestioned.

Such a legacy of a theology of prosperity also perpetuates an uncritical deference to the American myth of success. As the rhetoric of the "bootstrapper" and hard-working entrepreneur takes center stage, the imbalanced status of wealth distribution between contemporary Americans is no longer situated within the historical processes that nurture racial and economic inequality. Rather, the economic gap is incorrectly attributed solely to the "moral virtue" of hard work, savings, creativity, and thrift. What is also overlooked is that successive generations of African Americans have had to begin life with fewer and fewer material assets while being forced to confront barriers that prohibit economic development. This has been the case from the sedimentation of America's caste system extending from the days of slavery to the economic diversion of Jim Crow that prevented African American entrepreneurs from competing in an open market.[21] In fact, a leading research finding of a 2021 Brookings Institution study on the Black–white gap in multigenerational poverty found that poverty across three generations of Black and white Americans was over sixteen times higher among Black adults than white adults (21.3 percent and 1.2 percent, respectively).[22] In other words, the study states, "today one in five African Americans are experiencing poverty for the third generation in a row, compared to one in a hundred white Americans." Thus, while a legacy of a theology of prosperity has allowed for a heightened concern for personal liberation, social advancement, and economic empowerment, it also serves to frustrate the communal liberatory aims of the Black faith tradition and affirm social injustice and structures of dominance in America.[23]

Not only does such a legacy hinder the Black Church's ability to creatively engage Jesus's teachings on wealth and poverty. It also renders the Black faith community unable and ill-equipped to counter contemporary theologies of prosperity at the practical level and in ways that respond to Black people's needs and longing for a more abundant and better quality of life. What is needed, according to Douglas, is an imitation of Christ's prophetic role of challenging oppression and inequity wherever it is found in the struggle to attain wholeness. What is also needed is the creation of—and ultimately a theology that fosters—a nuanced understanding of salvation as social, and resource redistribution as a sacred act, alongside strategies that can facilitate the full realization of Black women's personhood and Black people's communal wholeness.

Delores Williams

Womanist God-Talk

Williams's work informs a discussion of social salvation and viable strategies. In *Sisters in the Wilderness: The Challenge of Womanist God-Talk*—the first book-length articulation of womanist theology—Williams addresses the alienation, ostracism, and oppression that invades Black women's lives and devalues their humanity and agency in their communities and the larger society. No other womanist theologian has either emphasized or articulated more thoroughly than Williams the theme of survival and survival strategies employed by Black Christian women.

Raising questions regarding who Black women say God is, and how they see God working in their lives, Williams critically explores and provides language, methodology, and a theoretical framework with which to critique Black women's multidimensional oppression of sexism, racism, classism, and heterosexism. Williams provides a nuanced rereading of the biblical story of Hagar (Gen 16, 21:8–21) to further articulate how God plays a role in the suffering and survival of Black women. Examining the symbolic relationship between Hagar's surrogacy and the historical role of surrogacy in Black women's lives, Williams draws a compelling analogy between Hagar and Black women's experiences, and their plights in resisting a multiplicity of oppressions, which include not only slavery, sexual exploitation, and racial and ethnic oppression, but also poverty.

Womanist God-Talk and Social Salvation

It is Williams's notion of social salvation,[24] which she defines in a manner that equates salvation with liberation,[25] as well as her reflections upon the survival strategies of Black women and her suggestion of using "in-house" strategies for the Black Church, that support the development of a theology of communal plenty. Williams asserts that the notion of salvation is both social and participatory and that a soteriology of the Black Church must attend to the needs of Black women at both the micro and macro level. She states, "elevating and healing Black women's self-esteem figures into womanist notions of what constitutes salvation for the oppressed African American community."[26] She also asserts that salvation must be concerned with more than just individual acts of sin. Noting that African Americans have long concerned themselves with wrongdoing at both the individual and social/communal level, Williams suggests that greater stress upon personal salvation may possibly have emerged as a result of their introduction to denominational Christianity[27] and "the impulse toward individualism that the dominating culture values, rewards, and encourages Americans to develop."[28]

However, nascent notions of sin and salvation in the African American community historically embodied a collective consciousness which seemed more concerned about the transformation of the community as a whole.[29] Williams writes, "[S]laves seem[ed] more concerned about a process of moving toward positive transformation and destination than with identifying individual acts as sinful."[30] It is this much larger notion of salvation—the social salvation of the Black community—that Black churches must attend to in order to rid themselves and society of the collective behaviors and social institutions that perpetuate and normalize devaluing and defiling Black women's bodies, humanity, wisdom, experience, and agency.

Williams argues that even Black women's devaluation of self and proclamations concerning their personal unworthiness as sin are linked to society's denigration of Black woman's humanity through a process that she calls "invisibilization—that is, invisibilizing the womanist character of Black women's experience and emphasizing the stereotypical images of Black women that are perpetuated in the larger society."[31] Thus, for Williams, what constitutes salvation for the Black community is the alleviation of the social sin committed by both individuals and groups of people within and outside the Black Church who participate in systems and ideologies that perpetuate and normalize behaviors that devalue and make invisible the very personhood of Black women.

In addition, salvation must deny any sacrifice or suffering in the body, and instead be located in a vision of, and actions toward, fostering right relationships between Black women and themselves, and Black women and Black men, white women, and the world at large. Salvation must come from humanity's embrace of Jesus's ministerial vision of teaching, healing, and identifying with the marginalized. Matching Black women's social-role surrogacy[32] with views of the atonement that cite Jesus's death as a vicarious sacrifice for a sinful humanity, Williams argues that Jesus's sacrifice should not be emulated by Black women:

> *In this sense, Jesus represents the ultimate surrogate figure; he stands in the place of someone else: sinful humankind. Surrogacy, attached to this divine personage, thus takes on an aura of the sacred. It is therefore fitting and proper for black women to ask whether the image of a surrogate-God has salvific power for black women or whether this image supports and reinforces the exploitation that has accompanied their experience with surrogacy. If black women accept this idea of redemption, can they not also passively accept the exploitation surrogacy brings?*[33]

Like the enslaved African Americans who fashioned their own theological responses and soteriological vision, today's Black churches will need to fashion a nuanced and adequate liberative theological response and vision of salvation for the Black community in order to address the plight of disenfranchised Black women, men, and children. If the Black Church is to be a place of transformation and transcendence, especially for poor, disenfranchised Black women, men, and children, its ecclesial vocation must include confronting the powers of domination that foster and sustain the multiplicity of destructive forces that impoverish and subordinate. It must question, as well, a soteriology that endorses inequity and values wealth acquisition over human life, equitable relations, and the well-being of all humans, all creatures, and the earth. And it will need to seriously reconsider its understanding of the salvific significance of Jesus's ministry, death, and resurrection, which Williams suggests many Black women and others are already doing:

> *Black women are intelligent people living in a technological world where nuclear bombs, defilement of the earth, racism, sexism and the economic injustice attest to the presence and power of evil in the world. Perhaps not many people today can believe that evil and sin were overcome by Jesus' death on the cross, that is, that Jesus took human sin upon himself and therefore saved humankind. Rather, it seems more intelligent to believe that redemption had to do with God, through Jesus, giving humankind new vision to see resources for positive, abundant relational life—a vision humankind did not have before.*[34]

Whether or not, or to what extent, Black women would agree with Williams's contention regarding Jesus's death on the cross is certainly arguable. However, her statement suggests that there is a diverse range of interpretations among Black women concerning the significance of Jesus's death, resurrection, and ministry for their lives. The fact is that Black woman *do* view Jesus's life and ministry as a model and impetus for seeking new realities for themselves and the Black community. Those new realities are characterized by justice, a better quality of life, and communal well-being. Black women have also found in Jesus's sacrificial act "compassionate solidarity"[35] with their own suffering and dehumanization and, through Jesus's resurrection, a God-affirmed "revelatory privilege"[36] that gives them the authority to speak of God's power and desire to preserve and affirm their own and all human life as sacred. Making room in Black churches for the critical engagement of Black women's lived experiences and soteriological understandings, especially those of poor Black women, is among the necessary first steps in fostering communal redemption and an inclusive soteriology.

Williams also insists that salvation is this-worldly because "there is only the material world in which to work out a place of salvation for Black people and the Black community."[37] She asserts that Black Christians and Black churches must learn to "leave heaven and 'otherworldly' pursuits to the business and judgment of God," while they work out a place of salvation for Black people on the temporal plane.[38] Thus, salvation, at both the micro (individual) and macro (social/communal) level is not about leaving social injustices untouched while trying to make it into heaven after death. Neither does it call for the most vulnerable and disenfranchised to live diminished and exploited lives so that others may thrive. Rather, salvation embraces the power of the resurrection and the life of Jesus in the here and now as that which empowers us to seek and weed out, as Jesus did, the root causes of marginalization, inequity, and oppression.

Salvation is about righting human relations and bringing them in alignment with Jesus's teachings. It requires our participation in the life and ministerial vision of Jesus as change agents who challenge norms, systems, institutions, and theologies that oppress, disempower, and disenfranchise any part of the human family, while finding meaning and fostering a quality of life here on earth.

Strengths, Insights, and Survival Strategies of Black Women

Williams's notion of survival and survival strategies also deserves the attention of Black churches, especially those seeking to serve as sites that promote flourishing and thriving for Black women and the entire Black community. No other womanist theologian has emphasized the theme of survival, or survival strategies employed by Black women, more than Williams. The category of survival is not used to glorify the oppression of Black women, but to allow for an honest evaluation of both Black women's oppression and their strength, insights, force, and strategies for living, persevering, and preserving community in spite of racism, sexism, heterosexism, poverty, and violence. While this category of understanding does not automatically lead to the development of an alternative model of existence that is life-enhancing, ascertaining the survival strategies of poor Black Christian women is paramount for arriving at any model for communal living that at once enhances Black women's quality of life and takes seriously their voices and varied experiences within the Black Church and society at large.

Williams highlights the survival strategies that Black women have developed to preserve their own lives, their churches, and the larger Black community. Use of the survival category has enabled Williams to point out that, while survival is a way of life for many Black women in the United States, it is an undesired way of life. Williams calls attention to the fact that

Black women's survival status is conditioned and sustained by external forces and structures that delimit the resources and power they need to ensure quality standards of living for themselves and their families. Nevertheless, poor and marginalized Black women often manage to develop survival strategies that help them to subvert, challenge, and transcend material deprivation, oppression, and relations of power.

Tracing the parallels between African American women's experiences and the biblical story of Hagar, the Egyptian enslaved girl and surrogate for Sarah (Gen 16, 21:8–21), Williams draws a compelling analogy between the two experiences. Noting parallels between the two with regard to resisting a multiplicity of oppressions (slavery, racial/ethnic oppression, poverty, and sexual exploitation), survival strategies, and continuously calling upon God to "make a way out of no way," she states:

> *the uncanny resilience of the mothering/nurturing/caring/enduring and resistance capacities of Hagar and black women has birthed a spirit of hope in the community. Historically, this spirit has kept the community alive as black women's spirituality and politics came together to design resistance strategies benefiting the entire community.*
>
> *Like Hagar when she and her child were thrown out of Abraham's house into the wilderness, black women in the "wilderness" of America had to learn how to survive. Neither Hagar nor African American women, in freedom, had enough resources for the survival of themselves and their families. Yet many black women, by the help of God, became very skilled at surviving. I supposed Hagar did too.*[39]

Williams then further delineates several survival strategies Black women have used to keep the community alive and hopeful, even in the midst of Black churches that often acted as sites of oppression and endurance rather than sites of liberation, change, and hope. Highlighting four strategies which she names the art of cunning, the art of encounter, the art of care, and the art of connecting,[40] Williams describes how Black women developed and used each strategy to defy and disrupt oppressive circumstances and ensured their own and their families' survival.

Drawing on the art of cunning enabled Black women to use their imagination and skill to exercise a "wholesome shrewdness that assures the survival of themselves and the entire community"[41] and devise economic strategies to foster the economic well-being of Black women and their families. Perfecting the art of encounter enabled Black women to know when to exercise resistance and when to engage in the act of endurance as defiant revolutionary moves against oppression. Williams notes that although African American denominational churches were often shaped by male preachers into "unproductive endurance structures"[42] with theologies and ecclesial practices that encouraged Black women's endurance of sexist oppression, Black women nevertheless used such a strategy to effectively inaugurate change.

The third strategy, the art of care, though often exploited by those within and beyond the Black community, allowed Black women to provide for the preservation of Black churches and the Black community through their commitment and charitable endeavors, while the fourth strategy, the art of connecting,[43] concludes Williams, is the most developed among many African American religious women. She states:

> *Harriet Tubman, Milla Granson and Mammy Pleasant knew with whom and how to connect in order to liberate slaves. Tubman connected with free Blacks, with white abolitionists and with slaves in order to effect political liberation. Milla Granson connected with a slave holder who taught her to read. Then she connected with other slaves, taught them to read and thereby effected their educational liberation. Because they learned to read, many of these slaves forged passes and escaped into Canada. Mammy Pleasant was advisor to the wealthy white men in California, increased her fortune considerably and used much of her money to secure the political and educational liberation of black people. In our own time, black women like Mary McLeod Bethune, Fannie Lou Hamer and Patricia Reeberg perfected the art of connecting with the people and with the relevant social, political and religious structures that could contribute to the educational, political and spiritual well-being of African American people: women, men and children.*[44]

Williams provides these strategies used by Black women to make meaning in their day-to-day lives and transcend debilitating conditions they encounter as a way to both elucidate and testify to Black women's historical resilience and faithful resourcefulness, even when they find themselves in the midst of Black churches steeped in sexist and heterosexist norms and practices. As Williams suggests, when the Black Church is not engaged in sociopolitical change, it does not mean that Black women who may be part of the Black Church are not engaged. These women embody their faith and forms of activism even when at times their church does not. Black women found ways to allow their imagination, intellect, ingenuity, and resources, however limited, to further such causes as educational, political, and economic justice and parity for Black women and the entire Black community.

Consider, for instance, Johnnie Tillmon, a pioneer in addressing the concerns of poor Black women and a welfare mother living in Los Angeles's Nickerson Projects, who helped found ANC (Aid to Needy Children) Mothers Anonymous of Watts in 1963, one of the first grassroots welfare mothers' organizations that fought to radically reimagine welfare. The organization was made up mostly of Black women, with organizers in Puerto Rican neighborhoods and on Native American reservations. ANC later became part of the National Welfare Rights Organization (NWRO), which was founded in 1966, and after the resignation of its first executive director in 1972, Tillmon was tapped to lead NWRO as its second executive director. Tillmon used both these organizations to advocate for women's equal pay, welfare rights, reproductive rights, childcare assistance, dignity, and democracy. She prioritized motherhood and challenged the welfare system at a time when recipients were subjected to punitive actions such as caseworker unannounced home visits—what became known as midnight raids[45]—as well as cancellation or alteration of benefits and, in some states, forced sterilization to prevent them from having more children. Tillmon would capture her audience by first identifying herself:

> *I'm a woman. I'm a black woman. I'm a poor woman. I'm a fat woman. I'm a middle-aged woman. And I'm on welfare. In this country, if you're any one of those things you count less as a human being. If you're all those things, you don't count at all. Except as a statistic.*[46]

Consider also the young women of Mamas of Color Rising, a grassroots collective of poor and working-class African American, Latino, Mexican, Asian, and other women of color who are young heterosexual and lesbian single mothers based in and around Austin, Texas. They address the lack of food, health, housing, education, living-wage jobs, and childcare available to poor women and their children. Through projects such as the Yo Mamas Catering Co-op and their provision of training for poor women to become DONA-certified doulas (birth companions)[47] free of charge in exchange for a commitment to serve as birth companions to other poor women of color at no cost, the collective endeavors to halt the experiences of deprivation experienced by poor women in their community by envisioning, advocating for, and building a more just, loving, and equitable world that provides them with economically viable, healthy choices and respects their desires, history, and indigenous cultural norms.[48]

Strategies for the Black Church

Black churches must find ways to join with and prioritize the strategies of poor and disenfranchised Black women in grappling with the increasing oppression that they and the entire Black community encounter. The Mamas of Color Rising collective employ what Williams calls "Black common sense."[49] It is this Black common sense that Williams avers the Black Church needs to engage to both retrieve and perpetuate "the collective consciousness, knowledge, wisdom and actions Black people used as they tried to survive, to develop productive quality of life and to be liberated from oppressive social, political, economic and legal systems."[50]

In order for Black churches to retrieve and perpetuate "Black common sense," Williams suggests implementing what she calls three "in-house strategies."[51] The first in-house strategy is the reactivation and upholding of the memory of Black heroines and heroes whose actions show how racism has historically oppressed Black people. Williams cites Angela Davis and Malcolm X as just two such examples. Committing to memory the knowledge and wisdom that Black history has borne out is critical for understanding "how the dominating White Western culture has been organized historically to oppress Black people."[52] Committing such knowledge and wisdom to memory is not only critical for appreciating how African Americans and others in the past exacted agency as they struggled against oppressive social, political, religious, legal, and economic systems. Such knowledge and wisdom can also inform our collective work in re-envisioning the Black Church as a site of liberation, rethinking our theologies of prosperity in light of Jesus's teachings, and reimagining what it will take for Black women, men, and children to survive and thrive today.

The second in-house strategy for effecting the social salvation of African Americans is the development of Black community consciousness and actions that assist Black people in moving from "can't do" to "can do" and transcending oppressive systems.[53] This strategy entails prodding memories and educating younger generations about groups and individuals who previously modeled and currently embody "can-do" attitudes and ideas. It helps the Black community inside and outside the church to connect the work they do in the religious, educational, economic, and political realms, reminding them that it was the "*past working* connections established between the Black Church, family, school and mutual aid societies . . . [that] saved Black people from utter despair and destruction, especially after the failure of the Reconstruction following the Civil War."[54] Such a strategy also encourages making social, political, religious, and economic alliances with non-Black groups and organizations that support Black advancement and flourishing on a communal level.

Lastly, Williams asserts, Black churches need to advance constructive critical thinking and planning. She posits that it is this strategy that can equip and lead people to uncover and challenge oppressive structures, systems, and norms, even dominating forms of leadership, in church and society. Such a strategy is useful in moving the Black faith community from venting to visioning to mapping a path toward their social salvation. Williams concludes, "If the church does not encourage and participate in the work of bringing salvation to the suffering and violated ones, it has no mission to speak of. It has no life in Christ."[55]

I concur with Williams. Salvation is social, and, because it requires the active participation of Black institutional churches in this realm, it is also this-worldly. When Black churches support the "quest for salvation here on earth,"[56] they not only support the historical beliefs of the Black community and the theologies of womanists and womanist-adjacent Black male liberation theologians. They also allow themselves to become both sacred spaces of transformation and transcendence for the entire Black community and makers of "Disciples of Christ" who are aligned with Jesus's call for radical inclusion.

However, in order for the Black Church to fully align itself with Jesus's call for radical inclusion, it must begin to elevate and take seriously the importance of Jesus's ministry and teachings on wealth, poverty, and radical sharing. In this era of hypercapitalism characterized by unbridled greed, acquisition, and exploitation of humans and material resources, Black churches must acknowledge that any redemptive process that sees as central the life and work of Jesus must involve not an escape from but a transformation of the ongoings of this world. Such a redemptive process requires not actions focused on acquisition and conquests, but actions grounded in liberation, or more precisely, deliverance from the exploitation, commodification, and devaluation of all that is sacred, which includes God, humans, human relations, the earth, and nature. Such a process must question ecclesial doctrine and traditions that privilege men over women, the individual over the communal, a spiritualized mindset over concern for and support of community, and centering the pursuit of the "high life"—more money, more power, more privilege—over the pursuit of the "good life," which entails a just and nonhierarchical world with egalitarian human relations. Furthermore, a redemptive process that has as its foundation Jesus's revaluation of wealth and poverty, even as it acknowledges complexities and ambiguities, must present as unambiguous in its alignment with Jesus's call to renounce stratified power, privilege, and inequity. It must reject prosperity theologies that equate salvation with material acquisition and celebrate individual wealth accumulation without challenging the exploitative norms, values, policies, and social structures that such a theology sustains.

Keri Day: The Black Church and Black Women's Poverty

Keri Day is the first womanist in the theological and ethical fields to provide an exploration of the realities of Black women's poverty and the potential role that Black churches can play in addressing the economic disenfranchisement and well-being of poor Black women. Day notes the complex history of Black churches and the various perceived roles the Black Church has held in the minds of its adherents—from being viewed as a liberating agent that fostered self-determination, spiritual formation, and political activism during the post-Emancipation and Reconstruction periods to being perceived by nineteenth- and early-twentieth-century Black scholars as a "failed institution that had plunged into political irrelevancy by the end of the Reconstruction period."[57]

The reluctance of the majority of Black churches across denominations to participate in the Civil Rights Movement bears witness to this reality. While a number of African American churches certainly played a pivotal role in the struggle for civil rights, the Black Church was not unanimous in its support of or involvement in the movement. An example of such, as Day points out, is the Church of God in Christ (COGIC) that, as a denomination, considered the methods of the Civil Rights Movement "unlawful."[58] They were not alone in their thinking. In fact, the National Baptist Convention ejected Martin Luther King Jr. from his position as vice president of NBC's National Sunday School and Baptist Training Union for what they deemed were "radical" views.

Day also notes that this complex history—saturated with historical tensions that make categorizing Black churches as "prophetic or priestly, progressive or conservative, radical or accommodationist"[59] difficult—includes Black churches' ambivalence toward engaging and being in solidarity with poor Black women. One can even find gaps between the religious language, ideology, and social justice rhetoric used by more "socially conscious black churches" and actual practices that not only support but transform poor Black women's lives. Further complicating the Black Church's efforts, even those that attempt to serve as "contexts of transcendence for their parishioners," is their failure to acknowledge and address "larger structural problems that generate and sustain deprivation among poor black women."[60]

Day rightly advers, "attention to structural obstacles that impede poor black women's sense of flourishing must be addressed, and many anti-poverty strategies within black churches inadequately address these structural dimensions."[61] While offering resources through food and clothing banks and other faith-based initiatives can certainly provide poor Black women with some needed resources and a sense of hope, these efforts do not address the social systems and structures that perpetuate poverty. Nor do they address "the particular destructive assumptions about poor black women, namely that these women are in need of moral reformation in order to improve their socioeconomic conditions."[62] Thus, as Day notes, while there are many Black churches that are sincere in their commitment to alleviate intergenerational poverty, realizing such a commitment will not happen without Black churches also addressing the socioeconomic and political structures that sustain Black women's poverty and deprivation.

I concur with Day. The Black Church must interrogate those larger issues of the American political economy that produce structural inequalities and perpetuate Black women's cycles of poverty. However, I would add that Black churches must also critically examine the theological presuppositions that perpetuate Western Christianity's ambivalence toward Jesus's statements on wealth, poverty, and radical sharing. If the Black Church is to be a transformative force in the lives of poor Black women, men, and children, it must engage in deconstructing and challenging those presuppositions that allegorize Jesus's teachings, trivialize inequitable socioeconomic arrangements, and value material acquisition over equitable human relations.

Day's work confirms Williams's argument that, given the history of violence perpetuated against Black churches and Black communities, the Black Church must develop a new theological understanding of itself that is relevant to and transformative for not only the Black Church but the Christian church as a whole.[63] This new self-understanding must emphasize prioritizing, supporting, and taking action to bring about the social salvation and flourishing of Black women, men, children, and all marginalized people. This is to say, alongside the original distinguishing marks of the universal Christian church—apostolicity, catholicity, unity, and holiness—the Black Church must provide a new mark, namely, opposition to all forms of violence against humanity, nature, and the earth.[64]

The need for Black churches to interrogate their theological views regarding systems, social norms, and even ideologies that produce and sustain poverty and economic inequity cannot be overstated. If the Black Church is to bring social salvation to the poor and disenfranchised, if it is to be seen as more than a sound signifying nothing, then it must engage in an examination of the Christian sacred texts and the deconstruction of theological traditions, liturgical practices, and ecclesial policies that support and sacralize various forms of violence against poor Black women—whether that violence is manifested as physical, economic, sexual, or gender oppression. So too must Black churches question how they have come to sanction American society's socioeconomic arguments that blame generations of Black women, men, and children for their own impoverishment and disenfranchisement.

While Day argues that "promoting socially-conscious capitalism among black businesses and capitalists, black churches can develop a theology of holistic prosperity that considers the thriving of all members within society,"[65] I posit that, in order for the Black Church to develop a theology that imbues poor Black women with a sense of hope and new possibilities for themselves and their families, Black churches must not only interrogate capitalist institutions and systems that perpetuate impoverishment for many Black women and their children. Black churches must also develop a vision of communal salvation that both counters prosperity theologies' capitalistic notions of progress and addresses Black people's legacy of longing and history of lack, while also bearing witness to Jesus's teachings on wealth, poverty, material redistribution, and concern for the poor.

6

REDEMPTIVE MODELS OF RESISTANCE AND TRANSCENDENCE

MOST OF AMERICA'S wealth continues to sit in the hands of 1 percent of Americans, who control more than the combined wealth of America's entire middle class. Meanwhile, the bottom 80 percent of Americans control barely 7 percent of the country's wealth. The bottom 50 percent of households hold between 2.5 percent and 3.5 percent of the total wealth, and there isn't an economist who will argue that this trend will change in any substantial manner.[1] This bottom 50 percent includes almost 20 percent, or close to one-fifth, of the total African American population, and nearly one out of three Black single mothers.[2] In fact, Black single women with children, along with Latina and Native American single mothers, are the fastest-growing groups in this sector of society.

The extreme disparities, displacement, and inequity coursing through America has induced public outcry and spurred such movements as Moral Mondays,[3] the new Poor People's Campaign,[4] Occupy Wall Street,[5] Occupy Faith,[6] and Union Theological Seminary of New York City's Poverty Initiative,[7] and groups like Mamas of Color Rising. These initiatives and others like them point to the growing number of persons across racial and class lines in faith-based and secular institutions that are now feeling the need to respond—through protest, political action, and in a myriad of other ways—to the widening disparity and growing oppression. Still the vast majority of Black churches and their leadership are largely absent from these endeavors.

Black churches must be willing to join in the struggle to seek out and craft viable solutions that address the suffering of the poor, disenfranchised, and vulnerable within the Black community, and beyond. Preaching a gospel of prosperity that uncritically advances a preoccupation with a personal quest for wealth and health promised by the myth of the American dream, while turning a blind eye to an increasingly inequitable American landscape, is not the answer. Nor can or should the Black Church preoccupy itself with preaching a message that calls for waiting on the hereafter or the coming eschaton. Instead, a radical revolution of values that supports our shifting from a wealth-oriented to a people-oriented society, honest discourse concerning Black people's continued suffering as a result of continuing oppression (racist, sexist, homophobic, political, and economic), and strategies geared to fostering communal transcendence and flourishing must be part of the Black Church's agenda and vision.

In an effort to help the Black Church begin such critical work, I offer what I deem redemptive models of resistance and transcendence—beginning with the life and work of activist Fannie Lou Hamer. Such models also include the work of several other women and men in our more contemporary times. I am aware of the limitations of lifting up a few individuals (or approaches) as the answer to all prayers. But I like to think of redemptive models of resistance and transcendence as sources, or rather, keys, that can help us enter onto new pathways for fostering communal remediation, transformation, abundance, and flourishing. Sometimes these keys help us ascertain what is on the horizon. Sometimes they unlock the hidden malignancies at work in ourselves and our socioreligious, political, and economic cultures. Sometimes they point to what is needed for our communal healing, remediation, transformation, and Black economic mobility.

Redemptive models of resistance and transcendence take seriously Douglas's sociopolitical analysis. They not only help Black churches to decipher the ways in which the adaptation of historic oppressive Western Christian religious traditions and theological underpinnings have continued to undermine the liberation of the Black community at the communal level. Such models also help the Black Church live into Douglas's admonishment to see Jesus as liberator, sustainer, and prophet who calls his followers to renounce oppression at every level and to imitate Jesus's prophetic role in addressing disenfranchisement, inequity, unjust norms, and dehumanizing practices. Such models help the Black community to see its way beyond, as Williams notes, merely fostering the undesirable state of surviving, to becoming sacred spaces of transformation and transcendence in which the work of challenging and redeeming unjust systems, ideologies, theologies, and norms is consistently practiced to ensure the agency, empowerment, well-being, and flourishing of Black women and the entire Black community.

Such redemptive models of resistance and transcendence can help Black churches seriously consider, as Day rightly avers they must do, the structural obstacles that hinder poor Black women's sense of flourishing as well as the anti-poverty strategies employed by Black churches that do not fully address these structural obstacles. This is not to say that food and clothing banks, and other faith-based initiatives employed by churches, do not provide poor Black women with some needed resources and a sense of hope. However, these efforts do not address the socioeconomic and political systems and structures that perpetuate poverty and deprivation, or the destructive assumptions about poor Black women.

Employing redemptive models of resistance and transcendence in Black churches for the communal remediation, transformation, and flourishing of Black women in particular and the Black community as a whole is about redeeming the minds, bodies, spirits, and agency of Black people who have been subjected to sexism, racism, colorism, heterosexism, patriarchy, and all "otherisms." It is about advocating for Black liberation, economic self-sufficiency, political self-determination, wholeness, wellness, and flourishing on a collective front. And it requires constructing new community narratives and practices that not only foster inclusion and inclusive attitudes toward human rights but also promote justice-informed outcomes and social norms.

The Life and Work of Fannie Lou Hamer

In order for Black churches to become places of communal transcendence and flourishing for Black women, men, and children, they need to prioritize and reinstate the radical faith tradition and praxis of African American women. Empowered by Jesus's earthly ministry and teachings, these women took the lead and acted as catalysts and creative initiators of revolutionary acts toward collective transformation, social change, and communal redemption. An outstanding Black woman within that tradition was Fannie Lou Hamer. Her leadership represented a necessary radical tendency within the Civil Rights Movement that sought the "Kin-dom" or commonwealth of God here on earth by exposing sociopolitical and economic inequity and the denial of distributive justice.

"To Make Democracy a Reality"[8]

A Mississippi sharecropper turned activist, who emerged as arguably the most compelling grassroots leader of the Civil Rights Movement, Hamer entered the movement in the summer of 1962 at the age of forty-four, after attending a Student Nonviolent Coordinating Committee (SNCC) mass meeting held in Williams Chapel Church, Ruleville, Mississippi.[9] This was not her first encounter with the work of civil rights activists as she was already an attendee of the annual meetings of the Regional Council of Negro Leadership, where she would hear such leaders as Thurgood Marshall and Medgar Evers speak about civil and voting rights. It was, however, at the SNCC meeting that her decision to do more and unseat injustice was crystallized. Throughout her fifteen years as an advocate for civil rights, Hamer worked to transform the brutally oppressive and unjust world of Blacks in the Mississippi Delta. Within that period, she registered thousands to vote, served as the field secretary of the SNCC (1963), founded the community development program, Delta Ministry (1963), and the Mississippi Freedom Democratic Party (1964), led a school desegregation movement (1968), created a farm cooperative (1969), ran for political office several times, and taught thousands about activism.[10]

The outcome of the 1964 Democratic National Convention in Atlantic City, where she and sixty-eight other Freedom Democrats boldly challenged the seating of the all-white Mississippi delegation as legitimate representatives of the state, had a critical impact on Hamer's evolution as an activist and on her agenda. Hamer, who was vice-chair of the MFDP, was invited along with the other officers to address the convention's Credentials Committee. Recounting the problems she encountered in registering to vote and her brutal near-death ordeal in jail in Winona, she concluded her speech on the verge of tears, and left her audience stunned by her final words:

> *All of this is on account we want to register, to become first-class citizens, and if the Freedom Democratic Party is not seated now, I question America. Is this America, the land of the free and home*

> *of brave where we have to sleep with our telephones off the hooks because our lives be threatened daily because we want to live as decent human beings—in America?*[11]

Attempting to divert press coverage from her speech, and fearing its impact on his nomination for president, President Lyndon B. Johnson called an emergency press conference, making the seven million Americans who were watching the hearings miss the final minutes of coverage. But national networks ran the speech in its entirety that evening. Support came pouring into the Credentials Committee for the MFDP from across the nation. When Democratic operatives headed by Senator Hubert Humphrey offered a compromise that would give the MFDP two non-voting seats, Hamer adamantly refused the compromise, stating,

> *Do you mean to tell me that your position is more important than four hundred thousand black people's lives? Senator Humphrey, I know lots of people in Mississippi who have lost their jobs trying to register to vote. I had to leave the plantation where I worked in Sunflower County, Mississippi. Now if you lose this job of Vice-President because you do what is right, because you help the MFDP, everything will be all right. God will take care of you. But if you take [the vice-presidential nomination] this way, why, you will never be able to do any good for civil rights, for poor people, for peace, or any of those things you talk about. Senator Humphrey, I'm going to pray to Jesus for you."*[12]

For Hamer it was not about making concessions to quickly advance some Mississippians. Instead, it was about the ascendancy of truth over politics and divine justice for all over the liberal shrewdness of some; about the creation of a New Kingdom here on earth not riddled with the sickness of the prevailing American ethos but infused with a new vision inspired by "the least of these." It was about, for Hamer, being faithful to her call.

When the convention modified the compromise from two non-voting to two-voting seats, the MFDP rejected the offer. Refusing what they considered a political handout, Hamer said, "We didn't come all this way for no two seats!"[13] Hamer and the delegation's demand for equality of representation for their state would help to usher in the Voting Rights Act of 1965 and a change in the Democratic Party seating of delegates four years later in Chicago, in 1968. Although defeated in her own bids for public office and in her 1964 and 1965 congressional challenges, Hamer became the first African American since Reconstruction to be seated as an official delegate at a national party convention, and the first woman ever to be seated from Mississippi.[14]

The experience in Atlantic City was both an end and a beginning. It was not only the cultivation of many months of canvassing, registering, and educating voters; it was the finale to a dramatic episode and it marked the start of a new chapter in Hamer's struggle for freedom.

Dreaming of New Beginnings in the Midst of a Nightmare

In September 1964, entertainer and civil rights activist Harry Belafonte arranged for Hamer and ten other SNCC leaders to travel to Guinea as a way to relieve stress and reinvigorate the organization. Realizing that reality in newly liberated Guinea was "so vice-versa [to] what I'd heard that I couldn't hardly believe it,"[15] Hamer spoke of experiencing for the first time what Black freedom could entail. Thus, coming on the heels of a disillusioning experience in Atlantic City, traveling to Africa gave her new and troubling insights about America. It solidified her skepticism of American claims about freedom and democracy. It lessened what little faith she had left in the willingness of the federal government and white Americans to push for racial change on the basis of appeals to conscience. The idea that the federal government would rectify the situation if it understood what was truly happening in Mississippi, and that white Americans would champion such a change if they were made aware of such, no longer held weight for Hamer:

> *I used to say when I was working so hard in the fields, if I could go to Washington—to the Justice Department—to the FBI—get close to let them know what was going on in Mississippi, I was sure that things would change in a week. Now that I have traveled across America, been to Congress, to the Justice Department, and to*

> *the FBI, I am faced with things I'm not too sure I wanted to find out. The sickness in Mississippi is not a Mississippi sickness. This is America's sickness.*[16]

Hamer's life mirrored her conviction that God's power and presence was with the poor and disenfranchised, calling them to make unambiguous ethical choices in an unethical world. Her understanding of Jesus's life and message led her to testify: "The churches have got to remember how Christ dealt with the people, like in the fourth chapter of St. Luke, and the eighteenth verse, when Jesus said, 'The spirit of the Lord is upon me, because he hath anointed me to preach the gospel to the poor; he hath sent me to heal the broken-heated, to preach deliverance to the captives, and recovering of sight to the blind, to set at liberty those that are bruised.'"[17] For Hamer, Jesus, the miraculous, resurrected Christ on the one hand, was also the historical and gritty revolutionary who on the other hand said "no" to the empire, and who empowered her to say no to Jim Crow. Thus, her unwavering faith, as witnessed in the spirituals, hymns, and freedom songs she constantly sang and strategically used in her voter registration, speeches, and other civil rights work, emboldened and kept her determined to work to bring about a new, just world in which poor Black women and men would have a say in every aspect of their lives.

The Freedom Farm Corporation and Black Economic Cooperation

Sociologist Monica White notes that African Americans have long connected land, food, and freedom as a way to garner community resilience and collective agency. She aptly argues, "The millions of men, women, and children who were kidnapped from their homelands in Africa and transported through the Middle Passage, the most extreme case of forced deportation in world history, possessed knowledge of microclimates and the particular kinds of crops that they could grow in the places where they would toil as enslaved."[18] Enslaved underfed Africans, looking to ward off starvation and stay alive, used their agricultural knowledge of crops from their own heritage, as well as the shared knowledge of indigenous communities about the crops available to them in their new environment, to sustain themselves by growing small food gardens.[19] They fostered their survival and Africanized plantation societies' foods by planting, for example, millet seeds and sorghum for grain and cereal crops, coffee, okra, watermelon, and "Asian" long beans or green beans—all native to Africa. These were brought to the Americas on slave ships as either food, medicines, or materials to make ropes and bedding.[20]

Hamer's unwillingness to waiver in her commitment to secure political and economic freedom and agency for the poor—Blacks and whites—both broadened the focus of the Civil Rights Movement across the nation and challenged capitalistic democracy. It was Hamer's personal experience with hunger, alongside her experience of unbridled racialized violence, gender oppression, and exploitation, that turned her into a staunch advocate not only for voting rights, but also for food security, home ownership, and other community-led development initiatives that would promote collective agency and redistribute economic justice. "You say you can't feed me," she said at the 1969 White House Conference on Hunger. "But you can take my son to Vietnam. And don't put this all on Mississippi people. There are hungry people right here in DC."

Expanding her efforts to include economic equity and self-reliance as part of her work, which she called her work for Christ,[21] in 1969 Hamer laid the foundation for the Freedom Farm Corporation, an elaborate project to initiate economic cooperative self-sufficiency among poor African Americans. Through her work with antipoverty projects associated with the farm, Hamer broadened the meaning of civil rights activism to include addressing African Americans' socioeconomic needs. Her vision had always included a focus on poverty, and her desire to run her own antipoverty organization independent of local, state, and federal government was now heightened. The exposure that resulted from her televised speech at the convention, particularly her account of the Winona jail beating which she suffered as a result of her voter registration efforts, broadened her base of supporters and her ability to start the project.[22]

The needs of African Americans in the Delta area were dire. According to the 1960 Census Report, in the county of Sunflower, Hamer's home county, more than five thousand families who lived below the poverty line earned less than $2,000 a year.[23] An overwhelming majority of that five thousand—4,300 to be exact—were Black. Sixty-eight percent of the county's residents existed on $1,000 a year or less. The median annual income of the county's Black residents was $456. Of the thirty-one thousand Black people in the county, only seventy-one owned any land; and while 70 percent of the homes were in a state of deterioration, 60 percent of the homes had no plumbing. The average educational accomplishment was a sixth-grade education—the actual grade which Hamer herself completed.[24]

To address this extreme poverty, Hamer initiated multiple projects as part of the Freedom Farm Corporation, starting with a project known as the "pig bank."[25] With the help of Sunflower County's office of the National Council of Negro Women (NCNW) who donated the first fifty pigs, Freedom Farm's pig bank was opened. The pig bank was available to any family which had the facilities to keep a pregnant female pig who would eventually have anywhere from nine to twenty baby pigs. The mother pig would then be returned to the pig bank, and the family who received the initial donation would then donate two of their female pigs, once they became pregnant, to another family in the chain. The objective was to breed and redistribute as many pigs as possible. In the first eighteen months of the pig bank's operation, roughly 135 families had received pigs,[26] and by the third year, at least three hundred families, with a yield of between two thousand and three thousand new pigs. In less than five years the project had assisted close to nine hundred families.[27]

The second program of Freedom Farm involved acquiring land on which to raise produce. While the first forty acres were initially used for the pig bank, within two years Freedom Farm had acquired more than 700 acres upon which were grown produce and cotton. This made Freedom Farm the owner of almost 33 percent of the 1,940 acres owned by Blacks in North Sunflower County. While proceeds from the sale of the cotton were used to pay for the land, buy seed, and cover administrative costs, the food grown was primarily shared among those in need, while a portion was sold to provide seed money for the third project of the Freedom Farm, which entailed helping families to secure housing.

The housing program of Freedom Farm involved providing poor families with their own homes via the farm purchasing and reselling homes, securing small loans from local banks, and using profits from the sale of its produce to make homeownership possible for many who had never experienced living in anything other than a shack. By 1972, three years after it began, Freedom Farm had built seventy affordable homes and expanded its housing program to include the construction of streets and alleys, the laying of sewage and water pipes, and the securing of electric and gas services.[28] Hamer proudly stated:

> *We decided to organize everybody who lived in a shack—which was most of us . . . and teach them how to take advantage of low-cost FHA and farm mortgages. Once we got started, we found that so many people wanted to take part that we didn't have time to give the organization a name. We just sort of call it The Co-op.*[29]

The two last official programs of Freedom Farm dealt with education and Black business development. Through its education component, Freedom Farm provided scholarships and grants to local students to start or complete their education. Its business component provided seed money and loans to start and support local businesses.

The above list of programs, however, does not detail in full the scope of the work of the Freedom Farm Cooperative, which served as a social service agency, a job referral service, a clothing bank, and an advocate on behalf of the community, participating in "picket lines and boycotts of local merchants that abused Black customers."[30]

Freedom Farm was operated as a cooperative with a $1 monthly membership fee, although few could afford to pay this and no one was denied participation as a result. The primary redistributive nature of the farm's programs and projects themselves grew out of Hamer's commitment to seek freedom for the most marginalized in her community. She envisioned the organization as one that would provide freedom "from hunger, poverty, and homes that did not adequately protect . . . families from the cold winds of 'Old Man Winter.'" The guiding philosophy was empowerment of a long-term nature at the communal level.

Despite efforts at reorganizing Freedom Farm, and seeking out new sources of funding, Hamer's declining health and the sudden death of her business partner, Joseph Harris, in 1974 took their toll on the cooperative.[31]

Practicing Communal Reliance, Redistribution, and Abundance

While the Freedom Farm was not the only one of its kind with regard to either being a cooperative or serving the poor within the Delta area, it was distinctive in three important ways. First, it was started not from the pooling of Black-owned land, but as a result of purchasing forty acres from one of the few Black farmers in the area, who was being threatened with foreclosure. While the significance may be lost to some, for Hamer it was anything but. For African Americans to be in a position to collaborate with, bargain with, and purchase land from each other when the whites had, for so long and at every turn, denied them such an opportunity, was a tremendous victory. As a result of Hamer's speaking engagements across the nation and her requests for donations, Freedom Farm would make an additional purchase of 640 acres of land between Drew and Ruleville, Mississippi, and use the land to expand their operation and start new initiatives, including a garment factory and Head Start.

Second, Freedom Farm Cooperative made a deliberate attempt to avoid receiving federal funding for its operation, even while it helped others to seek out such funding for their well-being. Hamer continued her advocacy efforts on multiple levels, while meeting the needs of the poor within the Sunflower County and holding government and businesses accountable.

Finally, the Freedom Farm Cooperative board, which included women not only in supportive roles but also in leadership positions, encouraged cooperative community practices in which human life, dignity, connectedness, and concern for the collective well-being of community was not sacrificed for privilege, wealth, and power. Such a model is instructive for creating a community in which the radical redistribution and sharing of resources, and the insurrectionary and revolutionary process of challenging the status quo and demanding equality and inclusion at every level, are all operative. It points to the imitation of Christ, as it did for Hamer, and the possibility of an inclusive community.

The Freedom Farm Cooperative not only marked a high point and a culmination of sorts in Hamer's grassroots organizing and activist career. It was a reflection as well of her belief in God's ability to "make a way out of no way" in the midst of deprivation and opposition. It was the manifestation of her resistance to the socioeconomic conditions in which she found herself and her community, her critique of the multiplicity of oppression of African Americans, and her attempt to develop strategies aimed at communal wholeness and social change. Her persistent response to Black people's deprivation served as a witness to her liberating, reconciling faith, shaped by an indefatigable belief in Jesus as friend and deliverer of the poor. It reflected Hamer's ability and capacity to recognize the "sickness in America" and yet reimagine it as a place that could be changed to meet the communal needs and longings of the disenfranchised. Her audacious refusal to succumb to the unbending resolve of white racism and the quiet acquiescence of those Black preachers who would shrink from salvation's hard demands is well documented. On one occasion, upon entering the Sunday morning service of one of these preachers and being welcomed by the preacher and asked to say a few words, Tracy Sugarman states:

> *Mrs. Hamer rose majestically to her feet. Her magnificent voice rolled through the chapel as she enlisted the Biblical ranks of martyrs and heroes to summon these folks to the Freedom banner. Her mounting, rolling battery of quotations and allusions from the Old and New Testaments stunned the audience . . . "Pharaoh was in Sunflower County! Israel's children were building bricks without straw—at three dollars a day!" Her voice broke, and tears stood in her eyes. "They're tired! And they're tired of being tired." Suddenly the rhetoric ceased . . . a silence rushed the room. . . . [S]he pointed to the shaken minister, and every eye fastened on the man in the pulpit. "And you, Reverend Tyler, must be Moses! Leadin' your flock out of the chains and fetters of Egypt—takin' them yourself to register—*tomorra'*—in Indianola!"*[32]

Hamer gives voice to a distinctive Christian discourse that takes seriously Jesus's life story and earthly countercultural ministry, as was evidenced in her creation of the Freedom Farm Cooperative. Her theological conviction that Jesus's ontological reality and atonement were of grave importance did not lead her to trivialize or devalue his existential reality and earthly ministry. Instead, it encouraged her to work for change and justice in a seemingly unchangeable, unjust world, privileging the voices of the poor and collaborating with others across lines of difference to eradicate inequity and effect poor Black people's (and white's) well-being and communal salvation.

Following in Hamer's Footsteps

There are no quick fixes or easy answers to righting the inequity in American society experienced by poor Black women, men, and children. Yet the suffering and yearning amongst the poor and disenfranchised for economic justice and an improved quality of life begs for a response; one that embodies the movement of Hamer which connected catastrophe with courage and compassion, while taking seriously Jesus's new vision for humanity to initiate communal flourishing and just human relations. It is exceedingly clear that the Black Church will not accomplish the eradication of poverty and oppression amongst poor Blacks by itself. However, Black churches in the twenty-first century have the opportunity to contribute mightily to the realization of the liberation of African Americans and the liberation of the larger human family. Perhaps it is time to take cues from some African American women (and men) who engage redemptive models of resistance and transcendence with a focus on fostering communal remediation, transformation, abundance, and flourishing.

Jamila Norman and Patchwork City Farms

In Atlanta, Jamila Norman began Patchwork City Farms, a 1.2-acre farm in the middle of the city, to address food insecurity and provide a viable alternative to the unhealthy food options to which she and her neighbors were subjected. Norman, the daughter of Caribbean parents whose history is rooted in agriculture, grew up in Queens, New York. In 2010, after working to help a church with its garden, she decided to start her own urban farm for her family, which expanded to serving her community. The farm's organic produce is now sold at local farmers' markets and has also become a source for local farm-to-table restaurants.

Norman also cofounded the Southwest Atlanta Growers Cooperative (SWAG), a farmer-based, community-supported food cooperative dedicated to building an economically sustainable urban food system. Supported by Southwest Atlanta's farmers and other food businesses and restaurants around the city of Atlanta, the cooperative works to raise awareness about and access to healthy and affordable foods within the Black community, while also fostering better health outcomes. SWAG also serves as a supportive community for cooperative members like Abiodun Henderson's Gangstas to Growers, a social enterprise that not only grows healthy foods for the Black communities it serves, but also provides opportunities for employment, empowerment, and agricultural entrepreneurship for at-risk and formerly incarcerated youth.

Abiodun Henderson's Gangstas to Growers

In 2016, Henderson started Gangstas to Growers with the aim of disrupting the cycle of generational poverty, ending recidivism, providing a space of healing, supporting a Black-run, Black-owned food system, and promoting communal wealth building and well-being. With the objective of developing economic empowerment and self-sufficiency, participants learn about food production and are employed by the program while being trained in how to grow crops and run their own businesses. They are then hired by nearby Black-owned farms or supported as they engage in other endeavors. Participants also make and sell Sweet Sol hot sauce, a product for which they grow and harvest the ingredients, and the sales revenue from which helps to fund the program.

Born in Brooklyn, New York, Henderson grew up with parents of Liberian and Trinidadian lineage who were advocates for change. Her mother, a Liberian-born social worker, psychology teacher, and entrepreneur who started a school and employment agency for immigrant women, died when Henderson was fourteen. It was her mother's diagnosis of AIDS and desire to improve her and her family's health by shifting to a vegan diet that initiated a dietary shift in Henderson.

In 1997, when her mother died, Henderson was sent to live with her father's family. Her practice of cutting classes to head for the library to read books by Black authors who were of interest to her led Henderson's family to send her to Piney Woods Country Life School, a historical African American boarding school in Mississippi. After graduating from Piney Woods and attending Dillard University, Henderson began waitressing in eateries, moved to Georgia, and found work in fine-dining restaurants. In 2011, three years after managing to save enough money to buy her first home in Atlanta, the bank foreclosed her home and her father died unexpectedly.

The loss of her father and the righteous discontent she held concerning the economic and social disparities that were impacting the Black community propelled Henderson to take action. She used her modest inheritance from her father to travel the country to take photos of the Occupy movement protests, which began in New York City on Wall Street as protests against corporate financial misdeeds and which spread across the United States. After encountering Occupy the Hood, an offshoot of the Occupy movement in Washington, DC, which sought to increase access to healthy foods in Black and low-income communities, Henderson returned to Atlanta committed to engaging in this work.

In 2012, Henderson began her foray into food justice work, first persuading a property owner in Atlanta's Westview neighborhood, where she was renting, to let her plant produce, then getting the neighborhood association to allow her to oversee their community garden, and finally recruiting young people living around the neighborhood to assist her with growing vegetables, a skill Henderson honed as a trainee with Truly Living Well, an urban farming nonprofit. Her efforts grew into an annual summer camp for kids and teens and set her on the path to win a $10,000 fellowship with Atlanta's Center for Civic Innovation to design her pilot for Gangstas to Growers.

Karen Washington and the Food Justice Movement

Karen Washington, a food justice activist and community organizer, coined the term *food apartheid.* Washington speaks of the need to address food apartheid rather than food deserts when discussing disparities in access to healthy food across racial and socioeconomic lines. The term *food desert*—defined as areas where residents' access to affordable, healthy food options (especially fresh fruits and vegetables) is restricted or nonexistent due to the absence of grocery stores within convenient traveling distance—fails to acknowledge the intersectional inequalities, such as race and income, that lead to inequitable food systems.[33] It also ignores the ways in which white supremacy has manipulated food availability in Black and brown neighborhoods—spaces that are not as empty or desolate as the word "desert" might lead one to think, but which are full of life, vibrancy, and resiliency, and agency. The word *apartheid*, used to refer to the enforced racial segregation in South Africa, when paired with the word "food" takes into consideration the root causes of food disparity—structural injustices, oppressive policies, and intentional actions—that impact African American and other communities of color.

Washington's commitment to turn empty lots in Bronx neighborhoods of New York City into community gardens is not only based on her desire to provide fresh vegetables to community members, but also on her commitment to create a more democratic food system and economy rooted in racial and gender equity. Before becoming a food justice activist, Washington, who received a master's degree in occupational biomechanics and ergonomics from New York University, worked as a physical therapist. Seeing many of her patients who were predominantly Black and brown suffering from diabetes, obesity, and hypertension, she wanted to find more preventive measures than the treatments available, which involved medication and surgery. Seeking a better, healthier, and more economical way to address their health issues, she became a vocal community gardener.

Washington's work highlights the intersectionality of oppressions; that is, the connection between the unjust food system in the United States, poverty, health disparities, crime, and other disenfranchising social issues. As a result, Washington became a community activist through the Northwest Bronx Community Clergy Coalition. She later teamed up with other community gardens to launch a local farmers' market and, in 2009, she cofounded the Black Urban Growers, an organization that supports urban and rural African American growers as a way to "engage people of African descent in critical food and farm-related issues that directly impact our health, communities, and economic security."[34]

Other organizations that Washington has cofounded include: the Black Farmers & Urban Gardeners (BUGS) Annual Conference, a national conference that cultivates Black agriculture and supports urban and rural African American growers, as well as Black leadership in the food movement; Farm School NYC, which leads workshops across the United States on growing fresh food and food justice; the Black Farmer Fund, which attends to the economic development and social capital of the Black community in regard to farming and food through providing loans, grants, and financial education to the food community; and the three-acre Rise and Root Farm, a farm in New York's Orange County that centers, is run by, and is focused on empowering those who are BIPOC (Black, Indigenous, People of Color) and LGBTQI+, and women—in farming, the food system, food justice movement, and what it takes to "uproot the underlying systems of oppression in order to create liberation."[35]

Reflecting Christ's Teachings Through Affordable Housing

In recent years, in an effort to transform communities by providing affordable housing, more and more large as well as small Black faith communities across the United States have begun to build affordable housing on their church property. Addressing the affordable housing crisis is a critical issue with which the Black Church must contend. This is paramount, given the fact that the Black religious landscape continues to change across the United States because of dwindling church attendance among younger generations who do not view the Black Church as an institution that is aligned with their desire to address social issues and engage in justice work,[36] population shifts due to gentrification, and Black and brown residents having to move a distance from their church homes as a result of being priced out of gentrifying housing markets across the country.

For instance, Washington, DC, once proudly labeled "Chocolate City," in recent years has experienced a dramatic drop in its Black population. During the 1970s and 1980s, Blacks made up 71 percent of the DC population. By 2000, their numbers had dropped to 60 percent, and by 2022, the population of African Americans in DC had slid to 41 percent,[37] while African Americans and persons of color who remain in the district struggle to find and keep affordable housing. Decades of racist local policies have set the stage for present-day displacement. A different kind of stewardship is needed—one that entails religious institutions developing their underused church-owned lands and buildings into permanent affordable housing to help parishioners afford to stay in their neighborhoods, as well as advocating for fair housing policies that label adequate affordable housing as a right and not a privilege, and encouraging cooperative home ownership among Black families to counter systems of inequity and serve the most vulnerable. Several churches are modeling how to move in this direction.

Joseph W. Daniels Jr. and Emory Fellowship

When Senior Pastor Reverend Dr. Joseph W. Daniels Jr. and Emory Fellowship, a United Methodist Church, covenanted with each other to engage in a different kind of stewardship, they decided part of that difference would entail building affordable housing for their surrounding community in Ward 4 of the Brightwood section of the Washington, DC. Their renovated church sits in the center of the $60-million-dollar Beacon Center complex, comprised of ninety-nine affordable housing units, a food pantry, culinary arts training center, and space for a restaurant, a health clinic, immigration clinics, a gymnasium, and community spaces available for lease by the community. The design of the refurbished church surrounded by its new affordable housing development symbolizes what Daniels believes is the congregation's commitment to work within and address the community's needs in a way that fosters flourishing. To develop the complex, the church's nonprofit, Emory Beacon of Light, partnered with The Community Builders, a nonprofit real estate developer.

In 2016, the Beacon broke ground after acquiring $17.2 million from the DC Department of Housing and Community Development's Housing Production Trust Fund (HPTF), $21.6 million in bonds from the DC Housing Authority, and $16 million from low-income housing tax credits. A recommendation was made by the DC Fiscal Policy Institute to grant the project an additional $200 million to keep up with the increasing construction costs and an additional $100 million was allocated for this purpose. The project also receives an annual allotment from the DC Housing Authority as rent supplement from its Local Rent Supplement Program funds to support units for formerly unhoused persons. In 2019, the Beacon opened and received its first tenants.

Reverend Daniels believes that such projects as this help the church to show up, "as the center of community life and let[s] people know, especially those who have been frustrated with our faith communities, that there is hope, that there are people who want to connect with people who are struggling and people who want to improve the lives of their sisters and brothers."[38]

William H. Lamar IV and Metropolitan AME Church

Across town near the White House, at the historic Metropolitan African Methodist Episcopal Church where Frederick Douglass in 1894 gave speeches and where the memorial service for Rosa Parks took place, Reverend William H. Lamar IV advocates for policies to counter the damaging effects of gentrification, which has pushed Blacks out of DC neighborhoods. Understanding how slavery, Jim Crow, racism, housing discrimination, and redlining in particular have prohibited African Americans from accumulating wealth, Lamar concludes,

> *The black pastor, like Jesus remains connected to the pain of the people, and when I have investigated because of the pain, I see that it lands squarely in economics, politics, and policy. That forces me and the Black Church in the best of our tradition to say, wait a minute. We can give people clothes and turkeys at Thanksgiving, but that does not fundamentally change their economic lot.*[39]

Lamar helps to lead the Black Equity Through Home Ownership Alliance, a program of the Washington Interfaith Network (WIN). The alliance consists of fifty African American churches seeking to build homes for Black residents of DC, create a fund for inherited homes to receive monies for repairs, facilitate home-ownership workshops, and advocate for affordable housing, including rental properties. Where religious leaders fight the lack of helpful policies by organizing Black homeowners in DC, Lamar's answer is to advocate for policies that foster equity, establish affordable housing as a right and not a privilege, and promote communal flourishing. As he states, "I don't want apologies. I want policy."

We Have Plenty

There are no quick fixes or easy answers to righting the legacy of prosperity theology in American society. This is evidenced by the long-standing structural inequalities, unjust policies, and economic inequity with which poor and disenfranchised Black women, men, and children have had to contend. Yet the suffering and yearning for economic justice and an improved quality of life begs for a theological response—one that embodies a communal vision of salvation and redemptive models of resistance and transcendence that allow communal healing, remediation, transformation, abundance, and flourishing within Black communities.

Such a vision of salvation, along with redemptive models of resistance and the Black Church's new distinguishing mark of identity that opposes all forms of violence, including structural inequities within the US economy, can not only foster a theology that takes seriously the concerns and holistic liberation of the poor. It can also help us to develop embodied practices that express what my maternal great-grandmother, Posey Mazyck-Warren, known as Honey, would say: "We have plenty." This was not a statement that Honey, born in 1915 to sharecropping parents, made because our family had an abundance of resources. Like her poor working-class neighbors, she struggled to make ends meet. Still, my great-grandmother believed that by developing supportive networks of women (and men) who could share resources, insights, and wisdom, the construction of a social fabric that would foster sustainability and communal well-being for Black families could be realized.

Even while my great-grandmother confronted oppressive structures and systems that were meant to derail her agency and eliminate resources she sought for her community, she continued to embody ways of fostering communal abundance in her daily living and across the span of her life. Her approach to modeling Jesus's teachings on material redistribution included opening her home and setting the table for family, friends, and strangers alike, building an extended network of support, and engaging in local politics, all while raising generations of children, including me and my siblings, and refusing to differentiate between family-by-blood and family-by-choice. She met catastrophe with courage and compassion, while taking seriously Jesus's new vision for humanity to initiate communal flourishing and just human relations.

While it is exceedingly clear the Black Church will not accomplish the eradication of poverty and oppression among poor African Americans as an institution by itself, it is clear that the Black Church has an opportunity to contribute mightily to the realization of the liberation of African Americans, and the liberation of the larger human family in ways that will make this world a better, more just, and more equitable place for all. This is my desire, hope, and fervent prayer for the Black Church, and for us all.

NOTES

Introduction

1 Although Black Americans account for roughly 14 percent of the US population, they make up half of the number of persons killed by on-duty officers. *The Washington Post* reported that in 2024, 1,172 African Americans were killed by on-duty police, which is most likely less than the actual total number. Hayden Godfrey et al., "Democracy Dies in Darkness: 1,172 People Have Been Shot and Killed by Police in the Past 12 Months," *Washington Post,* September 9, 2024, https://www.washingtonpost.com/graphics/investigations/police-shootings-database. A report by *NBC News* stated that the recorded numbers in the FBI database are lower than the number of killings because the federal government does not keep comprehensive counts of such, and because the 2019 FBI-created National Use of Force database is voluntary and self-reported by individual law agencies. Matthew Danbury, "Ten Years After Ferguson, Data on Police Killings Shows a Lack of Progress," *NBC News,* August 9, 2024, https://www.nbcnews.com/data-graphics/data-police-killings-changed-10-years-ferguson-rcna16384. See also Cristopher Ingraham, "Racial Inequality in Minneapolis Among the Worst in the Nation," *Washington Post,* May 30, 2020, https://www.washingtonpost.com/business/2020/05/30/minneapolis-racial-inequality, and Leslie Redmond and Curtiss Paul DeYoung, "White Privilege Shines with COVID-19," *Star Tribune,* April 23, 2020, https://www.startribune.com/white-privilege-shines-with-covid-19/569903692.

2 A phrase that Dr. Martin Luther King Jr. would come to use and define as a world based on community values of mutual aid, cooperation, interdependence, respect, and shared responsibility. See his speech, "Facing the Challenge of New Age," in *The Essential Writings and Speeches of Martin Luther King Jr.*, ed. James Melvin M. Washington (Harper San Francisco, 1991), 140.

3 Kate Bowler's brilliant mention of "hard prosperity" and "soft prosperity" helps us to think more deeply about the complexity and varieties

of prosperity gospel preaching. It cautions researchers against providing a simplistic definition of prosperity gospel preaching and beckons a deeper investigation into theologies of prosperity in the Christian tradition, which is what I offer in this text. See Kate Bowler, *Blessed: A History of the American Prosperity Gospel* (Oxford University Press, 2013).

4 These denominations include: the National Baptist Convention (NBC), the National Baptist Convention of America (NBCA), the Progressive National Baptist Convention (PNBC), the African Methodist Episcopal (AME), African Methodist Episcopal Zion (AMEZ), the Christian Methodist Episcopal (CME), and the Church of God in Christ (COGIC). See C. Eric Lincoln and Lawrence H. Mamiya, *The Black Church in the African-American Experience* (Duke University Press, 1990).

5 Kelley Brown Douglas and Ronald E. Hopson, "Understanding the Black Church: The Dynamics of Change," *Journal of Religious Thought* 56/57, no. 2/1 (2000–2001): 96.

6 Delores S. Williams, *Sisters in the Wilderness: The Challenge of Womanist God-Talk* (Orbis Books, 1993), 206.

7 Williams, *Sisters in the Wilderness*, 206.

8 Williams, *Sisters in the Wilderness*, 205–206.

Chapter 1: Black Folks, Prosperity Gospels, and a Legacy of Longing

1 Slaves created what came to be known as the "invisible institution." This institution, a precursor to the Black Church, allowed slaves to pray and worship their God in a way that was liberating for them. Out of mistrust of their masters' preachers, enslaved Africans resorted to holding their own meetings in the quiet, secluded spots often called "hush harbors." See Norma J. Lutz, *The History of the Black Church* (Chelsea House Publishers, 2001), 21ff.

2 Gayraud S. Wilmore, *Black Religion and Black Radicalism: An Interpretation of the Religious History of Afro-American People*, 2nd ed., rev. ed. (Orbis Books, 1983), 222.

3 Wilmore, *Black Religion and Black Radicalism*, 222.

4 See Albert J. Raboteau's essay, "The Black Experience in American Evangelicalism: The Meaning of Slavery," in *African American Religion: Interpretive Essays in History and Culture* (Routledge, 1997), 91–106.

5 Raboteau, "The Black Experience in American Evangelicalism." As Raboteau explains in his essay, one example of how Black and white

evangelicals drew differently upon biblical images can be seen in how they viewed the biblical account of the Exodus from Egypt motif. While white Protestants linked themselves to God's chosen people, the new Israel, liberated from the bondage of Great Britain, and linked America to the Promised Land, Black Protestants were inclined to identify themselves as the children of Israel whom the Lord would deliver from America—the land of their captivity and suffering—first, through an emancipation from an enslaved existence and then from an existence in which segregation and oppression seemed perpetual.

6 Raboteau, "The Black Experience in American Evangelicalism."

7 Jacquelyn Grant, *White Women's Christ and Black Women's Jesus: Feminist Christology and Womanist Response* (Scholars Press, 1989), 221.

8 This most enduring ideal promulgates that neither family lineage nor class can supplant an individual's ability to control one's destiny, that success is deemed as a reward for moral virtue and sublime personal character, and that demonstrating the appropriate character traits of hard work, thrift, honesty, and altruism can help one overcome adversity and drink from the fountains of American success. Traceable back to the Puritan tradition with its notion of the Protestant work ethic, this myth of success presupposes that American society is conducive to social mobility on a large scale. In the late nineteenth and early twentieth century, leaders in religion, business, and government formed alliances to impress this notion upon America popular consciousness, and the cultural heroes of the time, including Horatio Alger, Henry Ward Beecher, Andrew Carnegie, and even Booker T. Washington became known as "saints in the cult of success" with their rags-to-riches biographies. See Harold Vanderpool, "The American Success Syndrome," *The Christian Century* (1975): 820–823. Also see Conrad Cherry, *God's New Israel: Religious Interpretations of American Destiny*, rev. ed. (University of North Carolina Press, 1998), 220.

9 Larry Murphy, "Piety and Liberation: A Historical Exploration of African American Religion and Social Justice," in *Blow the Trumpet in Zion: Global Vision and Action for the 21st Century Black Church*, ed. Iva E. Carruthers, Frederick D. Haynes III, and Jeremiah A. Wright Jr. (Fortress Press, 2005), 37.

10 C. Eric Lincoln and Lawrence H. Mamiya, *The Black Church in the African American Experience* (Duke University Press, 1990), 249.

11 Lincoln and Mamiya, *The Black Church in the African American Experience*, 244–250.

12 Lincoln and Mamiya, *The Black Church in the African American Experience*, 240–241.

13 It was during the Poor People's Campaign, considered the second part of the Civil Rights Movement, that Dr. Martin Luther King Jr. and others began to call for what they considered a revolution of American values that included changing the narrative practices that perpetuated sociocultural and environmental racism, US imperialism, ultimately, an unjust US economic system that fostered inequity and extreme poverty. For more information on the Poor People's Campaign, see Sylvie Laurent's *King and the Other America: The Poor People's Campaign and the Quest for Economic Equality* (University of California Press, 2018).

14 Jill Watts, *God, Harlem, USA: The Father Divine Story* (University of California Press, 1992), 22–23. See also Beryl Satter's introduction in her text, *Each Mind a Kingdom: American Women, Sexual Purity and the New Thought Movement, 1875–1920* (University of California Press, 1999).

15 Stephanie Mitchem, *Name It and Claim It? Prosperity Preaching in the Black Church* (The Pilgrim Press, 2007), 52.

16 My definition of theological anthropology is taken from Dwight Hopkins, who states, "Theological anthropology defines and regulates what it means to be a human being in a religious system." See his essay, "Theologies in the USA," *Theologies and Cultures: Church and Empire* 2, no. 1 (June 2005): 79.

17 Milmon F. Harrison, *Righteous Riches: The Word of Faith Movement in Contemporary African American Religion* (Oxford University Press, 2005), 9.

18 Darnise C. Martin, *Beyond Christianity: African Americans in a New Thought Church* (New York University Press, 2005), 12–13.

19 Martin, *Beyond Christianity*, 13–14.

20 Both Milmon and Lee note that the origins of the Word of Faith evangelical Christian movement and prosperity theology developed as a US phenomenon after World War II.

21 Kenneth Copeland and Gloria Copeland, *Prosperity Promises* (Kenneth Copeland Publications, 1997), 57. See also Harrison, *Righteous Riches*, 8.

22 Harrison, *Righteous Riches*, 10.

23 Harrison, *Righteous Riches*, 97.

24 Harrison, *Righteous Riches*, 12.

25 Harrison, *Righteous Riches*, 11–12.

26 Harrison, *Righteous Riches*, 8–9. See also Kenneth Copeland, *Managing God's Mutual Funds—Yours and His: Understanding True Prosperity* (K. Copeland Productions, 1996), 7.

27 Creflo A. Dollar, *The Collar of Love: Understanding God's Answer to Racism, Separation, and Division* (Harrison House, 1997), 187–190.

28 Harrison, *Righteous Riches*, 13.

29 Harrison, *Righteous Riches*, 134.

30 Shayne Lee, *T. D. Jakes: America's New Preacher* (New York University Press, 2005), 35.

31 Anne Pinn and Anthony H. Pinn, *Fortress Introduction to Black Church History* (Fortress Press, 2004).

32 Such theology included: belief in an instantaneous conversion; an appreciation of ecstatic experiences; the Christian's ability to attain perfection through love of God and neighbor, resulting in freedom from sin (i.e., "being saved"); and the act of almsgiving without wealth renunciation or wealth redistribution. It should be noted that although Wesley would visit the American colonies and embark upon a brief preaching tour himself, it was his colleague and sometimes disputant George Whitefield who would be most effective in bringing English Evangelicalism and Calvinistic Methodism to the American colonies. Whitefield's Methodism was in large part Wesleyan, except in his adoption of Calvin's doctrine of predestination. See Walker et al., *A History of the Christian Church*, 4th ed. (Charles Scribner's Sons, 1985), 599ff.

33 Lee, *T. D. Jakes*, 35–36.

34 New Thought scholar Beryl Satter argues that it is difficult to pinpoint the origins of New Thought in the African American community (Satter, *Each Mind a Kingdom*, 16) and Kate Bowler includes in her list of African Americans who infused New Thought in their theologies such figures as Father George Hurley of Detroit's Universal Hagar's Spiritual Church, Reverend Clarence Cobbs of Chicago's First Church of Deliverance, radio evangelist Prophet James F. Jones, and Elder Solomon Lightfoot Michaux, revivalist and founder of the Church of God movement and the radio show, "The Radio Church of God" (Bowler, *Blessed*, 26–27). Each of these religious leaders adopted metaphysical religion to create their own innovative self-help religious response and practices to address African Americans' longing for the Good Life. However, not all of them explicitly preached material acquisition. In fact, Michaux preached against materialism in his broadcasts. I highlight the three religious leaders who explicitly admonished their followers to embrace material acquisition, and to understand the acquisition of such as a blessing from God.

35 The state of Maryland was among the five border states (Delaware, Maryland, West Virginia, Kentucky, and Missouri) that were

slave-holding states with legacies similar to the Confederate states. Like the Confederate states, these border states all attempted to establish laws that upheld racial segregation and voting restrictions for Black men between the 1880s and 1900s. However, disenfranchising Maryland Black voters was never attained to a significant degree during these years because of the large and increasing number of educated African Americans in Baltimore and other parts of Maryland who used their economic and political power to thwart disenfranchisement. For more information, see C. Fraser Smith, *Here Lies Jim Crow: Civil Rights in Maryland* (The Johns Hopkins University Press, 2008), 66.

36 Jill Watts, *God, Harlem, USA: The Father Divine Story* (University of California Press, 1992), 5–7.

37 Watts, *God, Harlem, USA*, 11–12.

38 Milton C. Sernett, *Bound for the Promised Land: African American Religion and the Great Migration* (Duke University Press, 1997). See also Albert J. Raboteau, *Canaan Land: A Religious History of African Americans* (Oxford University Press, 2001), 82.

39 Watts, *God, Harlem, USA*, 19–20.

40 Watts, *God, Harlem, USA*, 20.

41 Watts, *God, Harlem, USA*, 24.

42 Watts, *God, Harlem, USA*, 24.

43 See Watts, *God, Harlem USA*, and Robert Wiesbrot, *Father Divine and the Struggle for Racial Equality* (University of Illinois Press, 1983).

44 Watts, *God, Harlem, USA*, 33.

45 Watts, *God, Harlem, USA*, 61.

46 Hans A. Baer and Merrill Singer, *African American Religion in the Twentieth Century: Varieties of Protest and Accommodation* (University of Tennessee Press, 1992), 202.

47 See Johnnie Colemon's, "What We Believe" on the Johnnie Colemon Theological Seminary's "Our Beliefs" page, accessed January 8, 2025, https://ufbl.org/beliefs. See also Phillipe Matthews, "The First Lady of New Thought Metaphysics, The Reverend Doctor Johnnie Colemon," accessed January 8, 2025, http://thepmshow.tv/channel/spirtual-development/the-first-lady-of-new-thought-metaphysics-the-reverend-doctor-johnnie-colemon.

48 Influenced by the New Thought teachings of hypnotist and inventor Phineas Quimby, who advocated healing the body through using the mind (positive thinking), Myrtle and Charles Fillmore founded the Unity movement in the late 1880s, launching *Unity Magazine* (1889), the Unity School (1914), and the *Daily Word*. Jill Watts notes, in *God,*

Harlem USA, "Expounding the traditional New Thought line, Unity's founder argued that the mind was a powerful instrument that shaped human destiny. While sin, sickness, and misfortune resulted from negative thinking, awareness of God's internal presence and the power of positive thought allowed men and women to overcome adversity and actualize their desires. Fillmore took New Thought one step further, contending that positive thinking brought mortals close to divinity" (23).

49 See Johnnie Colemon Theological Seminary "Our Beliefs" page, https://ufbl.org/beliefs. See also Johnnie Colemon's set of five workbooks, *It Works If You Work It*, vol. 1, transcribed by Rosalie Jackson (Christ University Temple, n.d.), iii, and Phyllis Crinchlow et al., "The African American in Unity History June 19, 1993 Presentations" (26 Videos), https://www.truthunity.net/african-americans-in-unity/the-african-american-in-unity-history; and Glenn Mosley and Edie Skalitzy, "The History of Afro-Americans in the Unity Movement," *Association of Unity Churches Headquarters Highlights* 3, no. 1 (June/July 1993).

50 In an article by Phillippe Matthews, Colemon describes the racist treatment she experienced from the beginning of her association with the Unity School, stating, "I thought I was there to receive a healing for Johnnie Colemon. That was not the reason I was really there. I was there because the beautiful literature that they wrote then and still write was all about love and how much we must love each other. But, every night when my classes were over, I would have to drive from Lee's Summit to Kansas City, which was 15 miles in the morning and 15 miles in the evening because of the color of my skin, and I could not live on Unity Farm. I knew why I was there. I completely took the focus off of being healed and began to say, 'What am I suppose to do about this situation?' I began to ask God what am I suppose to do about this situation. However, my answer did not come immediately." Matthews, "The First Lady of New Thought Metaphysics." See also Johnnie Colemon, *It Works If You Work It, Jubilee Edition* (Universal Foundation for Better Living Press 2020).

51 See "Unity and Race: A Truthful History, Mistakes, Apologies, and Actions Through the Years," ed. Ellen Debenport, with contributions Jim Blake, Sandra Campbell, Charline Manuel, and Alexandra Scott, https://www.unity.org/en/article/unity-and-race-truthful-history.

52 Matthews, "The First Lady of New Thought Metaphysics."

53 Bruce Buursma, "Minister Practices What She Preaches, Her Gospel Is 'Success,'" *Chicago Tribune*, July 28, 1985, section 2, p. 3.

54 In her workbook, *It Works If You Work It*, vol. 1, Colemon insists that God is the substance of all things, including money, and while her definition of prosperity includes more than acquiring capital, she also states "it is a sin to be poor" (1), and "When we claim our divine inheritance, we begin to draw riches us. . . . You have to be willing to try to think only positive, rich, abundant thoughts . . . [if] You are going to bless that pocketbook and think—PLENTY!" (3). See Colemon's *It Works If You Work It*, vol. 1, iii.

55 Colemon, *It Works If You Work It*, 9.

56 Leonard Novarro, "Rev. Ike: Prophet or Pitch Man?," *The Tribune*, May 8, 1985.

57 Biographical information was gathered from Baer and Singer's *African American Religion in the Twentieth Century*, 200–202. Other sources include Beau Cutts, "Know Thyself, Says Rev. Ike," *The Atlanta Constitution*, March 29, 1973; Bille Chene Speed, "You Can't Lose, Rev. Ike Says," *The Atlanta Journal*, March 29, 1973; James K. Cazalas, "Resplendent Rev. Ike Says Man Is God, Heaven's Here," *The Boston Globe*, May 5, 1973; Renie Schapiro, "He Promises Pie in the Sky with Ice Cream on Top: Mr. Preacherman," *Sunday Times*, December 8, 1974; Clayton Riley, "The Golden Gospel of Rev. Ike," *New York Times*, March 9, 1979; and Teresa Hairston, "Rev. Ike: The Prosperity Pioneer," *Gospel Today*, September/October 2004.

58 Sernett, *Bound for the Promised Land*. See also Raboteau, *Canaan Land*, 82.

59 Riley, "The Golden Gospel of Rev. Ike."

60 Baer and Singer, *African American Religion in the Twentieth Century*, 201.

61 "Rev. Ike Speaks on His Philosophy," accessed January 8, 2025, https://www.revikelegacy.com.

62 Riley, "The Golden Gospel of Rev. Ike."

63 David Edwin Harrell, *Oral Roberts: An American Life* (Indiana University Press, 1985).

64 James Morris, *The Preachers* (St. Martin's Press, 1973), 184.

65 Morris, *The Preachers*, 176.

66 Delores S. Williams, *Sisters in the Wilderness: The Challenge of Womanist God-Talk* (Orbis Books, 1993), xii.

67 Jacquelyn Grant, *White Women's Christ and Black Women's Jesus: Feminist Christology and Womanist Response* (Scholars Press, 1989).

68 For an important essay on the naming process of Black female bodies, see Hortense Spillers, "Mama's Baby, Papa's Maybe," in *Black, White*

and in Color: Essays on American Literature and Culture (University of Chicago Press, 2003). The descriptive "God's leading lady," "anointed woman of God," and "Daddy's little girl" are the patriarchal terms commonly used by prosperity preacher T. D. Jakes (and two of the three are titles of his books) to describe God's relationship with African American women.

69 T. D. Jakes, *Behind Closed Doors* (Higher Dimension Ministries, 1992).

70 Lee, *T. D. Jakes*, 122ff.

71 T. D. Jakes, *The Great Investment: Faith, Family, and Finance to Build a Rich Spiritual Life* (Penguin, 2002), 13–14.

72 T. D. Jakes and Cornel West, "Preachers, Prophets and the Prophetic: The New Face of American Evangelicalism," lecture delivered as part of "Conversations," a public lecture series of Princeton University's Program in African American Studies, Princeton University, between Professor Cornel West and Bishop T. D. Jakes, Princeton University, October 26, 2005.

73 In his 2004 text, *He-Motions: Even Strong Men Struggle*, Jakes appears to problematize the "Strong Black Man" myth and rhetoric of hyper-masculinity he embraced in his earlier 1995 text, *Loose That Man & Let Him Go*, 2nd ed. (Bethany House Publishers, 2003). However, his continued depiction of women as the softer side of men and his notions of femininity both limit women's creative authority to define their own physicality, personal style, sexuality, and life options.

74 Jakes, *Loose That Man & Let Him Go*, 29.

75 Jakes, *Loose That Man & Let Him Go*, 42.

76 T. D. Jakes, *Woman, Thou Art Loosed: Healing the Wounds of the Past* (Destiny Image Publishers, 1993).

77 T. D. Jakes, *Man Power: Healing The Man* (Annual ManPower Conference Audio Tapes, 2012).

78 T. D. Jakes, *So You Call Yourself A Man? A Devotional for Ordinary Men with Extraordinary Potential* (Baker Publishing Group, 1997).

79 T. D. Jakes, "Real Men Pour In," sermon delivered on Father's Day, June 19, 2022. See The Potter's House T. D. Jakes YouTube Channel. https://www.youtube.com/@TPHDallas/search?query=June%2019%2C%202022.

80 T. D. Jakes, *The Lady, Her Lover, and Her Lord* (G.P. Putnam's Sons, 1998).

81 T. D. Jakes, *Daddy Loves His Little Girls* (Charisma House, 1996).

82 In June 2022 in a Sunday sermon entitled, "The Great Misunderstanding," Dollar publicly retracted his views on tithing, confessing that he

misled people with these teachings. Citing Romans 6:14 to substantiate that Christians now live under God's grace and not the laws of the Old Testament, Dollar told his listeners it is not biblically mandated to tithe. Rather, it is up to individuals to give according to their heart and ability.

83 Creflo A. Dollar Jr., *The Color of Love: Understanding God's Answer to Racism, Separation, and Division* (Harrison House, 1997).

84 Information retrieved from World Changers International website, https://cywn.tv.

85 See the chapter "Release Word out of Your Mouth to Unleash Prosperity," in Creflo A. Dollar, *Total Life Prosperity: 14 Practical Steps to Receiving God's Full Blessing* (T. Nelson Publishers, 1999).

86 Marla F. Frederick, *Between Sundays: Black Women and Everyday Struggles of Faith* (University of California Press, 2003), 135.

87 Taffi Dollar, "Far Above Rubies: The Price of a Virtuous Woman," *Changing Your World* 3, no. 5 (May 2001): 19.

88 Dollar, "Far Above Rubies," 19.

89 Dollar, "Far Above Rubies," 19.

90 Baer and Singer, *African-American Religion in the Twentieth Century*, 99ff.

Chapter 2: Jesus, Wealth, and Poverty

1 Brian K. Blount, *Then the Whisper Put on Flesh: New Testament Ethics in an African American Context* (Abingdon Press, 2001).

2 Redmond Mullin, *The Wealth of Christians* (Bookhouse Australia, 1983), 40.

3 Martin Hengel, *Property and Riches in the Early Church: Aspects of a Social History of Early Christianity*, trans. John Bowden (Fortress Press, 1974), 26–27.

4 Wolfgang Stegemann, *The Gospel and the Poor*, trans. Dietlinde Elliott (Fortress Press, 1984), 22–23.

5 Stegemann, *The Gospel and the Poor*, 23.

6 Stegemann, *The Gospel and the Poor*, 23.

7 Cf. John Dominic Crossman, *The Historical Jesus: The Life of a Mediterranean Jewish Peasant* (HarperSanFrancisco, 1992) and *Jesus: A Revolutionary Biography* (HarperSanFrancisco, 1994).

8 Sharon Ringe, *Jesus, Liberation, and the Biblical Jubilee: Images for Ethics and Christology* (Fortress Press, 1985), 52.

9 Blount, *Then the Whisper Put on Flesh*, 81.

10 Blount, *Then the Whisper Put on Flesh*, 81.
11 Gerhard von Rad, *Wisdom in Israel*, trans. James D. Martin (SCM Press, 1972), 85.
12 Robert Gordis, *Poets, Prophets, and Sages: Essays in Biblical Interpretation* (Indiana University Press, 1971), 163, 169.
13 I Kgs 10:14–20.
14 I Kgs 3:13.
15 Such sayings are throughout Psalms and Proverbs; Deut 28:3–12; and Lev 26:3–10.
16 David J. A. Clines, "The Book of Job," in *The Oxford Companion to the Bible*, ed. Bruce M. Metzger and Michael D. Coogan (Oxford University Press, 1993), 368.
17 Delores Williams reminds us through her work, *Sisters in the Wilderness*, that Hagar and African American women—the "Hagars" of our world—do not always experience God as liberator. Instead, God appeared for Hagar, and for many African American women in their life-threatening experiences, as sustainer and counselor—as "The One" who helps them make a way out of no way.
18 Theories differ on the origins and formation of the book of Job. Many contemporary final-form interpreters favor a holistic, that is literary, approach that shows the unifying elements within the book of Job as the product of a single, postexilic author even though they acknowledge the distinction between several parts of the text differentiated by genre, such as the prose that frames the narrative, the poetic dialogue between Job and his friends, Job's final defense, Elihu's speeches, and the speeches of God from the whirlwind. Mark Bartusch, in his article "The Formation of the Book of Job: The Priority of Poetry, the Primacy of Prose," provides readers with an excellent window into the book of Job's redactors and, in particular, how the final redactor privileges the patient, faithful, heroic Job who is rewarded over the angry, lamenting, and protesting Job who had experienced inexplicable suffering in search of understanding. As a result of the final redactor addition, Bartusch writes, "the once pious lament and protest became—in the final form of the book of Job—something less virtuous and more suspect (hence, the friends' arguments). [This led to] a great loss, insofar as it now undermines the audience's ability to be 'authentic' in the midst of life's uncertainty or most inexplicably tragic moments, leading readers to suppress or deny their profound experience of reality." See Mark Bartusch, "The Formation of the Book of Job: The Priority of Poetry, the Primacy of Prose," *Currents in Theology and Mission: The*

Theological Journal of the Lutheran School of Theology at Chicago and Wartburg Theological Seminary 46, no. 4 (July 2019), https://currents-journal.org/index.php/currents/article/view/206/233.

19 Rainer Albertz, *A History of Israelite Religion in the Old Testament Period*, vol. I, *From the Beginnings to the End of Monarchy*, trans. John Bowden (Westminster John Knox Press, 1994), 159–160.

20 Albertz, *A History of Israelite Religion*, 159–160.

21 Hans Walter Wolff, *Joel and Amos: A Commentary on the Books of the Prophets Joel and Amos* (Fortress Press, 1977), 104.

22 Willy Schottroff, "The Prophet Amos: A Socio-Historical Assessment of His Ministry," in *God of the Lowly: Socio-Historical Interpretations of the Bible*, trans. Matthew J. O'Connell, ed. Willy Schottroff and Wolfgang Stegemann (Orbis Books, 1984), 27–46.

23 Schottroff, "The Prophet Amos," 35.

24 Schottroff, "The Prophet Amos," 27.

25 Schottroff, "The Prophet Amos," 30.

26 Schottroff, "The Prophet Amos," 39.

27 Schottroff, "The Prophet Amos," 40.

28 Schottroff, "The Prophet Amos," 40.

29 Martin Hengel, *Property and Riches in the Early Church: Aspects of a Social History of Early Christianity*, trans. John Bowden (Fortress Press, 1974).

30 Hengel, *Property and Riches in the Early Church*, 20.

31 Peter Phan, "Social Thought," in *Message of the Fathers of the Church*, vol. 20, ed. Thomas Halton (Michael Glazier, 1984), 17.

32 Redmond Mullin, *The Wealth of Christians* (Orbis Books, 1983), 26–28.

33 I use the word "realm" instead of kingdom in recognition of Joanna Dewey's point that though "realm" is usually translated as "kingdom," the Greek word, *basileia*, refers to ruling in general, regardless of gender. See Dewey's essay, "The Gospel of Mark," in *Searching the Scriptures: A Feminist Commentary*, ed. Elisabeth Schüssler Fiorenza (Crossroad Publishing, 1994), 476.

34 Emerson B. Powery, "The Gospel of Mark," in *True to Our Native Land: An African American New Testament Commentary*, ed. Brian K. Blount et al. (Fortress Press, 2007), 123.

35 Powery, "The Gospel of Mark," 129.

36 H. B. Swete, *The Gospel According to St. Mark* (Macmillan, 1909), 116.

37 William L. Lane, *The Gospel According to Mark* (Wm. B. Eerdmans, 1974), 207.

38 Lane, *The Gospel According to Mark*, 207–208.

39 John Dominic Crossan, *Jesus: A Revolutionary Biography* (HarperOne, 1995), 132–133, 136. Crossan concludes, "We have, in the final analysis, no way of knowing for sure what Jesus knew about Cynicism, or whether he knew about it at all. That, however, is not really the point. Maybe he had never even heard of the Cynics and was just reinventing the Cynic wheel all by himself. But the differences as well as similarities between the Jesus and the Cynic preachers are instructive even if not derivative. Both are populists, appealing to the ordinary people; both are life-style preachers, advocating their position not only by word but by deed, not only in theory but in practice; both use dress and equipment to symbolize dramatically their message. But he [Jesus] is rural, they are urban; he is organizing a communal movement, they are following an individual philosophy; and their symbolism demands knapsack and staff, his no-knapsack and no-staff" (136–137).

40 Ernest Best, *Following Jesus: Discipleship in the Gospel of Mark* (JSOT, 1981) 28–29, 38–39. Best argues that the reference to the crowd suggests that Mark intends this passage to be more than simply specific instructions about martyrdom for the disciples and the words in 9:1 that follow suggest that death is not a necessary outcome for Jesus's followers. Womanists rightly warn us against using Jesus's words to validate the "redemptive" value of suffering in and of itself or put forth "spiritual" notions of "suffering for the sake of suffering" which are full of abusive potential. Cf. Delores S. Williams, "The Color of Feminism," *Christianity and Crisis* April 29 (1985): 164–165; "Black Women's Surrogacy Experience and the Christian Notion of Redemption," in *After Patriarchy: Feminist Transformations of the World Religions*, ed. Paula M. Cooey et al. (Orbis Books, 1991), 1–14; and her November 5 taped lecture at the "Re-Imagining Conference" (November 4–7, 1993). See also Jacquelyn Grant, "Womanist Jesus and the Mutual Struggle for Liberation," in *The Recovery of Black Presence: An Interdisciplinary Exploration*, ed. Randall C. Bailey and Jacquelyn Grant (Abingdon Press, 1995), 129–142; Emilie Townes, ed., *A Troubling in My Soul: Womanist Perspectives on Evil and Suffering* (Orbis Books, 1993); and Joanne Marie Terrell, *Power in the Blood? The Cross in African American Experience* (Orbis Books, 1998).

41 Numerous studies have been done to explain the actual evolution of this passage into its present form, as well as how this passage is to be understood in the present day. Luise Schottroff and Wolfgang Stegemann, in their text, *Jesus and the Hope of the Poor*, trans. Matthew J. O'Connell (Orbis Books, 1986), argue that it is impossible to follow Jesus as the disciples did, because Jesus is no longer on earth.

They further turn to a passage in Luke (22:35–38), which recalls the past sending of the disciples and instructs them to equip themselves with swords, to argue their point that past commandments, including renunciation for the disciples, are no longer relevant for the new age. Jack Kingsbury, in his work *Jesus Christ in Matthew, Mark and Luke: The New Testament Witnesses for Preaching* (Fortress Press, 1981), argues that the disciples must be prepared, if and when it becomes necessary, to renounce possessions and wealth. In R. W. Haskin's dissertation, "The Call to Sell All: A History of the Interpretation of Mark 10:17–23 and Parallels" (Columbia University, 1968), we find a complete study of this passage that is devoted just to the categorization of its schools of interpretation.

42 John Bowman, *The Gospel of Mark: The New Christian Jewish Passover Haggadah* (E. J. Brill, 1965), 214.

43 Powery, "The Gospel of Mark," 141.

44 Martin Dibelius, "The Motive for Social Action in the New Testament," in *Jesus: Study of the Gospels and an Essay on "The Motive for Social Action in the New Testament"* (SCM Press, 1963), 55.

45 The revaluation of wealth and poverty, along with the act of wealth redistribution as a prerequisite to discipleship, is found in both of these pericopes. Whereas in 8:34, Jesus states "whoever desires to come after me, let him deny himself, and take up his cross, and follow me," in 10:21, after hearing the man's positive response to his statement regarding the commandments prerequisite to discipleship, Jesus tells him, "one thing you lack: go your way, sell what you have and give to the poor, and you will have treasure in heaven; then come, follow me."

46 Frank J. Matera, *New Testament Ethics: The Legacies of Jesus and Paul* (Westminster John Knox Press, 1996), 28.

47 Ezra Palmer Gould, *A Critical and Exegetical Commentary on the Gospel According to St. Mark* (Charles Scribner's Sons, 1896), 239.

48 Gould, *A Critical and Exegetical Commentary*, 239.

49 Bowman, *The Gospel of Mark*, 238.

50 The Gospel According to Mark, 12:43–44 (NRSV).

51 Dewey, "The Gospel of Mark," 499.

52 R. S. Sugirtharajah, *The Bible and the Third World: Precolonial, Colonial, and Postcolonial Encounters* (Cambridge University Press, 2001), 263.

53 In the Deuteronomic law that demands a year of release from debt and servitude for the sake of the poor (15:1–12), it is stated that "there will never cease to be poor people" (v. 11). However, it is also recognized in that same pericope that if God's will were fully obeyed by God's

people, there would be no poverty and "no one in need among you" (vv. 3–5). Jesus is reiterating that same sentiment here with regard to the existence of poverty.

54 Allen Verhey, *The Great Reversal: Ethics and the New Testament* (Eerdmans, 1984), 18–19.

55 Dewey, "The Gospel of Mark," 501–502.

56 David L. Mealand, *Poverty and Expectations in the Gospels* (SPCK, 1977), 16, 92; G. D. Kilpatrick, *The Origin of the Gospel According to Matthew* (Clarendon Press, 1950), 124–125.

57 Thomas E. Schmidt, *Hostility to Wealth in the Synoptic Gospels* (JSOT Press, 1987), 121–122.

58 A more detailed examination of several of these Matthean passages (5:42, 6:19–24, 19:6–30) highlights wealth devaluation and redistribution as acts of true discipleship.

59 Schmidt, *Hostility to Wealth*, 125.

60 Schmidt, *Hostility to Wealth*, 125–126.

61 See Robert A. Guelich, *The Sermon on the Mount: Foundation for Understanding* (W Publishing Group, 1982), 329–332. See also David Hill, *The Gospel of Matthew* (Marshall Morgan and Scott, 1972), 142.

62 Willoughby C. Allen, *A Critical and Exegetical Commentary on the Gospel According to S. Matthew* (T & T Clark, 1912), 62. See also M. D. Goulder, *Midrash and Lection in Matthew: The Speaker's Lectures in Biblical Studies* (SPCK, 1974), 302.

63 This understanding can be found in Deut 15:9 and Prov 28:22. Although the NRVS version of Deut 15:9 reads, "be careful that you do not entertain a mean thought . . . and therefore view your needy neighbor with hostility and give nothing," the NKJ reads "beware lest there be a wicked thought in your heart, . . . and *your eye be evil against your poor brother* and you give him nothing . . ." In Prov 28:22, the same interpretation of the evil eye representing stinginess is given, as it states, "A man with an evil eye hastens after riches . . ."

64 Eduard Schweizer, *The Good News According to Matthew* (Westminster John Knox Press, 1975), 388.

65 Blount, *Then the Whisper Put on Flesh*, 69.

66 Blount, *Then the Whisper Put on Flesh*, 70.

67 Frank J. Matera, *New Testament Ethics: The Legacy of Jesus and Paul* (Westminster John Knox Press, 1996), 49.

68 Schmidt, *Hostility to Wealth*, 136–137.

69 Blount, *Then the Whisper Put on Flesh*, 87.

70 Joel B. Green, "Good News to Whom: Jesus and the 'Poor' in the Gospel of Luke," in *Jesus of Nazareth: Lord and Christ Essays on the*

Historical Jesus and New Testament Christology, ed. Joel B. Green and Max Turner (Eerdmans, 1994), 59.

71 Blount, *Then the Whisper Put on Flesh*, 86.

72 Alfred Plummer, *A Critical and Exegetical Commentary on the Gospel According to S. Luke*, 4th ed. (T & T Clark, 1901), 323.

73 John Navone, *Themes of St. Luke* (Gregorian University Press, 1970), 109.

74 G. B. Caird, *The Gospel of Luke* (Westminster Knox Press, 1963), 163.

75 The point being made here is that the unjust steward's actions are not, as some commentators have suggested, being praised by Jesus, but highlighted as indicators of his being not a son of God but a "son of this world," or rather of empire of his day whose illegitimate acts show his unconcern for God's teachings.

76 Stephanie Buckhanon Crowder, "The Gospel of Luke," in *True to Our Native Land: An African American New Testament Commentary*, ed. Brian K. Blount et al. (Fortress Press, 2007), 176.

Chapter 3: The Valuation of Poverty and Wealth in the Early Church

1 Nothing says more about Constantine's understanding of himself as the emperor empowered to rule the empire by God than his letter to Aelafius, a Christian official in North Africa, to whom he writes, "Since I am informed that you too are a worshipper of the Highest God, I will confess to your gravity that I consider it absolutely contrary to the divine law that we should overlook such quarrels and dissension [that is, between rival parties in the North African church], whereby the Highest Divinity may be moved to wrath not only against the human race, but against me myself, to whose care he has by his heavenly will committed the government of all earthly things" (preserved in Optatus *De Schismate Donatistarum*, App. III, 204–206, Mark Edwards's translation).

2 Though some scholars argue that locally the church changed little structurally, administratively, and theologically from the third to fourth to fifth centuries, Constantine's acknowledgment of the church did eventually bring about significant change in both its organizational structure and the function and status of its clergy. Bishops, in order to remain so, had to pander to the empire. In essence, they became peddlers of a different kind of gospel; a gospel of the empire—that followed Constantine. Christians such as the Arians were kicked out of the church as heretics. The Council at Nicaea was the place where many

of these changes were instituted. See W. Walker et al., *A History of The Christian Church*, 4th ed. (Charles Scribner's Sons, 1985), 183–186.

3 Cornel West, *Democracy Matters* (Penguin, 2004), 147–148.
4 West, *Democracy Matters*, 148.
5 West, *Democracy Matters*, 149.
6 West, *Democracy Matters*, 20.
7 West, *Democracy Matters*, 20–21.
8 West, *Democracy Matters*, 21.
9 Schmidt, *Hostility to Wealth*, 165.
10 Schmidt, *Hostility to Wealth*, 164–165.
11 Justo L. Gonzalez, *Faith & Wealth: A History of the Early Christian Ideas on the Origin, Significance and Use of Money* (Wipf & Stock, 1990), 159–161.
12 Gonzalez, *Faith & Wealth*, 159.
13 W. H. C. Frend, *The Rise of Christianity* (Fortress Press, 1984), 485–486.
14 Jane E. Merdinger, *Rome and the African Church in the Time of Augustine* (Yale University Press, 1997), 18.
15 See Augustine "Sermon 355," in Adolar Zumkeller, *Augustine's Ideal of the Religious Life* (Fordham University, 1986), 407.
16 James O'Donnell, *Augustine: A New Biography* (HarperCollins, 2005), 21.
17 O'Donnell, *Augustine*, 21.
18 As the fourth-century Christian church began to formalize its structure of governance, it relied heavily on, and ultimately came to resemble, the structure of the Roman Empire, incorporating its hierarchical structure of regions or prefectures, which were divided into twelve dioceses that were each ruled by a vicar selected by the emperor and whose regions were divided into even smaller units or provinces that were managed by a local minister or member of the senatorial aristocracy (better known as the "council of elders").
19 Pelagius, *Tractatus De Divitiis* P.L. 1383, 1397, 1401.
20 Alister E. McGrath, *Christian Theology: An Introduction* (Blackwell, 1994), 21–23.
21 Gerard Bonner, *St. Augustine of Hippo: Life and Controversies* (The Canterbury Press, 1986), 353.
22 Bonner, *St. Augustine of Hippo*, 353.
23 Frend, *The Rise of Christianity*, 674.
24 W. H. C. Frend, "Early Christianity and Society," *Harvard Theological Review* (1983): 76, 53–71.
25 Gonzalez, *Faith and Wealth*, 216.

26 In *Exposition on the Book of Psalms* 147.13, Augustine teaches that one should "set aside in their mind what they need to live, and think about who should have the rest, lest, trying to save in order to live, they will reap their own death."
27 Augustine, *Expositions on the Book of Psalms* 36.3.6.
28 Augustine, *Expositions on the Book of Psalms* 124.2.
29 Augustine, *Sermon* 39.4.6.
30 Augustine, "Letter 157.25," in *The Works of Saint Augustine: A Translation for the 21*st *Century, Part 2– Letters*, vol. 3, *Letters 156–210*, trans. Roland Teske, SJ, ed. Boniface Ramsey (New City Press, 2002), 31–32.
31 Augustine, "Letter 130," in *The Fathers of the Church, A New Translation: Saint Augustine Letters*, vol. 2, *Letters 83–130*, trans. Sister Wilfrid Parsons, SND (Fathers of the Church, 1953). See also "Letter 157" in *Augustine's Ideal of the Religious Life*, ed. A. Zumkeller (Fordham University Press, 1986).
32 Peter Brown, *Augustine of Hippo: A Biography* (University of California Press, 1969), 351.
33 Augustine, "Letter 157." Augustine wrote this letter as a rebuttal to Pelagius's literal interpretation of Matt 19:21, "sell what you have, and give to the poor" in his letter "On Riches."
34 Gonzalez, *Faith and Wealth*, 215–230.
35 Brown, *Augustine of Hippo*, 351.
36 Augustine, "Letter 130," 281–383.
37 Augustine, "Letter 130," 377.
38 Augustine, "Letter 130," 382; emphasis mine.
39 Augustine, "Letter 130," 400.
40 Augustine, "Letter 130," 400.
41 Augustine, "Letter 130," 387–392.
42 Augustine, "Letter 156," in *The Works of Saint Augustine*.
43 Augustine, "Letter 157."
44 Here Augustine references Gen 13:2, 26:13, 30:43.
45 Luke 16:19–20.
46 Luke 16:24–31.
47 Luke 16:24–31.
48 Luke 16:24–31.
49 Luke 16:24–31.
50 Augustine, "Letter 157," 31.
51 Matt 19:21.
52 1 Tim 6:17–19.

53 1 Tim 6:17–19.
54 Augustine, "Sermon 60.8," in *Sermons on Selected Lessons of the New Testament*, vol. 1, *S. Matthew, S. Mark, S. Luke* (John Henry Parker, 1984), 117.
55 Augustine, "Sermon 61.12," in *Sermons on Selected Lessons of the New Testament*, 122.
56 Augustine, "Sermon 53A," in *The Works of Saint Augustine*, 78.
57 Gonzalez, *Faith and Wealth*, 221.
58 The quote is taken from Augustine's "Letter 185.15," in which he condemns an uprising by the poor (who appear to be Donatists) against the rich landowners.
59 Augustine, *Concerning the City of God Against the Pagans: A New Translation by Henry Bettenson with an Introduction by John O'Meara* (Penguin, 1984), 8.1, 298.
60 Augustine, *Concerning the City of God*, 14.28, 593.
61 Augustine, *Concerning the City of God*, 14.28, 593.
62 Augustine, *Concerning the City of God*, 573.
63 Augustine, *Concerning the City of God*, 1.35, 45.
64 Augustine, *Concerning the City of God*, 15.1, 761.
65 Augustine, *Concerning the City of God*, 1.35, 46.
66 Augustine, *Concerning the City of God*, 19.26, 892.
67 Lester K. Little, "Pride Goes Before Avarice: Social Change and the Vices in Latin Christendom," *American Historical Review* 76 (1971): 46.
68 Little, "Pride Goes Before Avarice, 16–49.
69 Carter Lindberg, *Beyond Charity: Reformation Initiatives for the Poor* (Augsburg Press, 1993), 31.
70 Michel Mollat, *Poor in the Middle Ages: An Essay in Social History*, trans. Arthur Goldhammer (Yale University Press, 1986), 3–5.
71 Richard Hordern, "Luther's Attitude Towards Poverty: Theology and Social Reform," in *Festschrift: A Tribute to Dr. William Hordern*, ed. Walter Freitag (University of Saskatchewan, 1985), 94.
72 Lindberg, *Beyond Charity*, 33.
73 Lindberg, *Beyond Charity*, 33. The claim here is not that the church failed to give any alms to the poor, but that the lion's share of the ecclesial revenues went to support the church hierarchy and not the indigent.
74 Mollat, *Poor in the Middle Ages*, 121.
75 A. G. Little, *Studies in English Franciscan History* (Manchester University Press, 1917), 4. See also Malcolm D. Lambert, *Franciscan Poverty:*

The Doctrine of the Absolute Poverty of Christ and the Apostles in the Franciscan Order, 1210–1323 (SPCK, 1961), 103–115; Steven Ozment, *The Age of Reform (1250–1550): An Intellectual and Religious History of Late Medieval and Reformational Europe* (Yale University Press, 1980), 103.

76 In his exegesis of Psalm 22:26, which states, "the poor shall eat and be satisfied . . .," Martin Luther argues that the verse has nothing to do with physical hunger but refers to a desire to be filled with the Word of God and grace. See Lee Brummel, "Luther on Poverty and the Poor: A Study of Luther's Exegetical Understanding and Use of the Biblical Language of Poverty and the Poor" (PhD diss., Columbia University, 1979), 110–112, 114. See also Carter Lindberg, "'There Should Be No Beggars Among Christians': Karlstadt, Luther, and the Origins of the Protestant Poor Relief," *Church History* 46 (1977): 319.

77 See Lindberg, "'There Should Be No Beggars Among Christians,'" 319.

78 One of the biggest tragedies of the Reformation was when Luther applied his theology of the cross to the Peasants' War. A group of peasants, who were among Luther's most loyal supporters, requested that he respond to their list of grievances against their feudal lords. They asked for his support of their demands that: (1) each community determine, and if necessary, remove its pastor; (2) large tithes on grain be used to support the pastor and other community efforts while small tithes on livestock be altogether eliminated; (3) serfdom be abolished; (4) impositions on hunting reservations be instituted and provisions be made for use of the forest by the poor; (5) forced labor be regulated and compensation just; (6) just rents be instituted; (7) common lands previously seized be returned to indigenous communities; and (8) death taxes be eliminated. Luther critiqued their grievances and argued that the Bible had nothing to do with secular life and that the biblical language of poverty referred to the suffering and misery that people experienced spiritually in this life and not physically. Scripture, he argued, calls believers to "act like Christians" and in no way sanctions insurrection or a change in one's present social condition or status. Consequently, a whole sector of German society departed from Lutheranism and engaged in a war in which 100,000 peasants were killed, and unknown thousands more were disfigured and maimed by the feudal princes. Thus, his theology of the cross and his spiritualized understanding of poverty failed to recognize the abolition of the peasants' poverty as a biblical requirement and instead was

used to reinforce iniquity and economic injustice. See Lee Brummel, "Luther and the Biblical Language of Poverty," *The Ecumenical Review* 32 (1980): 40–58. See also Walker et al., *A History of the Christian Church*, 437.

79 Brummel, "Luther on Poverty and the Poor," 258–260.

80 Brummel, "Luther on Poverty and the Poor," 15.

81 Hugh T. Kerr, *Calvin's Institutes: A New Compend* (Westminster John Knox Press, 1989), 9.

82 Kerr, *Calvin's Institutes*, 83.

83 Alister E. McGrath, *A Life of John Calvin: A Study in the Shaping of Western Culture* (Blackwell, 1990), 235.

84 Will Durant, *The Reformation: The Story of Civilization* (Simon & Schuster, 1957), 6:474.

85 Pasquale Villari, *Life and Times of Girolamo Savonarola* (Scribner, 1888), 491.

86 One father was jailed for four days for naming his child Claude instead of Abraham. See Philip Schaff, *The Swiss Reformation* (Scribner, 1892), 2:492.

87 Durant, *The Reformation*, 474.

88 Schaff, *The Swiss Reformation*, 491.

89 Robert M. Kingdon, "Social Welfare in Calvin's Geneva," *American Historical Review* 76, no. 52 (1971): 50–69.

90 Kingdon, "Social Welfare in Calvin's Geneva," 59–60.

91 Kingdon, "Social Welfare in Calvin's Geneva," 64. The General Hospital was intended only to help native Genevans and transients who planned to spend a single night in Geneva, and could not handle the problems of the growing number of refugees. Calvin's fund, collected from wealthy French refugees in Geneva, tried to fill that gap.

92 E. Doumergue et al., "Jean Calvin," in *Calvin and the Reformation: Four Studies*, ed. William Park Armstrong (Fleming H. Revell, 1909), 258.

93 Doumergue et al., "Jean Calvin," 259.

94 Doumergue et al., "Jean Calvin," 276.

95 John Calvin, *Calvin's Commentaries: Commentary on II Corinthians* (Wm. B. Eerdmans, 1948), II Cor. 8:13–14.

96 See C. Gregg Singer, "Calvin and the Social Order; or Calvin as a Social and Economic Statesman," in *John Calvin: Contemporary Prophet*, ed. Jacob T. Hoogstra (Baker Book House, 1959), 227. Also see David W. Jones, "John Calvin's Financial Ethic of Usury," *Faith & Mission: A Theological Journal for Christians Engaged in Fulfilling The Great*

Commission 18, no. 3 (Summer 2001): 3–19. In addition, no analysis of Calvin's thoughts on wealth possession and acquisition or study of his financial ethics would be complete without mention of Max Weber's groundbreaking study, *The Protestant Ethic and the Spirit of Capitalism* (Scribner's, 1930), in which Weber proposed that Calvin's economic ethics was responsible for the rise of the economic theory of capitalism in the West. The "Weber Thesis," as it is known, is probably the most controversial and often mentioned theory concerning Calvin's financial ethics. His claim of a definitive influence of Calvin's teachings on wealth and poverty upon the development of Western capitalism has been deliberated upon and scrutinized by many major figures in the fields of history, economics, and sociology. This text rests upon a fresh and nuanced look at Calvin's influence on what I deem a legacy of a theology of prosperity within the Western Christian tradition.

97 The most famous of Calvin's letters on wealth acquisition is his letter to Claude de Sachinus, in *John Calvin, Calvin's Ecclesiastical Advice*, trans. Mary Beaty and Benjamin W. Farley (Westminster John Knox Press, 1991), in which Calvin discusses lending money at interest as permissible for Christians.

98 According to David Jones, there are four commentaries in which Calvin discusses wealth acquisition, particularly usury. These are his *Commentaries on the Four Last Books of Moses*, his *Commentary on the Book of Psalms*, his *Commentary on the First Twenty Chapters of the Book of Prophet Ezekiel*, and his *A Harmony of the Gospels Matthew, Mark, and Luke*. However, Calvin does address wealth and poverty as providential, and what he sees as the problematic of wealth redistribution, in several other writings, including in his *Commentary on II Corinthians*, *Commentary on Exodus*, and his *Commentaries on the Book of the Prophet Jeremiah and the Lamentations* ("for when anyone deals kindly with the poor, he may yet plunder the wealth of the rich, which cannot be deemed right . . .").

99 Donald K. McKim, *Readings in Calvin's Theology* (Baker Book House, 1984), 18.

100 William J. Bouwsma, *John Calvin: A Sixteenth Century Portrait* (Oxford University Press, 1988), 191–203.

101 Bouwsma, *John Calvin*, 232–233.

102 Bouwsma, *John Calvin*, 193.

103 In his Commentary on Daniel 7:25, Calvin asserts "in almost every age, the common people, although driven by wildness and barbarity, are less impious than the nobles or courtiers or other crafty men who think they excel others in talent and prudence."

104 Calvin, *Commentary on Isaiah* 3:5.
105 Bouwsma, *John Calvin*, 193.
106 Jones, "John Calvin's Financial Ethic of Usury."
107 McGrath, *A Life of Calvin*, 231.
108 See also Robert P. Maloney, "The Background of the Early Christian Teaching on Usury" (PhD diss., The Catholic University of America, 1969), in which he states that the idea of brotherhood is the "general context of the [biblical usury] legislation . . . Deuteronomy puts great emphasis on the brotherhood of God's People, so it forbids interest-taking among the brethren" (61, 68). Susan L. Buckley also notes, "These verses [Exod 22:25; Lev 25:35–38; Deut 23:19–20] also stress the concept of 'brotherhood/kinship' and the relational responsibilities, whether economic or social, that the small group engenders with regard to its sense of community." See Susan Buckley, *Teachings on Usury in Judaism, Christianity, and Islam: Texts and Studies in Religion* (Edwin Mellen Press, 2000), 4.
109 Edward Neufeld wrote, "This almost universally prevalent collective consciousness or solitary [*sic*] liability . . . lacks almost entirely the idea of ego-consciousness. . . . The average individual does not realize that he constitutes a personality different from the group to which he belongs. . . . The prohibition [of usury] in Exodus is a manifestation of [this] . . . concept of solitary [*sic*] liability." See Edward Neufeld, "The Prohibitions Against Loans at Interest in Ancient Hebrew Laws," *Hebrew Union College Annual* 26 (1955): 369–370, 407. Though I am not in total agreement with Neufeld's assertion regarding the average individual's ignorance of his/her individual status—because one operates as a collective does not necessarily mean that one does not realize one's individual status—there is validity in his statement concerning the primacy of a communal or collective consciousness over an individual ego-consciousness which leads to the elevation of group care in the Hebrew community.
110 Here, Calvin does not side with Augustine, whose response to usury was typical of the church fathers.
111 John Calvin, *Commentary on a Harmony of the Evangelists, Matthew, Mark and Luke*, vol. 1, *A New Translation I* (Wm. B. Eerdmans, 1949), 196–197.
112 John Calvin, "Commentary on Matthew 19:21," in *Commentary on a Harmony of the Evangelists by John Calvin*, trans. Rev. William Pringle (Wm. B. Eerdmans, 1949), 396–397.
113 Calvin, "Commentary on Matthew 19:21," 398.
114 Calvin, "Commentary on Matthew 19:23," 401.

115 See Calvin's comments on Matthew 19:21 in *Institutes of the Christian Religion in Two Volumes*, ed. John T. McNeill, trans. Ford Lewis Battles (The Westminster Press, 1960), 4.13.13; "Commentary on Matthew 19:16." See also "Commentary on Matthew 19:17."
116 Calvin, "Commentary on Matthew 19:17."
117 Calvin, *Institutes*, 4.13.13. Calvin states in his "Commentary on Matthew 19:20," "For if he had known himself thoroughly, as soon as he heard the mention of the law, he would have acknowledged that he was liable to the judgment of God; but now, when the bare words of the law do not sufficiently convince him of his guilt, the inward meaning is expressed by other words." Calvin argues the young man missed what the purpose of the law was for, namely, to reveal his sinfulness and *his poverty before God*; emphasis mine.
118 Calvin, "Commentary on Mark 10:21," 397.
119 Calvin, "Commentary on Mark 10:21," 397.
120 Calvin, "Commentary on Matthew 5:3," 260.
121 Calvin, "Commentary on Matthew 5:3," 260.
122 Calvin, "Commentary on Matthew 5:3," 269.
123 Calvin, "Commentary on Matthew 5:3," 269.
124 It is important to note that Calvin teaches that the lowly birth, suffering, and poverty of Christ forms a pattern of life for how the Christian life is to be lived and considers self-denial and bearing the cross fundamental to his doctrine of the Christian Life, as evidenced in book 3, chapter 7 of the *Institutes*, "The Sum of the Christian Life: Self Denial." In other words, one is called to imitate Christ, or to conform to his example, by bearing one's cross (i.e., poverty and other afflictions) and dying with Christ and experiencing regeneration; that is, by embracing an *inward* mortification of the flesh or allowing one's values and desires to be "crucified" with Christ by the Holy Spirit while outwardly enduring or suffering external afflictions and hardships. Such an experience, for Calvin, has the potential of becoming a vehicle of divine grace and blessing; bringing about a true knowledge of self and of God, by stripping away one's false sense of security and self-confidence and promoting instead self-doubt, a sense of vulnerability and dependence upon God's mercy. Thus, Calvin contends, poverty is one affliction through which God conforms the believer to Christ, imposing upon them such for their own good and "in the very act of inflicting us [believers] . . . He is providing for our own salvation" (*Institutes*, 3.8.11).

125 Calvin insists that God permits some to be poor and others God permits to remain wealthy to provide occasions to "know how to bear poverty peaceably and patiently, as well as to bear abundance moderately" (*Institutes*, 3.10.4). And since, for Calvin, it was to remain a mystery why some would be poor and others wealthy according to God's will, such a question was not even worth entertaining.
126 Calvin, "Commentary on Matthew," 25:2.
127 Calvin, "Commentary on Matthew," 6:19.
128 Calvin, "Commentary on Matthew," 19:23.
129 Calvin, "Commentary on Matthew," 25:40.
130 Calvin, "Commentary on Matthew," 25:35.
131 Calvin, "Commentary on Matthew," 25:35.
132 Calvin, "Commentary on Matthew," 25:35.
133 Calvin, "Commentary on Matthew," 19:20–22.
134 Calvin, "Commentary on Exodus," 11:2.
135 Sermon 95 on Deut 15:11–15. Translation of text taken from Fred Graham, *The Constructive Revolutionary: John Calvin and His Socio-Economic Impact* (John Knox, 1971), 69.
136 Calvin, "Commentary on II Corinthians," 8:23.
137 Calvin, "Commentary on II Corinthians," 8:15.
138 Calvin, "Commentary on II Corinthians," 8:9.
139 Calvin, "Commentary on II Corinthians," 8:15.
140 Calvin, "Commentary on II Corinthians," 8:15.
141 François Wendel, *Calvin* (William Collins, 1963), 122–123.
142 Wendel, *Calvin*, 124.
143 Prior to Calvin, the church councils and church fathers had been unified in rejecting the practice of usury.
144 Walker et al., *The History of the Christian Church*, 473.
145 Schaff, *The Swiss Reformation*, 328–335.
146 Calvin, *Institutes*, 1:35–40.
147 Calvin, *Institutes*, 1:241ff.
148 Calvin, *Institutes*, 1:161–162, 179–182, 183–184.
149 Albert Hyma, *Renaissance to Reformation* (Eerdmans, 1951), 443.
150 Calvin, *Institutes*, 1:699.
151 Calvin, *Institutes*, 1:408.
152 Calvin, *Institutes*, 2:910.
153 Calvin, *Institutes*, 1:698.
154 See Calvin, "Commentary on Ephesians 6:9," "Commentary on Psalms 41:2," "Sermon on Deut. 139," "Sermon on Deut. 94," and "Sermon on Deut. 95."

Chapter 4: The Legacy of a Theology of Prosperity on American Soil

1 This is not to suggest that there is no development in the thought of Rauschenbusch over the course of his career. However, this work essentially reflects on his prevailing theological suppositions.

2 It is important to note that while Puritanism laid the chief foundation for American religious life, by 1890 followers of the Wesleyan tradition, or Methodists, along with the Baptists, would become the two largest groups both numerically and theologically to provide the popular base for American Protestantism. They not only held in common an emphasis on free will and grace for all. They also proffered an individualistic understanding of conversion as the mark of a true Christian—an emphasis that would ultimately undermine concern for the commonwealth which the Puritans stressed—and perpetuated the notion that "it is only to the man of morality that wealth comes" even as they spoke of "the privilege of grateful service" and Christ's "precepts on the stewardship of wealth." See Sydney Ahlstrom, *A Religious History of the American People* (Yale University Press, 1972), 789, 842–848. See also Gail Kennedy, "The Relation of Wealth to Morals," in *Democracy and the Gospel of Wealth*, ed. Gail Kennedy (D. C. Heath, 1949), 68–76.

3 Ahlstrom, *A Religious History of the American People*, 789, 842–848. See also Kennedy, "The Relation of Wealth to Morals," 68–76.

4 While, as Ahlstrom notes, "nearly everyone agrees that [the social gospel] was more fully represented by Walter Rauschenbusch than anyone and that it gained classic utterance in 1907 with the publication of his *Christianity and the Social Crisis*," he was by no means alone. There was Washington Gladden, one of the early social gospelers, along with Francis Greenwood Peabody, and several others.

5 See Walter Rauschenbusch, *Christianizing the Social Order* (Macmillan, 1921).

6 Ronald H. Stone, *John Wesley's Life and Ethics* (Abingdon Press, 2001), 29–31.

7 Stone, *John Wesley's Life and Ethics*, 29. R. H. Stone notes here that because of their Calvinist heritage of dissent and religious and political loyalties, the religious–social tensions of the time almost caused a marital split between Wesley's parents when "Susan refused to say 'Amen' at the morning-prayer honoring King William III . . . [who] she regarded . . . as a usurper of the Crown . . . Samuel . . . declared that if

they served two different kings, they must have two different beds . . . both parents remained inflexible . . . until after King William . . . died . . . Susanna and Samuel accepted Queen Anne as sovereign . . . they reunited and their reconciliation led to John Wesley's birth."

8 Stone, *John Wesley's Life and Ethics*, 54–58.

9 Stone, *John Wesley's Life and Ethics*, 58ff.

10 Nehemiah Curnock, *The Journal of the Rev. John Wesley, A.M .*, 8 vols. (Charles H. Kelly, 1909–1916), 2:168–186. See also Élie Halévy, *The Birth of Methodism in England*, trans. and ed. by Bernard Semmel (The University of Chicago Press, 1971), 69.

11 John Wesley, *A Plain Account of Christian Perfection: As Believed and Taught by Rev. John Wesley from 1725–1777* (Eaton & Mains; Jennings & Pye, 1900), 3ff.

12 A description of England's political conditions can be found in Jay B. Botsford, *English Society in the XVIII Century: As Influenced by Overseas* (Octagon, 1965); Dorothy Marshal, *Industrial England 1776–1851* (Scribner's Sons, 1973); and Roy Porter, *English Society in the Eighteenth Century* (Penguin, 1992).

13 Goldman Smith, *England: A Short History* (Scribner's Sons, 1971), 138. The Poor Laws were seen as an encouragement to population growth among the poor because such laws helped large families and unmarried women to keep and feed their children. This type of thinking resulted in a Poor Law reform, the Act of Settlement and Removals, which made every town and parish responsible for taking care of their own poor, and which put the poor at the mercy of wealthy landowners who were prone to ignore them.

14 Thomas Malthus, *An Essay on the Principle of Population* (J. Johnson St. Paul's Church Yard, 1798), 132.

15 Adam Smith, *An Inquiry into the Nature and Causes of the Wealth of Nations* (W. Strahan and T. Cadell, 1776), 2:132.

16 M. C. Bauer, *Health, Wealth, and Population in the Early Days of Industrial Revolution* (Routledge & Kegan Paul, 1968), 43.

17 Bauer, *Health, Wealth, and Population*, 44.

18 Henry D. Rack, *Reasonable Enthusiast: John Wesley and the Rise of Methodism* (Abingdon Press, 1992), 10.

19 See E. Gordon Rupp, *Religion in England 1688–1791* (Clarendon Press, 1986), 25. See also Norman Sykes, *Church and State in England in the XVIII Century* (Archon, 1962), 92–146.

20 An example of Wesley's conviction is his letter to Miss J. C. March. Miss March was an educated woman of wealth who in 1760 became active

in the Methodist revival around 1760 and to whom Wesley wrote about pursuing salvation. Upon Miss March's admitting that she struggled with the idea of affiliating with the poor, whom she thought were of "lower character" or unrefined, Wesley reminded her not to consider herself just a gentlewoman, but one with a "higher character," as he directed her to "Go and see the poor and sick in their own poor little hovels. Take up your cross, woman! Remember the faith!" He further responded to her objections to associating with persons she thought were without tase and character by writing, "I have found some of the uneducated poor who have exquisite taste and sentiment; and many, very many, of the rich who have scarcely any at all. But I do not speak of this: I want you to converse more, abundantly more, with the poorest of the people, who, if they have not taste, have souls, which you may forward in their way to heaven. And they have (many of them) faith and the love of God in a larger measure than any persons I know." See John Telford, *The Letters of John Wesley* (Epworth Press, 1931), 6:88, 153–154.

21 For examples, see John Wesley's Sermon 87 (1781), "The Danger of Riches," in *The Works of the Rev. John Wesley, A.M.* (hereafter *Works*), 3rd ed., ed. Thomas Jackson, 14 vols. (Wesleyan Methodist Book Room, 1872; Baker Book House, 1979), 3:228–246; Sermon 61 (1783), "The Mystery of Iniquity," §34, *Works* 2:468; Sermon 68 (1784), "The Wisdom of God's Counsels," §§16–18, *Works* 2:560–563; "Thoughts upon Methodism" (1788), *Works* 9:527–530; Sermon 108 (1788), "On Riches," *Works* 3:519–528; Sermon 122 (1789), "Causes of the Inefficacy of Christianity," §§9, 17–18, *Works* 4:91, 95–96; Sermon 125 (1789), "On a Single Eye," *Works* 4:120–130; Sermon 126 (1790), "On Worldly Folly," *Works* 4:132–138; and Sermon 131 (1790), "The Danger of Increasing Riches," *Works*, 4:178–186. Cf. the discussion in Theodore W. Jennings Jr., *Good News to the Poor: John Wesley's Evangelical Economics* (Abingdon Press, 1990), 118ff.

22 Stone, *John Wesley's Life and Ethics*, 85.

23 Francis J. McConnell, *John Wesley* (Epworth Press, 1939), 96.

24 Ronald H. Stone, *John Wesley's Life and Ethics* (Abingdon Press, 2001), 76–89.

25 McConnell, *John Wesley*, 96.

26 Wesley left behind 151 sermons in print, 10 percent of which treat the subject of wealth and poverty at great length. I have chosen to provide an analysis of four of his sermons that are devoted entirely to the subject, as these four highlight his thoughts on wealth and poverty in great detail.

27 John Wesley, "On Riches, Discourse VII," *Works* 2:214–222.
28 Wesley, "On Riches, Discourse VII," 2:215.
29 Wesley, "On Riches, Discourse VII," 2:215.
30 Wesley, "On Riches, Discourse VII," 2:215.
31 See Wesley's "Sermon on the Mount, Discourse VIII," *Works* 5:368, in which he states, "How hard it is for them, whose every word is applauded, not to be wise in their own eyes. . . how hard for them not to think themselves better than the poor, base, undereducated herd . . ."
32 Wesley, "On Riches, Discourse VII," 2:215.
33 Wesley, "On Riches, Discourse VII," 2:215.
34 Wesley, "On Riches, Discourse VII," 2:220.
35 Wesley, "On Riches, Discourse VII," 2:217.
36 Wesley, "On Riches, Discourse VII," 2:218.
37 Wesley, "The Danger of Riches, Discourse VII," *Works* 2:13.
38 Wesley, "The Danger of Riches, Discourse VII," 2:13.
39 Wesley, "The Danger of Riches, Discourse VII," 2:14.
40 Wesley, "The Danger of Riches, Discourse VII," 2:14.
41 Wesley, "The Danger of Riches, Discourse VII," 2:14.
42 Wesley, "The Use of Money," *Works* 6:126. See also "On the Danger of Increasing Riches," *Works* 7:355; "Sermon on the Mount, Discourse VIII," 5:369.
43 Wesley, "On the Danger of Increasing Riches," 7:355–356.
44 Wesley, "On the Danger of Increasing Riches," 7:355.
45 Wesley, "On the Danger of Increasing Riches," 7:355.
46 Wesley, "On the Danger of Increasing Riches," 7:355.
47 Wesley, "On the Danger of Increasing Riches," 7:355.
48 John Wesley, *Fifty-Three Sermons* (Wesleyan Methodist Book Press, 1771), 702.
49 Wesley, *Fifty-Three Sermons*, 703.
50 Wesley, *Fifty-Three Sermons*, 703.
51 Wesley, *Fifty-Three Sermons*, 703.
52 Wesley, *Fifty-Three Sermons*, 703.
53 Wesley, *Fifty-Three Sermons*, 704.
54 Wesley, *Fifty-Three Sermons*, 705.
55 Wesley, *Fifty-Three Sermons*, 705.
56 Wesley, *Fifty-Three Sermons*, 705.
57 Wesley, *Fifty-Three Sermons*, 706–708.
58 Wesley, *Fifty-Three Sermons*, 710.
59 Wesley, *Fifty-Three Sermons*, 710.

60 Wesley's position on spending on luxuries is quite in opposition to Calvin's, who believed the rich should live more abundantly than the poor and that it was natural for the poor to eat "course bread and a scanty diet" while the rich live "more abundantly, according to their circumstances." See Calvin, *Commentary on II Corinthians* 8:15.

61 Wesley, *Fifty-Three Sermons*, 710.

62 Wesley, *Fifty-Three Sermons*, 711.

63 Wesley, *Fifty-Three Sermons*, 711–712.

64 Wesley, *Fifty-Three Sermons*, 712.

65 Wesley, *Fifty-Three Sermons*, 713.

66 Wesley, *Fifty-Three Sermons*, 713.

67 It is important to note that while Puritanism laid the chief foundation for American religious life, by 1890 followers of the Wesleyan tradition, or Methodists, along with the Baptists, would become the two largest groups both numerically and theologically to provide the popular base for American Protestantism. They not only held in common an emphasis on free will and grace for all. They proffered an individualistic understanding of conversion as the mark of a true Christian—an emphasis that would ultimately undermine concern for the commonwealth which the Puritans stressed—and perpetuated notion that "it is only to the man of morality that wealth comes" even as they spoke of "the privilege of grateful service" and Christ's "precepts on the stewardship of wealth." See Ahlstrom, *A Religious History of the American People*, 789, 842–848. See also "The Relation of Wealth to Morals," in *Democracy and the Gospel of Wealth*, ed. Gail Kennedy (D. C. Heath, 1949), 68–76.

68 Ahlstrom, *A Religious History of the American People*, 789, 842–848. See also "The Relation of Wealth to Morals," 68–76.

69 While, as Ahlstrom notes, "nearly everyone agrees that [the social gospel] was more fully represented by Walter Rauschenbusch than anyone and that it gained classic utterance in 1907 with the publication of his *Christianity and the Social Crisis*," he was by no means alone. Washington Gladden, one of the early social gospelers, along with Francis Greenwood Peabody.

70 Walter Rauschenbusch, *The Social Principles of Jesus* (Association Press, 1916), 52.

71 Walter Rauschenbusch, *A Theology for the Social Gospel* (Westminster John Knox Press, 1997), 142; emphasis mine.

72 Rauschenbusch, *A Theology for the Social Gospel*, 99.

73 Rauschenbusch, *Christianizing the Social Order*, 114.

74 Rauschenbusch, *Christianizing the Social Order*, 116.

75 Rauschenbusch, *A Theology for the Social Gospel*, 239.
76 Walter Rauschenbusch, *Walter Rauschenbusch: Selected Writings*, ed. Winthrop S. Hudson (Paulist Press, 1984), 141.
77 Robert T. Handy, *The Social Gospel in America 1870–1920* (Oxford University Press, 1966), 254–255.
78 Walter Rauschenbusch, quoted by Harry Emerson Fosdick in the introduction to *A Rauschenbusch Reader*, ed. Benson Y. Landis (Harper, 1957), xv–xvi.
79 Paul M. Minus, *Walter Rauschenbusch, American Reformer* (Macmillan, 1988), 51.
80 Minus, *Walter Rauschenbusch*, 2.
81 Rauschenbusch accepted the call from the Second German Baptist Church in New York City after his appointment by the American Baptist Foreign Missionary Society to an educational post in India had been blocked by one of his professors at Rochester, who was disturbed by Rauschenbusch's liberal views.
82 Klaus Jaehn, "The Formation of Walter Rauschenbusch's Social Consciousness as Reflected in His Early Life and Writings," [Part I] *Foundations* 16, no. 4 (October–December 1973): 295.
83 Donovan E. Smucker, "The Origins of Walter Rauschenbusch's Social Ethics" (PhD diss., University of Chicago, 1957), 317. Smucker deals with the pietistic influence in the life and work of Rauschenbusch at length (62–79), focusing on the areas of discontinuity as well as continuity in his introduction (316–319).
84 Minus, *Walter Rauschenbusch*, 51, 103. After the official end of slavery in 1865, the emancipated were promised a type of reparations in the form of "40 acres and a mule." However, with the assassination of President Abraham Lincoln, his successor Andrew Johnson rescinded the order, forcing Blacks into quasi-slavery in the form of vagrancy laws, sharecropping, and convict leasing.
85 Rauschenbusch's vision would mature in the ensuing decade in which he would publish *A Theology for the Social Gospel* (1917). Many consider this publication his most important work.
86 Raymond A. Mohl, *The New City: Urban America in the Industrial Age, 1860–1920* (Harlan Davidson, 1985), 3.
87 Mohl, *The New City*, 16. Arthur M. Schlesinger, in *The Rise of the City 1878–1898: A History of American Life* (New Viewpoints Edition, Franklin Watts; originally published by Macmillan, 1933), 10:79, states, "In America in the eighties urbanization for the first time became a controlling factor in national life. Just as the plantation was the typical product of the antebellum Southern system and the small farm of the

Northern agricultural order, so the city was the supreme achievement of the new industrialism. In its confines were focused all the new economic forces: the vast accumulations of capital, the business and financial institutions, the spreading railway yards, the gaunt smoky mills, the white-collar middle classes, the motley wage-earning population."

88 Adna F. Weber, a social scientist of the period, quoted in Mohl, *The New City*, 2.

89 Mohl, *The New City*, 12, 15.

90 Blake McKelvey, *The Urbanization of America, 1860–1915* (Rutgers University Press, 1963), 65; Minus, *Walter Rauschenbusch*, 50.

91 Henry May, *Protestant Churches and Industrial America* (Harper, 1949), 112.

92 Quoted in Mohl, *The New City*, 65–66.

93 William Crowell Trench, "The Social Gospel and the City: Implications for Theological Reconstruction in the Work of Washington Gladden, Josiah Strong, and Walter Rauschenbusch" (PhD diss., Boston University, 1986), 53. Numerous books were written during the period by those concerned with the problems and needs of the city. Among these, the following are helpful in giving a contemporary perspective on the issues: Jacob A. Riis, *How the Other Half Lives: Studies Among the Tenements of New York* (Charles Scribner's Sons, 1932. Digitized by the Internet Archive Digital Library of Free & Borrowable Texts, 2013); William T. Stead, *If Christ Came to Chicago* (Laird & Lee, 1894); Robert Woods, *The Poor in Great Cities* (Charles Scribner's Sons, 1895; repr. Arno Press & *The New York Times*, 1971); Josiah Strong, *Our Country: Its Possible Future and Its Present Crisis* (American Home Missionary Society, 1885); and Josiah Strong, *The Challenge of the City* (NY Missionary Education Movement, 1907).

94 Trench, "The Social Gospel and the City," 53.

95 Mohl, *The New City*, 50.

96 William T. Elsing, "Life in the New York Tenement-House as Seen by a City Missionary," in *The Poor in Great Cities: Their Problems and What Is Doing to Solve Them*, by Robert A. Woods et al. (Charles Scribner's Sons, 1895), 43.

97 Roy Lubove, *The Progressives and the Slums: Tenement House Reform in New York City, 1890–1917* (University of Pittsburgh Press, 1962), 43.

98 Riis, *How the Other Half Lives*, 4, 201–205.

99 Correspondence, July 13, 1886, quoted in Klaus Jaehn, "The Formation of Walter Rauschenbusch's Social Consciousness as Reflected in His Early Life and Writings," *Foundations* 16, no. 4 (October–December 1973): 294–326 [I]; and 17, no. 1 (January–March 1974): 68–85 [II].

100 Ronald C. White and C. Howard Hopkins, *The Social Gospel: Religion and Reform in Changing America, with an Essay by John C. Bennett* (Temple University Press, 1976), 63.
101 Louise Bolard More, *Wage-Earners' Budgets: A Study of Standards and Costs of Living in New York City* (1907; repr. Arnos Press, 1971), 268. This 1907 study was based on two hundred families in a working-class tenement in the district of Greenwich Village.
102 More, *Wage-Earners' Budgets*, 247.
103 Charles B. Sphar, *An Essay on the Present Distribution of Wealth in the United States* (Crowell & Co., 1896), 69, 129.
104 Samuel P. Hays, *The Response to Industrialism, 1885–1914*, 2nd ed. (University of Chicago Press, 1995), 64–66; Neville Kirk, *Labour and Society in Britain and the USA*, vol. 1, *Capitalism, Custom and Protest, 1780–1850* (Scholar Press, 1994), 131–155.
105 Hays, *The Response to Industrialism*, 45.
106 Hays, *The Response to Industrialism*, 45.
107 Hays, *The Response to Industrialism*, 48–54.
108 Martin J. Sklar, *The Corporate Reconstruction of American Capitalism, 1890–1916: The Market, The Laws and the Politics* (Cambridge University Press, 1988), 4, 20, 23, 431.
109 Sklar, *The Corporate Reconstruction of American Capitalism*, 4–5.
110 Kirk, *Labour and Society in Britain and the USA*, 244–245.
111 Riis, *How the Other Half Lives*, 151.
112 A detailed discussion of this attitude can be found in Martin E. Marty, *Righteous Empire* (HarperCollins, 1977), 144ff.
113 It should be noted that this fact is the source of differing modern interpretations of Rauschenbusch. His interpreters disagree on where the emphasis should be laid with regard to examining Rauschenbusch's complex relationship to pietism, evangelicalism, and liberalism.
114 Charles Howard Hopkins, *The Rise of the Social Gospel in American Protestantism, 1865–1915* (Yale University Press, 1940), 37–47.
115 Gary Dorrien, *Breaking White Supremacy: Martin Luther King Jr. and the Black Social Gospel* (Yale University Press, 2018), 35.
116 For more on the Black Women's Club movement, see Evelyn Brooks Higginbotham, *Righteous Discontent: The Women's Movement in the Black Baptist Church, 1880—1920* (Harvard University Press, 1993); E. Frances White, *Dark Continent of Our Bodies: Black Feminism and the Politics of Respectability* (Temple University Press, 2001); and Martha Jones, *All Bound Up Together: The Woman Question in African American Public Culture, 1830–1900* (University of North Carolina Press, 2007).

117 For Black club women, racial uplift insisted on acquiescence to a social code that they considered valuable in deconstructing and pushing passed social structures that barred Black economic prosperity and precluded an honorable reputation among the white population. As they understood it, their charge to better the race meant taking on the responsibility of making learners out of the illiterate and depending on respectability politics as well as a strict adherence to certain social standards to function and counter being consigned to an inferior social status by whites. They stressed racial uplifting to both counter the public perception of African Americans as socially inept and improve their economic status. They provided free or subsidized education and developed programs that trained African Americans in skills marketable for employment, launched institutions such as the National Association of Colored Women's Clubs, and gave speeches and published writings to arouse public sympathy for Black women and Black victims of lynching. Alongside, and at times in spite of, their African American male counterparts, they outlined new boundaries for the interpretation of the social gospel in which issues of gender and race were identified as factors in the movement.
118 Hopkins, *The Rise of the Social Gospel in American Protestantism*, 15.
119 Hopkins, *The Rise of the Social Gospel in American Protestantism*, 14.
120 Minus, *Walter Rauschenbusch*, 55.
121 Augustus Hopkins Strong, Rochester Seminary's president and professor of biblical theology during Rauschenbusch's tenure as a student, "proceeded like the seventeenth century architects of Protestant scholasticism . . . (his) key tenets . . . were the holiness of God, human depravity, Christ's substitutionary death, the election of some for salvation, the baptism and gathering of the elect into the church, the final sanctification of the elect, and the final destruction of the wicked." See Minus, *Walter Rauschenbusch*, 42.
122 Van A. Harvey, *A Handbook of Theological Terms* (Macmillan, 1964), 71.
123 Harvey, *A Handbook of Theological Terms*, 150–151.
124 David Roy Harry, "Two Kingdoms: Walter Rauschenbusch's Concept of the Kingdom of God Contrasted with the Theology of Revivalism in Early Twentieth Century America" (PhD diss., Southwestern Baptist Theological Seminary, 1993), 93.
125 H. Richard Niebuhr, *The Kingdom of God in America* (Harper, 1935), 36.
126 Niebuhr, *The Kingdom of God in America*, 127.

127 Minus, *Walter Rauschenbusch*, 56.
128 Harry, "Two Kingdoms," 25. For a description of the elements of German Pietism Rauschenbusch received from his father, see Donovan E. Smucker, *The Origins of Walter Rauschenbusch's Social Ethics* (McGill-Queen's University Press, 1994), 25.
129 See, e.g., David Allen McClintock, "Walter Rauschenbusch: The Kingdom of God and the American Experience" (PhD diss., Case Western Reserve University, 1975), 195, 226.
130 Harry, "Two Kingdoms," 95–96.
131 William G. McLoughlin, *Revivals, Awakenings, and Reform: An Essay on Religion and Social Change in America, 1607–1977* (University of Chicago Press, 1978), 144–145.
132 Harry, "Two Kingdoms," 139–140.
133 Harry, "Two Kingdoms," 15.
134 Smucker, *The Origins of Walter Rauschenbusch's Social Ethics*, 28, 49. See also Minus, *Walter Rauschenbusch*, 18, 61, 149–150.
135 Hopkins, *The Rise of the Social Gospel*, 15.
136 Stanley Hauerwas, *Dispatches from the Front: Theological Engagements with the Secular* (Duke University Press, 1994), 97.
137 It should be noted that although Rauschenbusch himself was an American Baptist working with a German-speaking American Baptist congregations, his frustration was broader than his denomination.
138 Walter Rauschenbusch, "The Kingdom of God," in *The Social Gospel in America*, ed. Robert T. Handy, 266–267. First published in 1913, cf. Dores Robinson Sharpe, *Walter Rauschenbusch*, with an introduction by Harry Emerson Fosdick (Macmillan, 1942), 232.
139 Handy, *The Social Gospel in America*, 266.
140 Rauschenbusch, *Christianizing the Social Order*, 41.
141 Rauschenbusch, *Christianizing the Social Order*, 42.
142 Rauschenbusch, *Christianizing the Social Order*, 42.
143 Rauschenbusch, *Christianizing the Social Order*, 43–46.
144 Rauschenbusch, *Christianizing the Social Order*, 46.
145 Rauschenbusch, *Christianity and the Social Crisis*, 3.
146 Rauschenbusch, *Christianity and the Social Crisis*, 4.
147 Rauschenbusch, *Christianity and the Social Crisis*, 6.
148 Rauschenbusch, *Christianity and the Social Crisis*, 11.
149 Rauschenbusch, *Christianity and the Social Crisis*, 12.
150 Rauschenbusch, *Christianity and the Social Crisis*, 34.
151 Rauschenbusch, *Christianity and the Social Crisis*, 45.
152 Rauschenbusch, *Christianity and the Social Crisis*, 35.

153 Rauschenbusch, *Christianity and the Social Crisis*, 49.
154 Rauschenbusch, *Christianity and the Social Crisis*, 51.
155 Rauschenbusch, *Christianity and the Social Crisis*, 53.
156 Rauschenbusch, *Christianity and the Social Crisis*, 49.
157 Rauschenbusch, *Christianity and the Social Crisis*, 53.
158 Rauschenbusch, *Christianity and the Social Crisis*, 85.
159 Rauschenbusch, *Christianity and the Social Crisis*, 47.
160 Rauschenbusch, *Christianity and the Social Crisis*, 150.
161 Rauschenbusch, *Christianity and the Social Crisis*, 75.
162 Rauschenbusch, "Revelation: An Exposition," *Biblical World* X, no. 2 (August 1897): 101.
163 Rauschenbusch, *The Social Principles of Jesus* (Association Press, 1916), introduction.
164 Rauschenbusch, *The Social Principles of Jesus*, 34–35.
165 Rauschenbusch, *The Social Principles of Jesus*, 38–39.
166 Rauschenbusch, *The Social Principles of Jesus*, 40.
167 Rauschenbusch, *The Social Principles of Jesus*, 120.
168 Rauschenbusch, *The Social Principles of Jesus*, 120.
169 Rauschenbusch, *The Social Principles of Jesus*, 121.
170 Rauschenbusch, *Christianity and the Social Crisis*, 75.
171 Rauschenbusch, *Christianity and the Social Crisis*, 76.
172 Rauschenbusch, *Christianity and the Social Crisis*, 76–77.
173 Rauschenbusch, *Christianity and the Social Crisis*, 76–77.
174 Rauschenbusch, *Christianity and the Social Crisis*, 77.
175 Rauschenbusch, *Christianity and the Social Crisis*, 79.
176 Rauschenbusch, *Christianity and the Social Crisis*, 79.
177 Rauschenbusch, *The Social Principles of Jesus*, 118.

Chapter 5: Womanist Sources for a Redemptive Response

1 *Proto-womanist* is a term that refers to those Black women who placed the lived experience and unique social location of Black women at the center of their theological interpretations, sociopolitical understandings, and activism. Their work on behalf of Black women, children, and men anticipated and laid the essential groundwork the emergence of womanist enterprise.
2 Williams, *Sisters in the Wilderness*, xii.
3 Keri Day, *Unfinished Business: Black Women, the Black Church, and the Struggle to Thrive in America* (Orbis Books, 2012).
4 The first scholar in theological studies to articulate an academic womanist perspective was ethicist Katie G. Cannon (see *Black Womanist*

Ethics [Oxford University Press, 1988]), who examined the life and literature of Zora Neale Hurston for indigenous cultural norms, standards, and resources expressing a womanist ethical perspective. Jacquelyn Grant published her work, *White Woman's Christ, Black Woman's Jesus* (1989), presenting a critical review of white feminist Christology and introducing a womanist Christology informed by Black women's tridimensional oppression as victims of racism, sexism, and classism. Delores Williams's *Sisters in the Wilderness* (1993), the first book-length articulation of womanist theology, and Emilie Townes's anthology, *A Troubling in My Soul* (1993), the first published collection of writing by womanist scholars, represent two more major breakthroughs in womanist theological scholarship, while second- and third-generation womanist theologians, ethicists, and biblical scholars have also participated in the development of womanist theory and methodology.

5 Kelly Brown Douglas, *The Black Christ* (Orbis Books, 1994), 78ff.
6 Douglas, *The Black Christ*, 85.
7 Douglas, *The Black Christ*, 19.
8 Douglas, *The Black Christ*, 30ff.
9 Luke 4:16–20 (NRSV).
10 Douglas, *The Black Christ*, 85.
11 Douglas, *The Black Christ*, 112–113.
12 Douglas, *The Black Christ*, 113.
13 Douglas, *The Black Christ*, 107.
14 Douglas, *The Black Christ*, 85.
15 Douglas, *The Black Christ*, 87.
16 Douglas, *The Black Christ*, 104.
17 Douglas, *The Black Christ*, 107.
18 Kelly Brown Douglas, *What's Faith Got to Do with It? Black Bodies/Christian Souls* (Orbis Books, 2005), 28.
19 Douglas, *What's Faith Got to Do with It?*, 149.
20 Douglas, *What's Faith Got to Do with It?*, 214.
21 Melvin L. Oliver and Thomas M. Shapiro, *Black Wealth/White Wealth: A New Perspective on Racial Inequality* (Routledge, 1995), 45–50.
22 Scott Winship et al., "Long Shadows: The Black–White Gap in Multigenerational Poverty," Brookings Institution, June 10, 2021, 3, https://www.brookings.edu/articles/long-shadows-the-black-white-gap-in-multigenerational-poverty.
23 The rhetoric of self-choice, controlling one's destiny, and seizing economic opportunities available in the "promised land" of America's capitalist economy has long been the rhetoric of those preaching prosperity, including contemporary African American prosperity preachers

who appear to regard the nineteenth-century economic theories of Booker T. Washington as a neoteric approach to personal liberation, social transformation, and economic empowerment for the African American community in the twenty-first century. Professing that the time is now for African Americans to cast down their buckets and quench their thirsts from the vast ocean of American opportunity, they ignore the fact that America's capitalist economy is more concretized than ever before and that, despite the dramatic economic growth of the 1990s, economic inequality intensified over the final quarter of the twentieth century up to our age. That is to say, while the top 10 percent of Americans dramatically increased their monopoly on America's capitalist economy—moving from controlling over 50 percent of all wealth in 1976 to controlling nearly 70 percent of the same in 2021—the remaining 90 percent of Americans went from controlling 50 percent to less than a third. Nor does such rhetoric take into consideration the racial caveat that African American income and private family wealth continue to lag far behind that of white households. Since wealth, unlike income, develops over generations, and since African American income is still trying to catch up with that of its white counterparts in this post–civil rights era—even while during the same period the wage value of workers across the board has dwindled—African Americans are fighting a dual battle within the contemporary capitalist economy. That is, they are fighting the vestiges of racial discrimination and income disparity along with contesting the declining value of labor in America. See Chuck Collins et al., *Economic Apartheid in America: A Primer on Economic Inequality & Insecurity*, 2nd rev. ed. (New Press; distributed by W.W. Norton, 2005), 51. See also Matthew Desmond, *Poverty, By America* (Crown, 2023); Oliver and Shapiro, *Black Wealth/White Wealth*; and Richard W. Stevenson, "In a Time of Plenty; the Poor Are Still Poorer," *New York Times*, January 23, 2000.

24 Delores S. Williams, "Straight Talk, Plain Talk: Womanist Words About Salvation in a Social Context," in *Embracing the Spirit: Womanist Perspectives on Hope, Salvation & Transformation*, ed. Emilie M. Townes (Orbis Books, 1997), 98.

25 Broadly speaking, Williams deems liberation to be full realization of a people or society that is free from sexism, racism, classism, colorism, heterosexism, and any other humanly sanctioned category or force that prevents persons from flourishing, experiencing wholeness, and realizing one's full potential.

26 Delores S. Williams, "A Womanist Perspective on Sin," in *A Troubling in My Soul: Womanist Perspectives on Evil and Suffering*, ed. Emilie M. Townes (Orbis Books, 1993), 147.

27 Williams, "A Womanist Perspective on Sin," 137.
28 Williams, "A Womanist Perspective on Sin," 137.
29 Williams suggests that while emancipation, among other historical moments, may have exacted the move toward individualism in the Black community, when, "slaves became responsible for their individual, economic welfare—providing for their own clothes, their own food, their families, finding their own jobs, and their own shelter," coupled with "the splintering of the ex-slave religious community into many institutional denominations (churches) stressing personal salvation," a collective consciousness and desire for communal transformation was not lost, but began to exist in tension with individualistic awareness and goals. Williams, "A Womanist Perspective on Sin," 137.
30 Williams, "A Womanist Perspective on Sin," 134.
31 Williams, "A Womanist Perspective on Sin," 146. Using the writings of nineteenth-century Black women to make her point, Williams concludes that the elevation of white womanhood, the consequent devaluation of Black womanhood, and the fact that the exploitation of Black of women's bodies (through rape, lynching, and surrogacy) was ignored by the American legal system, were sources that fed into the unworthiness felt by Black women, their devaluation of self.
32 Williams identifies two kinds of surrogacy in Black women's experiences—coerced and voluntary surrogacy. During slavery, Black women's surrogacy was coerced. White men and women forced Black women to provide labor and children, exploiting the biological functions of Black women in order to generate a steady supply of slaves for the developing capitalist economy, gratify sexual desires, and supply wet-nurse services for suckling white babies. Black women not only managed white people's homes, cooking, cleaning, and caring for their children, they also labored in the fields. Their labor was in substitution for the work of white women, white men, and Black men. Many Black women continue to be circumscribed to subservient positions and constitute a class of servants to white America as they choose voluntary surrogacy because of economic and social constraints.
33 Williams, *Sisters in the Wilderness*, 162.
34 Williams, "Black Women's Surrogacy Experience and the Christian Notion of Redemption," 13.
35 Douglas, *What's Faith Got to Do with It*, 100.
36 Douglas, *What's Faith Got to Do with It*, 96.
37 Williams, "Straight Talk, Plain Talk," 98.
38 Williams, "Straight Talk, Plain Talk," 98.
39 Williams, *Sisters in the Wilderness*, 235–236.
40 Williams, *Sisters in the Wilderness*, 235–239.

41 Williams, *Sisters in the Wilderness*, 236.
42 Williams, *Sisters in the Wilderness*, 237.
43 Williams, *Sisters in the Wilderness*, 237–238.
44 Williams, *Sisters in the Wilderness*, 238.
45 See Dorothy Roberts, *Killing the Black Body: Race, Reproduction, and the Meaning of Liberty* (Pantheon, 1997).
46 Premilla Nadasen, *Welfare Warriors: The Welfare Rights Movement* (Routledge, 2005).
47 The acronym "DONA" stands for Doulas of North America. The word "doula" comes from ancient Greek meaning "a woman who serves," and is now used to refer to a trained professional who provides continuous physical, emotional, and informational support to a mother before, during, and just after birth, or who provides emotional and practical support during the postpartum period.
48 See the "About Us" statement of purpose for the collective "Mamas of Color Rising" on their website: http://mamasofcolorrising.wordpress.com/about. For information on their birth companion project, go to http://mamasofcolorrising.wordpress.com/2011/03/04/kick-off-sxsw-by-supporting-mocrs-birth-companion-project.
49 Williams, "Straight Talk, Plain Talk," 99.
50 Williams, "Straight Talk, Plain Talk," 105.
51 Williams, "Straight Talk, Plain Talk," 104.
52 Williams, "Straight Talk, Plain Talk," 105.
53 Williams, "Straight Talk, Plain Talk," 111.
54 Williams, "Straight Talk, Plain Talk," 114.
55 Williams, "Straight Talk, Plain Talk," 120.
56 Williams, "Straight Talk, Plain Talk," 117.
57 Day, *Unfinished Business*, 19.
58 Day, *Unfinished Business*, 19.
59 Day, *Unfinished Business*, 21.
60 Day, *Unfinished Business*, 30.
61 Day, *Unfinished Business*, 30.
62 Day, *Unfinished Business*, 42.
63 Williams, "Straight Talk, Plain Talk," 118.
64 Williams, "Straight Talk, Plain Talk," 118.
65 Day, *Unfinished Business*, 145.

Chapter 6: Redemptive Models of Resistance and Transcendence

1 In the last twenty-five years, 82 percent of America's wealth has gone to the top 1 percent. In the last ten years, 100 percent of income growth

has gone to the top 10 percent. Data provided by the Federal Reserve shows that from 1990 to 2022 the wealth of the top 20 percent of US households increased by ten percentage points (from less than 61 percent of all wealth to 71 percent). This increase was driven in large part by the highest earning 1 percent of Americans who held 67 percent of the total household wealth in the first quarter of 2024. The bottom 50 percent of households held only 2.5 percent of the total wealth (a drop from 3.6 percent). See Statista Research Department, "Wealth Distribution in the United States in the First Quarter of 2024," Statista.com, August 21, 2024, https://www.statista.com/statistics/203961/wealth-distribution-for-the-us. See also US Census Bureau, "Distribution of Poverty by Race Using Official Poverty Measure: 2022," https://www.census.gov/content/dam/Census/library/visualizations/2023/demo/p60-280/figure3.pdf, and "Income and Poverty in the United States: 2020," https://www.census.gov/library/publications/2021/demo/p60-273.html, accessed August 24, 2024.

2 For a historical look at the racial wealth gap, see E. N. Wolff, "Recent Trends in Household Wealth in the United States: Rising Debt and the Middle-Class Squeeze: An Update to 2007," Working Paper no. 589 (The Levy Economics Institute of Bard College, March 2010). For current poverty statistics on African American, Latina, and Native American single women with children, see Shengwei Sun, "National Snapshot: Poverty Among Women & Families in 2022," November 8, 2023, https://nwlc.org/resource/national-snapshot-poverty-among-women-families.

3 Moral Mondays refers to a campaign founded and launched in 2013 in North Carolina by Reverend Dr. William J. Barber, II, head of North Carolina NAACP. The grassroots campaign, now known as the Forward Together Moral Mondays movement, is a movement that helped elect a democratic governor in North Carolina and spawned grassroots Moral Mondays social justice movements in states across the United States, including in South Carolina, Georgia, Florida, Alabama, Mississippi, Arkansas, Indiana, Ohio, New York, Pennsylvania, Tennessee, Wisconsin, and Illinois.

4 Reverend Dr. Barber and Reverend Dr. Liz Theoharis joined forces with other faith-based and community activists and organizations to intentionally address systemic racism, America's growing poverty and widening economic disparities, environmental degradation, the negative impact of war and war economies, and the call for fundamental human rights. Their effort draws on the history and unfinished work of the Reverend Dr. Martin Luther King Jr.'s 1967–1968 Poor People's Campaign, which called for America to stand against what King called the "triplets of evil"—systemic racism, poverty, and militarism.

5 Occupy Wall Street (OWS) refers to the protest movement that began on September 17, 2011, in Zuccotti Park, in New York City's Wall Street financial district to address social and economic inequality, greed, corruption, and the perceived undue influence of corporations on government—particularly from the financial services sector. The OWS slogan, "We are the 99 percent," refers to income inequality and wealth distribution in the United States between the wealthiest 1 percent and the rest of the population.

6 Occupy Faith is a group of select pastors who organized in New York City and in various urban locales around the United States to support the Occupy Wall Street movement and each other's social justice endeavors.

7 The mission of Union's Poverty Initiative is a mission to "raise up generations of religious and community leaders committed to building a movement to end poverty." The Poverty Initiative educates destitute community members through its Poverty Scholars Program, while organizing poverty-conscious religious leaders through theological education courses. See Union Theological Seminary's website: www.utsnyc.edu.

8 These words are taken from the title of the speech, "To Make Democracy a Reality," which Hamer delivered at the Vietnam War Moratorium Rally in Berkeley, California, October 15, 1969. See Maegan Parker Brooks and Davis W. Houck, eds., *The Speeches of Fannie Lou Hamer: To Tell It Like It Is* (University Press of Mississippi, 2011), 99–103.

9 Charles Marsh, *God's Long Summer: Stories of Faith and Civil Rights* (Princeton University Press, 1997), 10.

10 Chana Kai Lee, "Anger, Memory, and Personal Power," in *Sisters in the Struggle: African American Women in the Civil Rights–Black Power Movement*, ed. Bettye Collier-Thomas and V. P. Franklin (New York University Press, 2001), 139–170.

11 Lee, "Anger, Memory, and Personal Power," 139–170.

12 Lee, "Anger, Memory, and Personal Power," 39–40.

13 Fannie Lou Hamer, interview with Neil McMillen, April 14, 1972, University of Southern Mississippi Oral History Program, http://www.lib.usm.edu/~spcol/crda/oh/hamertrans.htm.

14 Clayborne Carson, *In Struggle: SNCC and the Black Awakening of the 1960s* (Harvard University Press, 1981), 124–125.

15 Fannie Lou Hamer, "To Praise Our Bridges," in *Mississippi Writers: Reflections of Children and Youth*, ed. Dorothy Abbott (University Press of Mississippi, 1985), 327.

16 Fannie Lou Hamer cited in "Foreword" to Tracy Sugarman, *Stranger at the Gates* (Hill & Wang, 1966), ix.

17 Fannie Lou Hamer, "Sick and Tired of Being Sick and Tired," *Katallagate*, Fall 1968, 27, 25.

18 Monica M. White, *Freedom Farmers: Agricultural Resistance and the Black Freedom Movement* (University of North Carolina Press, 2019), 11.

19 Judith A. Carney and Richard Nicholas Rosomoff, *In The Shadow of Slavery: Africa's Botanical Legacy in the Atlantic World* (University of California Press, 2011), 122.

20 Carney and Rosomoff, *In The Shadow of Slavery*, 122.

21 Marsh, *God's Long Summer*, 46.

22 Marsh, *God's Long Summer*, 13–24.

23 Chana Kai Lee, *For Freedom's Sake: The Life of Fannie Lou Hamer* (University of Illinois Press, 2000), 147.

24 Lee, *For Freedom's Sake*, 147.

25 Franklynn Peterson, "Pig Banks Pay Dividends," *Commercial Appeal Mid-South Magazine*, January 7, 1973, 32, Fannie Lou Hamer Vertical File, Mississippi Department of Archives and History, Jackson, MI.

26 Franklynn Peterson, "Brief History of the Freedom Farm," 4, Fannie Lou Hamer Papers, box 11, folder 23.

27 Peterson, "Pig Banks Pay Dividends"; Freedom Farm Papers Progress Report, n.d. (1972–1973), "Projects," Fannie Lou Hamer Papers, box 11, folder 23; and "Freedom Farm Corporation," 2 (c. March. 1973).

28 Peterson, "Pig Banks Pay Dividends," 34.

29 Peterson, "Pig Banks Pay Dividends," 34.

30 Lee, *For Freedom's Sake*, 151.

31 Lee, *For Freedom's Sake*, 159–161.

32 Marsh, *God's Long Summer*, 32.

33 Studies have shown that as poverty rates increase, supermarket availability decreases, and the availability of small convenience stores and fast-food options with limited healthful food options increases. See Kelly M. Bower et al., "The Intersection of Neighborhood Racial Segregation, Poverty, and Urbanicity and Its Impact on Food Store Availability in the United States," *Preventive Medicine* 58 (2014): 33–39, https://www.sciencedirect.com/science/article/abs/pii/S0091743513003988. See also Alison Hope Alkon et al., eds., *A Recipe for Gentrification: Food, Power, and Resistance in the City* (NYU Press, 2020).

34 Anna Brones, "Food Apartheid: The Root of the Problem with America's Groceries," *The Guardian*, May 15, 2018, https://www.theguardian.com/

society/2018/may/15/food-apartheid-food-deserts-racism-inequality-america-karen-washington-interview.

35 Taken from the Rise & Root Farm website, "Who We Are," https://www.riseandrootfarm.com/rise-and-root-farm, accessed August 1, 2024.

36 Besheer Mohamed et al., "Faith Among Black Americans," The Pew Research Center, February 16, 2021, https://www.pewresearch.org/wp-content/uploads/sites/20/2021/02/PF_02.16.21_Black.religion.report.pdf. See also Christina Turner, "Where Does the Black Church Fit in Today's Black Lives Matter Movement?," PBS.com, March 30, 2021, https://www.pbs.org/newshour/nation/where-does-the-black-church-fit-in-todays-black-lives-matter-movement.

37 Campbell Gibson and Kay Jung, "Historical Census Statistics on Population Totals by Race, 1790 to 1990, and by Hispanic Origin, 1970 to 1990, for the United States, Regions, Divisions, States," United States Census Bureau, https://www.census.gov/content/dam/Census/library/working-papers/2002/demo/POP-twps0056.pdf.

38 Lorena M. Parrish, "Interview Conducted with Reverend Dr. Joseph A. Daniels Jr.," Washington, DC, June 4, 2024.

39 J. C. Whittington and Monica Akhtar, "DC's Black Churches Are Losing Their Congregations: Blame Gentrification," interview with Reverend William H. Lamar IV, Politico.com, April 15, 2022, https://www.politico.com/news/magazine/2022/04/15/black-pastors-gentrification-washington-dc-00024460.

BIBLIOGRAPHY

Ahlstrom, Sydney E. *A Religious History of the American People*. Yale University Press, 1972.

Albertz, Rainer. *A History of Israelite Religion in the Old Testament Period*. Vol. I, *From the Beginnings to the End of Monarchy*. Translated by John Bowden. Westminster John Knox Press, 1994.

Alkon, Alison Hope, Yuki Kato, and Joshua Sbicca, eds. *A Recipe for Gentrification: Food, Power, and Resistance in the City*. NYU Press, 2020.Allen, Willoughby C. *A Critical and Exegetical Commentary on the Gospel According to St. Matthew*. The International Critical Commentary on the Holy Scriptures of the Old and New Testaments. T & T Clark, 1912. Reprint, 1977.

Augustine. "Answer to Letters of Petilian, Bishop of Cirta." In *The Nicene and Post-Nicene Fathers*. Vol. 4, *St. Augustine: The Writings Against the Manicheans and Against the Donatist*, translated by J. R. King and Chester D. Harttranft. Wm. B. Eerdmans, 1976.

Augustine. *The City of God Against the Pagans*. Translated and edited by R. W. Dyson. Cambridge University Press, 1998.

Augustine. *Concerning the City of God Against the Pagans: A New Translation by Henry Bettenson with an Introduction by John O'Meara*. Penguin, 1984.

Augustine. *Expositions on the Books of Psalms*. Translated with notes and indices. A Select Library of the Nicene and Post-Nicene Fathers of the Christian Church. Edited by Philip Schaff, DD, LLD. T & T Clark, 1891.

Augustine. "Letter 130." In *The Fathers of the Church: New Translation. Saint Augustine Letters*. Vol. II, *Letters 83–130*, translated by Sister Wilfrid Parsons, SND. Fathers of the Church, 1953.

Augustine. "Letter 262." In *The Fathers of the Church, A New Translation: Saint Augustine Letters*. Vol. V, *Letters 204–270*, translated by Sister Wilfrid Parsons, SND. Fathers of the Church, 1956.

Augustine. "Letters 156, 157 and 185." In *The Works of Saint Augustine: A Translation for the 21st Century, Letters 156–210*, translated and notes by Roland Teske, SJ, edited by Boniface Ramsey. New City Press, 2002.

Augustine. *Saint Augustine Commentary on the Lord's Sermon on the Mount with Seventeen Related Sermons*. Translated by Denis J. Kavanagh, OSA. Fathers of the Church, 1951.

Augustine. "Sermon 53A." In *The Works of Saint Augustine: A Translation for the 21st Century*. Part III, Vol. 5, *Sermons 148–183*, translated and notes by Edmund Hill, OP, edited by John E. Torelle, OSA. New City Press, 2002.

Augustine. "Sermon 60." In *Sermons on Selected Lessons of the New Testament*. Vol. I, *S. Matthew, S. Mark, S. Luke*. John Henry Parker, 1984.

Augustine. "Sermon 61." In *Sermons on Selected Lessons of the New Testament*. Vol. I, *S. Matthew, S. Mark, S. Luke*. John Henry Parker, 1984.

Baer, Hans A., and Merrill Singer. *African American Religion in the Twentieth Century: Varieties of Protest and Accommodation*. University of Tennessee Press, 1992.

Barrick, Audrey. "Black Believers Debate Prosperity Gospel." *Christian Post Reporter*, August 29, 2007.

Bauer, M. C. *Health, Wealth, and Population in the Early Days of Industrial Revolution*. Routledge & Kegan Paul, 1968.

Bennet, G. V. *The Tory Crisis in Church and State, 1688–1730*. Oxford University Press, 1976.

Best, Earnest. *Following Jesus: Discipleship in the Gospel of Mark*. JSOT, 1981.

Blake, John. "Black Pastors Choose Sides of Direction of Black Church." *The Atlanta Journal-Constitution, Home Edition*, February 15, 2005.

Blomberg, Craig L. *Neither Poverty nor Riches: A Biblical Theology of Material Possessions*. Inter Varsity Press, 1999.

Blount, Brian K. *Then the Whisper Put on Flesh: New Testament Ethics in an African American Context*. Abingdon Press, 2001.

Bonner, Gerard. *St. Augustine of Hippo: Life and Controversies*. The Canterbury Press, 1986.

Botsford, Jay B. *English Society in the XVIII Century: As Influenced by Overseas*. Octagon, 1965.

Bouwsma, William J. *John Calvin: A Sixteenth Century Portrait*. Oxford University Press, 1988.

Bower, Kelly M., Roland J. Thorpe Jr., Charles Rohde, and Darrell Gaskin. "The Intersection of Neighborhood Racial Segregation, Poverty, and Urbanicity and Its Impact on Food Store Availability in the United States." *Preventive Medicine* 58 (January 2014): 33–39. https://doi.org/10.1016/j.ypmed.2013.10.010.

Bowler, Kate. *Blessed: A History of the American Prosperity Gospel*. Oxford University Press, 2013.

Bowman, John. *The Gospel of Mark: The New Christian Jewish Passover Haggadah*. E. J. Brill, 1965.

Brady, Thomas A. *Ruling Class, Regime and Reformation at Strasbourg, 1520–1555*. Studies in Medieval and Reformation Thought 22. E. J. Brill, 1978.

Brones, Anna. "Food Apartheid: The Root of the Problem with America's Groceries." *The Guardian*, May 15, 2018. https://www.theguardian.com/society/2018/may/15/food-apartheid-food-deserts-racism-inequality-america-karen-washington-interview.

Brown, Peter. *Augustine of Hippo: A Biography*. University of California Press, 1969.

Brooks, Maegan Parker, and Davis W. Houck, eds. *The Speeches of Fannie Lou Hamer: To Tell It Like It Is*. University Press of Mississippi, 2011.Brummel, Lee. "Luther and the Biblical Language of Poverty." *The Ecumenical Review* 32 (1980): 40–58.

Brummel, Lee. "Luther on Poverty and the Poor: A Study of Luther's Exegetical Understanding and Use of the Biblical Language of Poverty and the Poor." PhD diss., Columbia University, 1979.

Buckley, Susan L. *Teachings on Usury in Judaism, Christianity, and Islam*. Texts and Studies in Religion. Edwin Mellen Press, 2000.

Burnaby, John. *Amor Dei: A Study of the Religion of St. Augustine*. With a foreword by Oliver O'Donovan. The Canterbury Press, 1938.

Buursma, Bruce. "Minister Practices What She Preaches, Her Gospel Is 'Success.'" *Chicago Tribune*, July 28, 1985, section 2, p. 3.

Caird, G. B. *The Gospel of Luke: Westminster Pelican Commentaries*. Westminster John Knox Press, 1963.

Calvin, John. *Calvin's Commentaries: Commentaries on the Book of Exodus*. Wm. B. Eerdmans, 1948.

Calvin, John. *Calvin's Commentaries: Commentaries on Genesis*. Wm. B. Eerdmans, 1948.

Calvin, John. *Calvin's Commentaries in 21 Vols*. Translated by William Pringle. Calvin Translation Society, 1843; reprint, Baker Book House, 1989.

Calvin, John. *Calvin's Ecclesiastical Advice*. Translated by Mary Beaty and Benjamin W. Farley. Foreword by John H. Leith. Westminster John Knox Press, 1991.

Calvin, John. *Commentaries on the Four Last Books of Moses Arranged in the Form of a Harmony*. 4 vols. Translated from the original Latin and compared with the French edition; with annotations, by the Rev. Charles Williams Bingham, MA, Rector of Melcombe-Horsey, Dorset, and formerly Fellow of New College, Oxford. Calvin Translation Society, 1852.

Calvin, John. "Commentary on Matthew." In *Commentary on a Harmony of the Evangelists, Matthew, Mark and Luke by John Calvin, Vol. Second*. Translated by Rev. William Pringle. Wm. B. Eerdmans, 1949.

Calvin, John. "Commentary on II Corinthians." In *Calvin's Commentaries: Commentary on II Corinthians*. Wm. B. Eerdmans, 1948.

Calvin, John. *Institutes of the Christian Religion in Two Volumes.* Edited by John T. McNeill. Translated by Ford Lewis Battles. The Westminster Press, 1960.

Calvin, John. *Sermons on Deuteronomy.* Sixteenth–Seventeenth Century Facsimile Editions. Translated by Arthur Golding. Banner of Truth, 1987.

Cannon, Katie Geneva. *Black Womanist Ethics.* American Academy of Religion Academy Series 60. Oxford University Press, 1988.

Carnegie, Andrew. *The Gospel of Wealth.* Originally published in *The North American Review*, June 1889. Applewood Books, 1998.

Carney, Judith A., and Richard Nicholas Rosomoff. *In The Shadow of Slavery: Africa's Botanical Legacy in the Atlantic World.* University of California Press, 2011.

Carson, Clayborne. *In Struggle: SNCC and the Black Awakening of the 1960s.* Harvard University Press, 1981.

Cazalas, James K. "Resplendent Rev. Ike Says Man Is God, Heaven's Here." *The Boston Globe*, May 5, 1973.

Cherry, Conrad. *God's New Israel: Religious Interpretations of American Destiny.* Rev. ed. University of North Carolina Press, 1998.

Chrysostom, S. John. "Homilies on Timothy, Homily XII." In *The Nicene and Post-Nicene Fathers of the Christian Church.* Vol. XIII, *St. Chrysostom: Homilies*, edited by Philip Schaff, DD, LLD. Wm. B. Eerdmans, 1979.

Chrysostom, S. John. "Second Sermon on Lazarus and the Rich Man." In *St. John Chrysostom on Wealth and Poverty*, translated by Catharine P. Roth. St. Vladimir's Seminary Press, 1984.

Chrysostom, S. John. *On Wealth and Poverty.* Translated by Catharine P. Roth. St. Vladimir's Seminary Press, 1984.

Clement. *Quis Dives, Salvetur.* In *Clement of Alexandria: The Exhortation to the Greeks*, edited by G. W. Butterworth. Loeb Classical Library. Harvard University Press, 1919.

Clines, David J. A. "The Book of Job." In *The Oxford Companion to the Bible.* Oxford University Press, 1933.

Colemon, Johnnie. *It Works If You Work It.* Vols. 1–5. Transcribed by Rosalie Jackson. Christ University Temple, n.d.

Colemon, Johnnie. *Open Your Mind and Be Healed.* Foreword by Della Reese. DeVorss and Company, 2004.

Colemon, Johnnie. "What We Believe." Johnnie Colemon Theological Seminary, "Our Beliefs." 2024. https://ufbl.org/beliefs.

Collins, Chuck, and Felice Yeskel, with United for a Fair Economy. *Economic Apartheid in America: A Primer on Economic Inequality & Insecurity.* The New Press, 2005. First published 2000.

Collins, William Ross. *Calvin and the Libertines of Geneva*. Edited by F. D. Blackley. Clarke, Irwin & Company, 1968.

Conwell, Russell H. *Acres of Diamonds*. Temple University Press, 2002.

Copeland, Kenneth. *Managing God's Mutual Funds — Yours and His: Understanding True Prosperity*. Kenneth Copeland Productions, 1996.

Copeland, Kenneth, and Gloria Copeland. *Prosperity Promises*. Kenneth Copeland Publications, 1997.

Crawford, Vicki L., Jacqueline Anne Rouse, and Barbara Woods, eds. *Women in the Civil Rights Movement: Trailblazers and Torchbearers, 1941–1965*. Carlson Publishing, 1990.

Crinchlow, Phyllis, Joanna Thompson Gabriel, Jim Lee, and James Trapp. "The African American in Unity History, June 19, 1993, Presentations" (26 Videos). https://www.truthunity.net/african-americans-in-unity/the-african-american-in-unity-history.

Crossan, John Dominic. *The Historical Jesus: The Life of a Mediterranean Jewish Peasant*. HarperSanFrancisco, 1992.

Crossan, John Dominic. *Jesus: A Revolutionary Biography*. HarperOne, 1995.

Crowder, Stephanie Buckhanon. "The Gospel of Luke." In *True to Our Native Land: An African American New Testament Commentary*, edited by Brian K. Blount, Cain Hope Felder, Clarice J. Martin, and Emerson B. Powery. Fortress Press, 2007.

Cutts, Beau. "Know Thyself, Says Rev. Ike." *The Atlanta Constitution*, March 29, 1973.

Day, Keri. *Unfinished Business: Black Women, the Black Church, and the Struggle to Thrive in America*. Orbis Books, 2012.

Danbury, Matthew. "Ten Years After Ferguson, Data on Police Killings Shows a Lack of Progress." *NBC News*, August 9, 2024. https://www.nbcnews.com/data-graphics/data-police-killings-changed-10-years-ferguson-rcna16384.

Debenport, Ellen, ed., with contributions from Jim Blake, Sandra Campbell, Charline Manuel, and Alexandra Scott. "Unity and Race: A Truthful History, Mistakes, Apologies, and Actions Through the Years." Accessed December 30, 2024. https://www.unity.org/en/article/unity-and-race-truthful-history.

Dewey, Joanna. "The Gospel of Mark." In *Searching the Scriptures: A Feminist Commentary*, edited by Elisabeth Schüssler Fiorenza. Crossroad Publishing, 1994.

Dibelius, Martin. *Jesus: Study of the Gospels and an Essay on "The Motive for Social Action in the New Testament."* Translated by Charles Baker Hedrick and Frederick Charles Grant. Appended essay translated by Dorothea M. Barton. SCM Press, 1963.

Dollar, Creflo A. *The Collar of Love: Understanding God's Answer to Racism, Separation, and Division*. Harrison House, 1997.

Dollar, Creflo A. *Total Life Prosperity: 14 Practical Steps to Receiving God's Full Blessing.* Thomas Nelson Publishers, 1999.

Dollar, Taffi. "Far Above Rubies: The Price of a Virtuous Woman." *Changing Your World* 3, no. 5 (May 2001): 19.

Douglas, Kelly Brown. *The Black Christ.* Orbis Books, 1994.

Douglas, Kelly Brown. *What's Faith Got to Do With It? Black Bodies/Christian Souls.* Orbis Books, 2005.

Douglas, Kelly Brown, and Ronald E. Hopson. "Understanding the Black Church: The Dynamics of Change." *Journal of Religious Thought* 56–57, no. 2/1 (Spring 2000–Fall 2001): 95–113.

Doumergue, Emile, with August Lang, Herman Bavinck, and Benjamin B. Warfield. *Calvin and the Reformation: Four Studies.* Edited by William Park Armstrong. Fleming H. Revell Company, 1909.

Durant, Will. *The Reformation: A History of European Civilization from Wyclif to Calvin, 1300–1564.* Simon & Schuster, 1957.

Dyson, R. W. "Introduction." In *Augustine: The City Against the Pagans.* Cambridge University Press, 1998.

Elsing, William T. "Life in the New York Tenement-House as Seen by a City Missionary." In *The Poor in Great Cities: Their Problems and What Is Doing to Solve Them* by Robert A. Woods, W. T. Elsing, Jacob A. Riis et al. Charles Scribner's Sons, 1895. Digitized on the Internet Archive Digital Library of Free & Borrowable Texts. https://archive.org.

Frend, W. H. C. "Early Christianity and Society: A Jewish Legacy in the Pre-Constantinian Era." *Harvard Theological Review* 76, no. 1 (1983): 53–71.

Frend, W. H. C. *The Rise of Christianity.* Fortress Press, 1984.

Eikerenkoeffer, Frederick. "Rev. Ike Speaks on His Philosophy." https://www.revikelegacy.com.

Frederick, Marla F. *Between Sundays: Black Women and Everyday Struggles of Faith.* The George Gund Foundation Imprint in African American Studies. University of California Press, 2003.

Fulop, Timothy E., and Albert J. Raboteau, eds. *African American Religion: Interpretive Essays in History and Culture.* Routledge, 1997.

Gibson, Campbell, and Kay Jung. "Historical Census Statistics on Population Totals by Race, 1790 to 1990, and by Hispanic Origin, 1970 to 1990, for the United States, Regions, Divisions, States." Working Paper No. 56. *United States Census Bureau,* September 2002. https://www.census.gov/content/dam/Census/library/working-papers/2002/demo/POP-twps0056.pdf.

Gonzalez, Justo L. *Faith and Wealth: A History of the Early Christian Ideas on the Origin, Significance and Use of Money.* Wipf & Stock, 1990.

Gordis, Robert. *Poets, Prophets and Sages: Essays in Biblical Interpretation.* Indiana University Press, 1971.

Godfrey, Hayden et al. "Democracy Dies in Darkness: 1,172 People Have Been Shot and Killed by Police in the Past 12 Months." *Washington Post*, September 9, 2024. https://www.washingtonpost.com/graphics/investigations/police-shootings-database.

Gordon, Barry. "Rich, Poor and Slave in the Socioeconomic Thought of the Later Church Fathers." In *On the Condition of Labor and Social Question One Hundred Years Later: Commemorating the 100th Anniversary of Rerum Novarum, and the Fiftieth Anniversary of the Association for Social Economics*, edited by Thomas O. Nitsch, Joseph M. Phillips Jr., and Edward L. Fitzsimmons. The Edwin Mellen Press, 1994.

Gould, Ezra Palmer. *A Critical and Exegetical Commentary on the Gospel According to St. Mark.* Charles Scribner's Sons, 1922. First published 1896 by Charles Scribner's Sons.

Goulder, M. D. *Midrash and Lection in Matthew: The Speaker's Lectures in Biblical Studies.* SPCK, 1974.

Graham, Fred. *The Constructive Revolutionary: John Calvin and His Socio-Economic Impact.* John Knox Press, 1971.

Grant, Jacquelyn. *White Women's Christ and Black Women's Jesus: Feminist Christology and Womanist Response.* American Academy of Religion Series 64. Scholars Press, 1989.

Grant, Jacquelyn. "Womanist Jesus and the Mutual Struggle for Liberation." In *The Recovery of Black Presence: An Interdisciplinary Exploration*, edited by Randall C. Bailey and Jacquelyn Grant. Abingdon Press, 1995.

Green, Joel B. "Good News to Whom: Jesus and the 'Poor' in the Gospel of Luke." In *Jesus of Nazareth: Lord and Christ Essays on the Historical Jesus and New Testament Christology*, edited by Joel B. Green and Max Turner. Eerdmans, 1994.

Guelich, Robert A. *The Sermon on the Mount: A Foundation for Understanding.* Word Publishing Group, 1982.

Hairston, Teresa. "Rev. Ike: The Prosperity Pioneer." *Gospel Today*, September/October 2004.

Hamer, Fannie Lou. Interview with Neil McMillen, April 14, 1972. *University of Southern Mississippi Oral History Program.* http://www.lib.usm.edu/~spcol/crda/oh/hamertrans.htm.

Hamer, Fannie Lou. "To Praise Our Bridges." In *Mississippi Writers: Reflections of Children and Youth*, edited by Dorothy Abbott. University Press of Mississippi, 1985.

Hamer, Fannie Lou. "Sick and Tired of Being Sick and Tired." *Katallagate* (Fall). Committee of Southern Churchman, 1968.

Handy, Robert T. *The Social Gospel in America 1870–1920*. Oxford University Press, 1966.

Harrell, David Edwin. *Oral Roberts: An American Life*. Indiana University Press, 1985.

Harrison, Milmon F. *Righteous Riches: The Word of Faith Movement in Contemporary African American Religion*. Oxford University Press, 2005.

Harry, David Roy. "Two Kingdoms: Walter Rauschenbusch's Concept of the Kingdom of God Contrasted with the Theology of Revivalism in Early Twentieth Century America." PhD diss., Southwestern Baptist Theological Seminary, 1993.

Harvey, Van A. *A Handbook of Theological Terms*. Macmillan, 1964.

Haskin, Richard W. "The Call to Sell All: The History of the Interpretation of Mark 10:17–23 and Parallels." PhD diss., Columbia University, 1968.

Hauerwas, Stanley. *A Better Hope: Resources for a Church Confronting Capitalism, Democracy, and Postmodernity*. Brazos, 2000.

Hauerwas, Stanley. *Dispatches from the Front: Theological Engagements with the Secular*. Duke University Press, 1994.

Hays, Samuel P. *The Response to Industrialism, 1885–1914*. 2nd ed. University of Chicago Press, 1995.

Hengel, Martin. *Property and Riches in the Early Church: Aspects of a Social History of Early Christianity*. Translated by John Bowden. Fortress Press, 1974.

Hill, David. *The Gospel of Matthew*. New Century Bible Commentary. Marshall Morgan & Scott, 1972.

Hopkins, Charles Howard. *The Rise of the Social Gospel in American Protestantism, 1865–1915*. Yale University Press, 1940.

Hopkins, Dwight. "Theologies in the USA." *Theologies and Cultures: Church and Empire* 2, no. 1 (June 2005): 73–84.

Hordern, Richard. "Luther's Attitude Towards Poverty: Theology and Social Reform." In *Festschrift: A Tribute to Dr. William Hordern*, edited by Walter Freitag. University of Saskatchewan, 1985.

Hudson, Winthrop S. *Religion in America*. Charles Scribner's Sons, 1965.

Hyma, Albert. *Renaissance to Reformation*. Eerdmans, 1951.

Ingraham, Cristopher. "Racial Inequality in Minneapolis Among the Worst in the Nation," *Washington Post*, May 30, 2020. https://www.washingtonpost.com/business/2020/05/30/minneapolis-racial-inequality.

Isichei, Elizabeth. *A History of Christianity in Africa: From Antiquity to the Present*. Africa World Press, 1995.

Jaehn, Klaus. "The Formation of Walter Rauschenbusch's Social Consciousness as Reflected in His Early Life and Writings." *Foundations* 16, no. 4

(October–December 1973): 294–326 [Part I]; 17, no. 1 (January–March 1974): 65–85 [Part II].

Jakes, T. D. *Behind Closed Doors*. Higher Dimension Ministries, 1992.

Jakes, T. D. *Daddy Loves His Little Girls*. Charisma House, 1996.

Jakes, T. D. *The Great Investment: Faith, Family, and Finance to Build a Rich Spiritual Life*. Penguin, 2002.

Jakes, T. D. *He-Motions: Even Strong Men Struggle*. Foreword by Max Lucado. G. P. Putnam's Sons, 2004.

Jakes, T. D. *The Lady, Her Lover, and Her Lord*. G. P. Putnam's Sons, 1998.

Jakes, T. D. *Loose That Man & Let Him Go!* 2nd ed. Bethany House Publishers, 2003.

Jakes, T. D. *Man Power: Healing the Man*. Annual ManPower Conference Audio Tapes, 2012.

Jakes, T. D. "Real Men Pour In." Sermon delivered on Father's Day, June 19, 2022. The Potter's House Dallas T. D. Jakes Ministries YouTube Channel. https://www.youtube.com/@TPHDallas/search?query=June%20 19%2C%202022.

Jakes, T. D. *So You Call Yourself a Man? A Devotional for Ordinary Men with Extraordinary Potential*. Baker Publishing Group, 1997.

Jakes, T. D. *Woman, Thou Art Loosed: Healing the Wounds of the Past*. Destiny Image Publishers, 1993.

Jakes, T. D., and Cornel West. "Preachers, Prophets and the Prophetic: The New Face of American Evangelicalism." Lecture delivered as part of "Conversations," a public lecture series of Princeton University's Program in African American Studies, Princeton University. Princeton University Chapel, October 26, 2005.

Jennings, Theodore W., Jr. *Good News to the Poor: John Wesley's Evangelical Economics*. Abingdon Press, 1990.

Jones, David W. "John Calvin's Financial Ethic of Usury." *Faith & Mission: A Theological Journal for Christians Engaged in Fulfilling the Great Commission* 18, no. 3 (Summer 2001): 3–19.

Kennedy, Gail, ed. "The Relation of Wealth to Morals." In *Democracy and the Gospel of Wealth*. D. C. Heath, 1949.

Kerr, Hugh T., ed. *Calvin's Institutes: A Compend*. Westminster John Knox Press, 1989.

Kilpatrick, G. D. *The Origins of the Gospel According to Matthew*. Clarendon Press, 1950.

Kingdon, Robert M. "Social Welfare in Calvin's Geneva." *American Historical Review* 76 (1971): 50–69.

Kingsbury, Jack. *Jesus Christ in Matthew, Mark and Luke: The New Testament Witnesses for Preaching*. Fortress Press, 1981.

Kirk, Neville. *Labour and Society in Britain and the USA*. Vol. 1, *Capitalism, Custom and Protest, 1780–1850*. Scholar Press, 1994.

Lambert, Malcolm D. *Franciscan Poverty: The Doctrine of the Absolute Poverty of Christ and the Apostles in the Franciscan Order, 1210–1323*. SPCK, 1961.

Landis, Benson Y., comp. *A Rauschenbusch Reader: The Kingdom of God and the Social Gospel*. With an interpretation of the life and work of Walter Rauschenbusch by Harry Emerson Fosdick. Harper & Brothers, 1957.

Lane, William. *The Gospel According to Mark: The New International Commentary on the New Testament*. Wm. B. Eerdmans, 1974.

Laurent, Sylvie. *King and the Other America: The Poor People's Campaign and the Quest for Economic Equality*. University of California Press, 2018.

Lee, Chana Kai. "Anger, Memory, and Personal Power." In *Sisters in the Struggle: African American Women in the Civil Rights–Black Power Movement*, edited by Bettye Collier-Thomas and V. P. Franklin. New York University Press, 2001.

Lee, Chana Kai. *For Freedom's Sake: The Life of Fannie Lou Hamer*. University of Illinois Press, 2000.

Lee, Shayne. *T. D. Jakes: America's New Preacher*. New York University Press, 2005.

Lightfoot, J. B., trans. "The Shepherd of Hermas." In *The Apostolic Fathers*. Macmillan, 1890.

Lincoln, C. Eric, and Lawrence H. Mamiya. *The Black Church in the African American Experience*. Duke University Press, 1990.

Lindberg, Carter. *Beyond Charity: Reformation Initiatives for the Poor*. Augsburg Press, 1993.

Lindberg, Carter. "'There Should Be No Beggars Among Christians': Karlstadt, Luther, and the Origins of the Protestant Poor Relief." *Church History* 46, no. 3 (1977): 313–334.

Little, A. G. *Studies in English Franciscan History*. Manchester University Press, 1917.

Little, Lester K. "Pride Goes Before Avarice: Social Change and the Vices in Latin Christendom." *American Historical Review* 76 (1971): 46.

Lubove, Roy. *The Progressives and the Slums: Tenement House Reform in New York City, 1890–1917*. University of Pittsburgh Press, 1962.

Lutz, Norma J. *The History of the Black Church*. Chelsea House Publishers, 2001.

Maloney, Robert P. "The Background of the Early Christian Teaching on Usury." PhD diss., The Catholic University of America, 1969.

Malthus, Thomas. *An Essay on the Principle of Population*. J. Johnson St. Paul's Church Yard, 1798.

Marsh, Charles. *God's Long Summer: Stories of Faith and Civil Rights*. Princeton University Press, 1997.

Marshal, Dorothy. *Industrial England 1776–1851*. Charles Scribner's Sons, 1973.

Martin, Darnise C. *Beyond Christianity: African Americans in a New Thought Church*. New York University Press, 2005.

Marty, Martin E. *Righteous Empire: The Protestant Experience in America*. HarperCollins, 1977.

Matera, Frank J. *New Testament Ethics: The Legacies of Jesus and Paul*. Westminster John Knox Press, 1996.

Matthews, Philippe. "The First Lady of New Thought Metaphysics—The Reverend Dr. Johnnie Colemon." *Philippe Matthews Show* (online). Accessed December 4, 2024. http://thepmshow.tv/channel/spirtual-development/the-first-lady-of-new-thought-metaphysics-the-reverend-doctor-johnnie-colemon.

May, Henry. *Protestant Churches and Industrial America*. Harper & Brothers, 1949.

McConnell, Francis J. *John Wesley*. Epworth Press, 1939.

McGrath, Alister E. *Christianity Theology: An Introduction*. Blackwell, 1994.

McGrath, Alister E. *A Life of John Calvin: A Study in the Shaping of Western Culture*. Blackwell, 1990.

McGuckin, J. A. "The Vine and the Elm Tree: The Patristic Interpretation of Jesus' Teachings on Wealth." In *Studies in Church History 24: The Church and Wealth*, edited by W. J. Sheils and Diana Woods. Blackwell, 1987.

McKelvey, Blake. *The Urbanization of America, 1860–1915*. Rutgers University Press, 1963.

McKim, Donald K. *Readings in Calvin's Theology*. Baker Book House, 1984.

McLoughlin, William G. *Revivals, Awakenings, and Reform: An Essay on Religion and Social Change in America, 1607–1977*. University of Chicago Press, 1978.

Mealand, David L. *Poverty and Expectations in the Gospels*. SPCK, 1977.

Merdinger, J. E. *Rome and the African Church in the Time of Augustine*. Yale University Press, 1997.

Minus, Paul M. *Walter Rauschenbusch: American Reformer*. Macmillan, 1988.

Mitchem, Stephanie Y. *Name It and Claim It? Prosperity Preaching in the Black Church*. Pilgrim Press, 2007.

Mohamed, Besheer, Kiana Cox, Jeff Diamant, and Claire Gecewicz. "Faith Among Black Americans." The Pew Research Center, February 16, 2021. https://www.pewresearch.org/wp-content/uploads/sites/20/2021/02/PF_02.16.21_Black.religion.report.pdf.

Mohl, Raymond A. *The New City: Urban America in the Industrial Age, 1860–1920.* Harlan Davidson, 1985.

Mollat, Michel. *Poor in the Middle Ages: An Essay in Social History.* Translated by Arthur Goldhammer. Yale University Press, 1986.

Monter, E. William. *Calvin's Geneva.* Wiley, 1967.

More, Louise Bolard. *Wage-Earners' Budgets: A Study of Standards and Costs of Living in New York City.* H. Holt, 1907. Reprint, Arnos Press, 1971.

Morris, James. *The Preachers.* St. Martin's Press, 1973.

Mosley, Glenn, and Edie Skalitzy. "The History of Afro-Americans in the Unity Movement." *Association of Unity Churches Headquarters Highlights: News for the Field* 3, no. 1. (June/July 1993). https://s3.amazonaws.com/truthunity/assets/video/the-african-american-in-unity-history-1993/the-african-american-in-unity-history-auc-newsletter-and-transcript.pdf.

Mullin, Redmond. *The Wealth of Christians.* Bookhouse Australia, 1983.

Murphy, Larry. "Piety and Liberation: A Historical Exploration of African American Religion and Social Justice." In *Blow the Trumpet in Zion: Global Vision and Action for the 21st Century Black Church*, edited by Iva E. Carruthers, Frederick D. Haynes III, and Jeremiah A. Wright Jr. Fortress Press, 2005.

Nadasen, Premilla. *Welfare Warriors: The Welfare Rights Movement.* Routledge, 2005.

Naphy, William G. *Calvin and the Consolidation of the Genevan Reformation with a New Preface.* Westminster John Knox Press, 1994.

Navone, John. *Themes of St. Luke.* Gregorian University Press, 1970.

Neufeld, Edward. "The Prohibitions Against Loans at Interest in Ancient Hebrew Laws." *Hebrew Union College Annual* 26 (1955): 355–412.

"The New Black Spirituality." *Ebony Magazine* 60, no. 2 (December 2004): 135–166.

"The New Mega Churches: Huge Congregations with Spectacular Structures Spread Across America." *Ebony Magazine* 57, no. 2 (December 2001).

Niebuhr, H. Richard. *The Kingdom of God in America.* Harper & Brothers, 1935.

Novarro, Leonard. "Rev. Ike: Prophet or Pitch Man?" *The Tribune*, May 8, 1985.

O'Connell, Patricia, ed. "Online Extra: Church of the Mighty Dollar: How Do Rolls-Royces Fit into God's Plan? The Founder of the World Changers Church International Explains All." *Bloomberg Business Week*, May 23, 2005.

O'Donnell, James. *Augustine: A New Biography.* HarperCollins, 2005.

Oliver, Melvin L., and Thomas M. Shapiro. *Black Wealth/White Wealth: A New Perspective on Racial Inequality.* Routledge, 1995.

Optatus, Bishop of Milevis. *Optatus: Against the Donatists*. Translated and edited by Mark Edwards. Translated Texts for Historians Series. Liverpool University Press, 1998.

Origen. *Commentaire sur l'Evangile selon Matthieu*. Editions du Cerf, 1970.

Ozment, Steven. *The Age of Reform (1250–1550): An Intellectual and Religious History of Late Medieval and Reformational Europe*. Yale University Press, 1980.

Pelagius. "On Riches." In *The Letters of Pelagius and His Followers*, edited by B. R. Rees. Boydell Press, 1991.

Peterson, Franklynn. "Freedom Farm Corporation." Fannie Lou Hamer Papers, c. March 1973.

Peterson, Franklynn. "Pig Banks Pay Dividends." *Commercial Appeal Mid-South Magazine*, January 7, 1973, 32. Fannie Lou Hamer vertical file, Mississippi Department of Archives and History, Jackson, MI.

Peterson, Franklynn. "Pig Banks Pay Dividends." *Freedom Farm Papers Progress Report*, n.d. (1972–1973), "Projects." Fannie Lou Hamer Papers, box 11, folder 23.

Phan, Peter. *Social Thought*. Vol. 20, *Message of the Fathers of the Church*. Edited by Thomas Halton. Michael Glazier, 1984.

Pinn, Anne, and Anthony H. Pinn. *Fortress Introduction to Black Church History*. Fortress Press, 2004.

Plummer, Alfred. *A Critical and Exegetical Commentary on the Gospel According to S. Luke*. 4th ed. T & T Clark, 1901.

Porter, Roy. *English Society in the Eighteenth Century*. Penguin, 1992.

Power, Kim. *Veiled Desire: Augustine on Women*. Continuum, 1996.

Powery, Emerson B. "The Gospel of Mark." In *True to Our Native Land: An African American New Testament Commentary*, edited by Brian K. Blount, Cain Hope Felder, Clarice J. Martin, and Emerson B. Powery. Fortress Press, 2007.

Raboteau, Albert J. *Canaan Land: A Religious History of African Americans*. Oxford University Press, 2001.

Rack, Henry D. *Reasonable Enthusiast: John Wesley and the Rise of Methodism*. Abingdon Press, 1992.

Rauschenbusch, Walter. *Christianity and the Social Crisis*. Macmillan, 1916.

Rauschenbusch, Walter. *Christianizing the Social Order*. Macmillan, 1921.

Rauschenbusch, Walter. "The Genesis of 'Christianity and the Social Crisis.'" *Rochester Theological Seminary Bulletin: The Record* 69 (November 3, 1918): 51–52.

Rauschenbusch, Walter. *A Gospel for the Social Awakening: Selections from the Writings of Social Walter Rauschenbusch*. Compiled by Benjamin E. Mays with an introduction by C. Howard Hopkins. Association Press, 1950.

Rauschenbusch, Walter. "Revelation: An Exposition." *Biblical World* X, no. 2 (August 1897): 94–103.

Rauschenbusch, Walter. *The Righteousness of the Kingdom*. Abingdon Press, 1968.

Rauschenbusch, Walter. *The Social Principles of Jesus*. College Voluntary Study Courses, Fourth Year—Part I. Written under the direction of Sub-Committee on College Courses, Sunday School Council of Evangelical Denominations, and Committee on Voluntary Study, Council of North American Student Movements. Association Press, 1916.

Rauschenbusch, Walter. *A Theology for the Social Gospel*. Introduction by Donald W. Shriver Jr. Westminster John Knox Press, 1997.

Rauschenbusch, Walter. *Walter Rauschenbusch: Selected Writings*. Edited by Winthrop S. Hudson. Paulist Press, 1984.

Redmond, Leslie, and Curtiss Paul DeYoung. "White Privilege Shines with COVID-19." *Star Tribune*, April 23, 2020. https://www.startribune.com/white-privilege-shines-with-covid-19/569903692.

Reid, W. Stanford, ed. *John Calvin: His Influence in the Western World*. Zondervan, 1982.

Richardson, Nicole Marie, Krissah Williams, and Hamil R. Harris. "The Business of Faith." *Black Enterprise Magazine* 36, no. 10 (May 2006): 102–114.

Riis, Jacob A. *How the Other Half Lives: Studies Among the Tenements of New York*. Charles Scribner's Sons, 1932. Digitized by the Internet Archive Digital Library of Free & Borrowable Texts, 2013. https://archive.org.

Riley, Clayton. "The Golden Gospel of Rev. Ike." *The New York Times*, March 9, 1979.

Ringe, Sharon. *Jesus, Liberation, and the Biblical Jubilee: Images for Ethics and Christology*. Fortress Press, 1985.

Rupp, E. Gordon. *Religion and England 1688–1791*. Clarendon Press, 1986.

Satter, Beryl. *Each Mind a Kingdom: American Women, Sexual Purity and the New Thought Movement, 1875–1920*. University of California Press, 1999.

Schaff, Philip. *The Swiss Reformation*, vol. 2. Scribner, 1892.

Schapiro, Renie. "He Promises Pie in the Sky with Ice Cream on Top: Mr. Preacherman." *Sunday Times*, December 8, 1974.

Schlesinger, Arthur Meier. *The Rise of the City 1878–1898: A History of American Life*, vol. 10. New Viewpoints Edition, Franklin Watts, 1971. Originally published by Macmillan, 1933.

Schmidt, Thomas E. *Hostility to Wealth in the Synoptic Gospels*. Journal for the New Testament Supplement Series 15. JSOT Press, 1987.

Schottroff, Luise, and Wolfgang Stegemann, eds. *God of the Lowly: Socio-Historical Interpretations of the Bible*. Translated by Matthew J. O'Connell. Orbis Books, 1984.

Schottroff, Luise, and Wolfgang Stegemann, eds. *Jesus and the Hope of the Poor*. Translated by Matthew J. O'Connell. Orbis Books, 1986.

Schweizer, Eduard. *The Good News According to Matthew*. Westminster John Knox Press, 1975.

Seccombe, D. "Possessions and the Poor in Luke-Acts." PhD diss., Cambridge University, 1978.

Sernett, Milton C. *Bound for the Promised Land: African American Religion and the Great Migration*. C. Eric Lincoln Series on the Black Experience. Duke University Press, 1997.

Sharpe, Dores Robinson. *Walter Rauschenbusch*. Introduction by Harry Emerson Fosdick. Macmillan, 1942.

"The Shepherd of Hermas." In *The Apostolic Fathers*, translated by Joseph B. Lightfoot. Macmillan, 1890.

Singer, C. Gregg. "Calvin and the Social Order; or Calvin as a Social and Economic Statesman." In *John Calvin: Contemporary Prophet*, edited by Jacob T. Hoogstra. Baker Book House, 1959.

Sklar, Martin J. *The Corporate Reconstruction of American Capitalism, 1890–1916: The Market, the Laws, and the Politics*. Cambridge University Press, 1988.

Smith, Adam. *An Inquiry into the Nature and Causes of the Wealth of Nations*, vol. 2. W. Strahan and T. Cadell, 1776.

Smith, C. Fraser. *Here Lies Jim Crow: Civil Rights in Maryland*. The Johns Hopkins University Press, 2008.

Smith, Goldman. *England: A Short History*. Scribner's Sons, 1971.

Smits, Luchesius. *Saint Augustine dans l'oeuvre de Jean Calvin*. 2 vols. Van Gorcum, 1957–1958.

Smucker, Donovan E. "The Origins of Walter Rauschenbusch's Social Ethics." PhD diss., University of Chicago, 1957.

Smucker, Donovan E. *The Origins of Walter Rauschenbusch's Social Ethics*. McGill-Queen's University Press, 1994.

Snyder, Howard. *Models of the Kingdom: Gospel, Culture and Mission in Biblical and Historical Perspective*. Abingdon Press, 1991.

"Sojourners." December 1982, 11.

Speed, Bille Chene. "You Can't Lose, Rev. Ike Says." *The Atlanta Journal*, March 29, 1973.

Sphar, Charles B. *An Essay on the Present Distribution of Wealth in the United States*. Crowell & Co., 1896.

Spillers, Hortense. "Mama's Baby, Papa's Maybe." In *Black, White and in Color: Essays on American Literature and Culture*. University of Chicago Press, 2003.

Statista Research Department. "Wealth Distribution in the United States in the First Quarter of 2024." Statista.com, August 21, 2024. https://www.statista.com/statistics/203961/wealth-distribution-for-the-us.

Stead, William T. *If Christ Came to Chicago*. Laird & Lee, 1894.

Stegemann, Wolfgang. *The Gospel and the Poor*. Translated by Dietlinde Elliott. Fortress Press, 1984.

Stevenson, Richard W. "In a Time of Plenty; the Poor Are Still Poorer." *New York Times*, January 23, 2000.

Stone, Ronald H. *John Wesley's Life and Ethics*. Abingdon Press, 2001.

Strong, Josiah. *The Challenge of the City*. NY Missionary Education Movement, 1907.

Strong, Josiah. *Our Country: Its Possible Future and Its Present Crisis*. American Home Missionary Society, 1885.

Sugarman, Tracy. *Stranger at the Gates: A Summer in Mississippi*. American Century Series. Hill & Wang, 1966.

Sugirtharajah, R. S. *The Bible and the Third World: Precolonial, Colonial, and Postcolonial Encounters*. Cambridge University Press, 2001.

Sun, Shengwei. "National Snapshot: Poverty Among Women & Families in 2022." November 8, 2023. https://nwlc.org/resource/national-snapshot-poverty-among-women-families.

Swete, H. B. *The Gospel According to St. Mark*. 3rd ed. MacMillan, 1909.

Sykes, Norman. *Church and State in England in the XVIII Century*. Archon, 1962.

Terrell, JoAnne Marie. *Power in the Blood? The Cross in the African American Experience*. Bishop Henry McNeal Turner/Sojourner Truth Series in Black Religion 15. Orbis Books, 1998.

Tertullian. *The Apology of Tertullian for Christians*. Translated with Introduction, Analysis, and Appendix Containing the Letters of Pliny and Trajan Respecting the Christians by T. Herbert Bindley. Parker & Co., 1890.

Thomas, Bettye Collier, and V. P. Franklin, eds. *Sisters in the Struggle: African American Women in the Civil Rights-Black Power Movement*. New York University Press, 2001.

Townes, Emilie M., ed. *A Troubling in My Soul: Womanist Perspectives on Evil and Suffering*. Bishop Henry McNeal Turner Studies in North American Black Religion 8. Orbis Books, 1993.

Trench, William Crowell. "The Social Gospel and the City: Implications for Theological Reconstruction in the Work of Washington Gladden, Josiah Strong, and Walter Rauschenbusch." PhD diss., Boston University, 1986.

Turner, Christina. "Where Does the Black Church Fit in Today's Black Lives Matter Movement?" PBS.com. March 30, 2021. https://www.pbs.org/newshour/nation/where-does-the-black-church-fit-in-todays-black-lives-matter-movement.

US Census Bureau. "Distribution of Poverty by Race Using Official Poverty Measure: 2022." https://www.census.gov/content/dam/Census/library/visualizations/2023/demo/p60-280/figure3.pdf.

US Census Bureau. "Income and Poverty in the United States: 2020." https://www.census.gov/library/publications/2021/demo/p60-273.html.

Vanderpool, Harold. "The American Success Syndrome." *The Christian Century*, September 24, 1975, 820–823.

Verhey, Allen. *The Great Reversal: Ethics and the New Testament.* Wm. B. Eerdmans, 1984.

Villari, Pasquale. *Life and Times of Girolamo Savonarola*. Translated by Linda Villari. Charles Scribner's Sons, 1888.

von Rad, Gerhard. *Wisdom in Israel.* Translated by James D. Martin. SCM Press, 1972.

Walker, Williston, Richard A. Norris, David W. Lotz, and Robert T. Handy. *A History of the Christian Church.* 4th ed. Charles Scribner's Sons, 1985.

Wallace, Ronald S. *Calvin's Doctrine of the Christian Life.* Wipf & Stock, 1997.

Washington, James Melvin, ed. *The Essential Writings and Speeches of Martin Luther King Jr.* Harper San Francisco, 1991.

Watts, Jill. *God, Harlem, USA: The Father Divine Story.* University of California Press, 1992.

Weber, Max. *The Protestant Ethic and the Spirit of Capitalism.* Charles Scribner's Sons, 1930.

Weaver, Rebecca H. "Wealth and Poverty in the Early Church." *Interpretation* 41, no. 4 (1987): 368–381.

Wendel, François. *Calvin: The Origins and Development of His Religious Thought.* Translated by Philip Mairet. Baker Books, 1963.

Werner, Wellman J. *The Wesleyan Movement in the Industrial Revolution.* Longmans, 1930.

Wesley, John. "The Character of a Methodist." In *The Works of John Wesley,* edited by Thomas Jackson. Felix Farley, 1872.

Wesley, John. "On the Danger of Increasing Riches." In *The Works of the Rev. John Wesley, A.M.*, vol. 7, edited by Thomas Jackson. 3rd ed. 14 vols. Wesleyan Methodist Book Room, 1872; reprinted by Baker Book House, 1979.

Wesley, John. *Fifty-Three Sermons.* London: Wesleyan Methodist Book Press, 1771.

Wesley, John. "On Riches, Discourse VII." In *The Works of the Rev. John Wesley, A.M.*, vol. 2, edited by Thomas Jackson. 3rd ed. 14 vols. Wesleyan Methodist Book Room, 1872; reprinted by Baker Book House, 1979.

Wesley, John. "Sermon on the Mount, Discourse VIII." In *The Works of the Rev. John Wesley, A.M.*, vol. 5, edited by Thomas Jackson. 3rd ed. 14 vols. Wesleyan Methodist Book Room, 1872; reprinted by Baker Book House, 1979.

Wesley, John. "The Use of Money, Discourse VI." In *The Works of the Rev. John Wesley, A.M.*, vol. 6, edited by Thomas Jackson. 3rd ed. 14 vols. Wesleyan Methodist Book Room, 1872; reprinted by Baker Book House, 1979.

Wesley, John. *The Works of John Wesley, Volume XII Letters, The First Complete Unabridged Edition in Nearly 100 Years.* Zondervan, 1872.

Wesley, John. *The Works of the Rev. John Wesley, A.M.* Edited by Thomas Jackson. 3rd ed. 14 vols. Wesleyan Methodist Book Room, 1872; reprinted by Baker Book House, 1979.

West, Cornel. "Black Theology and Marxist Thought." In *African American Religious Thought: An Anthology*, edited by Eddie S. Glaude Jr. and Cornel West. Westminster John Knox Press, 1993; reprinted 2003.

West, Cornel. *Democracy Matters: Winning the Fight Against Imperialism.* Penguin, 2004.

West, Cornel. *Race Matters.* Vintage Books, 1994.

White, Monica M. *Freedom Farmers: Agricultural Resistance and the Black Freedom Movement.* University of North Carolina Press, 2019.

White, Ronald C., and C. Howard Hopkins. *The Social Gospel: Religion and Reform in Changing America, with an Essay by John C. Bennett.* Temple University Press, 1976.

Whittington, J. C., and Monica Akhtar. "DC's Black Churches Are Losing Their Congregations: Blame Gentrification. Interview with Reverend William H. Lamar IV." Politico.com, April 15, 2022. https://www.politico.com/news/magazine/2022/04/15/black-pastors-gentrification-washington-dc-00024460.

Wilkerson, Isabel. "A Dollar and a Dream: Pastors Creflo and Taffi Dollar Have Built a Multi-Million Dollar Megachurch Empire by Practicing What They Preach." *Essence*, December 2005.

Williams, Delores S. "Black Women's Surrogacy Experience and the Christian Notion of Redemption." In *After Patriarchy: Feminist Transformations of the World Religions*, edited by Paul M. Cooey, William R. Eakin, and Jay B. McDaniel. Orbis Books, 1991.

Williams, Delores S. "The Color of Feminism." *Christianity and Crisis* 45, no. 7 (April 29, 1985): 164–165.

Williams, Delores S. "Re-Imagining Jesus." Taped recording of a paper presented on November 5, 1993, at the Re-Imaging Conference (November 4–7, 1993), held in Minneapolis, Minnesota.

Williams, Delores S. *Sisters in the Wilderness: The Challenge of Womanist God-Talk*. Orbis Books, 1993.

Williams, Delores S. "Straight Talk, Plain Talk: Womanist Words About Salvation in a Social Context." In *Embracing the Spirit: Womanist Perspectives on Hope, Salvation & Transformation,* edited by Emilie M. Townes. Orbis Books, 1997.

Williams, Delores S. "A Womanist Perspective on Sin." In *A Troubling in My Soul: Womanist Perspectives on Evil and Suffering*, edited by Emilie M. Townes. Orbis Books, 1993.

Wilmore, Gayraud S. *Black Religion and Black Radicalism: An Interpretation of the Religious History of African American People*. 2nd ed. Orbis Books, 1983.

Winship, Scott, Christopher Pulliam, Ariel Gelrud Shiro, Richard V. Reeves, and Santiago Deambrosi. "Long Shadows: The Black–White Gap in Multigenerational Poverty." Brookings Institution, June 10, 2021, 3. https://www.brookings.edu/articles/long-shadows-the-black-white-gap-in-multigenerational-poverty.

Wolff, E. N. "Recent Trends in Household Wealth in the United States: Rising Debt and the Middle-Class Squeeze: An Update to 2007." Working Paper no. 589. The Levy Economics Institute of Bard College, March 2010.

Wolff, Hans Walter. *Joel and Amos: A Commentary on the Books of the Prophets Joel and Amos (Hermeneia: A Critical & Historical Commentary on the Bible)*. Translated by Waldemar Janzen. Edited by Dean McBride. Fortress Press, 1977.

Woods, Robert A. *The Poor in Great Cities*. Charles Scribner's Sons, 1895. Reprint, Arno Press & New York Times, 1971.

Wrigley, E. A., and R. S. Schonfield, eds. *The Population History of England 1542–1871: A Reconstruction*. Cambridge University Press, 1993.

Zumkeller, Adolar, OSA, ed. *Augustine's Ideal of the Religious Life*. Translated by Edmund Colledge, OSA. Fordham University Press, 1986.

INDEX